Elijah
Prophet of Carmel

In friendship,
Jane

Elijah
Prophet of Carmel

Jane Ackerman

ICS Publications
Institute of Carmelite Studies
Washington, D.C.
2003

ICS Publications
2131 Lincoln Road, NE
Washington, DC 20002-1199
(800) 832-8489
www.icspublications.org

Illustrations from ICS library holdings.
Cover design by Rosemary Moak, OCDS.

Typeset and produced in the United States of America.

Library of Congress Cataloging-in-Publication Data

Ackerman, Jane, 1948–
  Elijah, Prophet of Carmel / Jane Ackerman.
    p. cm.
  Includes bibliographical references (p.   ).
  ISBN 0-935216-30-8
  1. Elijah (Biblical prophet). 2. Carmelites—Spiritual Life. 3.
Spirituality—Catholic Church—History. I. Title.
  BS580.E4A35 2003
  222'.5092—dc21
                                              2003000041

Contents

Acknowledgments

I would like to express my appreciation to many Carmelites in both branches of the Order for their support as I have completed this book. Carmelite historian Keith Egan, T.O.Carm., originally suggested that I inquire into Elijah's influence on the Order and guided me to key sources as I began the project. The O.Carm. community at Whitefriars in Washington, D.C., received me hospitably on numerous occasions. Within that group, I especially thank Fr. Lukas Schmidt, the former prior, for his wisdom. Fr. Patrick McMahon graciously oriented me to the Biblioteca Carmelitana housed at Whitefriars. In many ways, my work depends on research conducted in this important archive. I am also grateful to Fr. John Welch for an invitation to present part of my work on early Carmelite documents at a Carmelite Study week in Washington, D.C.

Many people have offered scholarly guidance and critical clarity during the years I have written this book. I am thankful to Frs. Joachim Smet, Richard Copsey, and Paul Chandler, all O.Carms. living at distant points of the globe who provided helpful suggestions. Fr. Chandler generously commented on the draft of chapter 4 and provided precise Latin translations of several passages from early documents. The most important of these is the *Rubrica prima*, the earliest story we have in which Carmelites mention their relationship to Elijah.

Among the Discalced Carmelites of the Washington, D.C., community, I would like to thank Frs. Kieran Kavanaugh and John Sullivan who lent me scholarly guidance both in person and through their writings. Fr. Steven Payne gave a much-needed extension on completion

of the book manuscript and enriched my understanding with materi-
als from their community archives. Br. Joseph Girouard helped improve the work with some careful copyediting. Over the years and in
many informal ways, members of both branches of the Order have
shown me what it means to be a Carmelite "zealous with zeal for the
Lord God of Hosts."

Friendly support did not lack at home. The Office of Research at
The University of Tulsa funded a trip to Whitefriars for archival research. Especially John Bowlin and Russell Hittinger, but also all my
colleagues in The Department of Philosophy and Religion at The
University of Tulsa, encouraged me in the project.

I thank my parents and friends for their love.

Colophon, Ceremonial of Carmelite Nuns, Antwerp 1656

Chapter 1
Elijah in the Books of the Kings

The word of Yahweh came to him: "Why are you here,
Elijah?" "Because of my great zeal for Yahweh the God
of Hosts," he replied. (1 Kings 19:9–10).[1]

A powerful prophet appeared in the northern kingdom of Israel in
the ninth century B.C.E. He was not alone in his calling. Some sixty
years before he arose, another messenger had condemned King
Jeroboam's shocking requirement that his people worship gold-
en calves. As Jeroboam stood by his altar sacrificing to his idols,
surrounded by a priesthood whose ranks he had filled, the man of
God roared his denunciation of the offense to the God of Hosts, and
Jeroboam's altar was torn down (1 Kings 12:25–13:5). Prophets continued to appear in waves in the northern kingdom. Twenty years later,
Jehu denounced the usurper then on the throne for leading his country into apostasy. As did the words that the man of God had
uttered to King Jeroboam, Jehu's prophecy of King Baasha's doom
came true. In 876 B.C.E., Baasha's commander of chariots Zimri
slaughtered the whole royal house and seized the throne himself
(1 Kings 16:8–10).

---

1. Biblical passages will be taken from the Revised Standard Version,
with the exception of one word. The RSV and most recent English translations of the Bible render the divine tetragrammaton ("YHWH" or
"Yahweh," in Roman letters) as "the LORD," capital letters distinguishing that name from "the Lord," meaning "Adonai." Throughout this book,
"Yahweh" is used in place of "the LORD," to draw attention to the specific uses of that name in Scripture. The Hebrew Bible testifies to one
Lord of Creation but says repeatedly that the Israelites especially knew
him through the name and actions of Yahweh.

Thus when Elijah the Tishbite began to prophesy around 870 B.C.E., it was far from the first time that messengers of God had surfaced in the turbulent country. Others before him had uttered words of chastisement and calls to the straight path. Later prophets, such as Amos, Hosea, and Elijah's disciple Elisha, would vigorously intervene in national life, warning of evils to come because of northern Israel's sins. None appear in the pages of Scripture with more power than does Elijah, called by God to wrest the kingdom from worship of the Canaanite fertility god Baal.

Although time erases details of memory, Elijah left his mark. Stories of his prophetic actions reached the version read today in the books of 1 and 2 Kings in the sixth century B.C.E., some three centuries after the events they describe. Many scholars think that a long oral tradition about the messenger preceded the composition of the biblical books and that oral tales of the stormy prophet were probably gathered into documents that the sixth-century redactors of 1–2 Kings consulted as they produced the biblical accounts of Elijah. If knowledge of the historical prophet's deeds survived in this way—first in the oral recitation of memories, then collected and cared for in documents, and finally edited into what can be now read—it means that Elijah was remembered for a long time indeed. Something was powerfully attractive in the original man, to begin such a line of storytelling.

The personal lives of other prophets active in the region were forgotten. The prophet Jehu retains his symbolic name in the Bible but no real signs of distinctiveness: whoever he was, Scripture remembers him only as a messenger who described God's action in history. Despite his memorable confrontation with King Jeroboam, even the personal name of Elijah's biblical predecessor, the man of God, dropped away. He, too, is remembered for God's action through him, nothing else. How different Elijah seems to be from his peers. First and Second Kings describe his gestures, vocabulary, and people's specific reactions to him in striking anecdotes that his editors strung into a story and, as later chapters in this book will show, in many new legends about him that sprang up as time passed.

Elijah's personality in the pages of 1–2 Kings is also more vivid than that of other great biblical figures. The book of Exodus says that Moses' anger at the Hebrews' sin burned hotly, but nowhere did Moses act with such personal ferocity as Elijah did when he slaughtered the 450 prophets of Baal in the valley of Kishon. Moses, Samuel, and Abraham argued with God for others, but no one is recorded in the Bible as having been audacious enough to demand of Yahweh what Elijah did. Scriptures record that ancient prophets were bodily as well as mentally conscripted into their calling—Ezekiel in a vision, for example, was pulled to his feet and obliged to eat a scroll—but who can think of a story of a prophet in the Hebrew Bible who used his bodily power more than Elijah? The Hebrew Bible says that the great Moses' arms tired and had to be propped up for the Hebrews to continue to win on the battlefield. Elijah, in contrast, threw his whole body into the resuscitation of a widow's son and into prayer to God to break a drought.

He always seems to have done, said, and dared more than others. Even his recorded experiences of the divine are extraordinary. Isaiah once saw God on his throne, "high and lifted up" in heaven, but 1 Kings records that Elijah was bodily transported to that realm, a most unusual thing for God to have done to a human being according to the Hebrew Bible. In the New Testament only Jesus exceeds Elijah in bodily power. In Jewish tradition, Elijah is exceeded only by the Messiah, whom he comes to resemble. In Islam, only Muhammad, Jesus, and the archangels best what the Bible says the northern Israelite prophet achieved. Elijah stood out spectacularly in a profession in which powerful gestures were the norm.

The prophet's vivid identity in 1–2 Kings may be understood in several ways. The first has already been suggested. His powerful personality may be explained as the effect of a historical life that was so impressive that traces of it are still visible in what the Bible says about him. This attractive thought cannot be investigated in modern ways. Evidence is too slight to make a historical case that Elijah's stories were inspired by an especially powerful man. No comment about him appears in Scripture earlier than 1–2 Kings. The books of 1–2 Chronicles borrow from 1–2 Kings, but no other document dated anywhere near the time of the composition of 1–2 Kings mentions the prophet. Additional comments about Elijah only begin appearing in the books of Malachi and Ecclesiasticus (Sirach), composed centuries after the final redaction of 1–2 Kings. It must be noted, however, that there is no basis for rejecting the possibility that the biblical stories of the fiery prophet reflect a remarkable life.

In *The Elijah Legends and Jehu's Coup*, Marsha White advances a second explanation for the distinctiveness of the prophet that would seem to undermine belief that 1–2 Kings describes the life of a man who once lived. Compiling scriptural passages that comment on Jehu (the king whose actions are described in later pages of 2 Kings and 1–2 Chronicles, not the earlier-mentioned prophet), Moses, Elihu, and David's prophet Nathan, White shows how comments about Elijah in the books of Kings parallel passages describing these other figures. She believes that most of the 1–2 Kings description of Elijah was created by deliberately imitating earlier traditions having to do with the four figures, "leaving the Elijah of the drought legend as the only reliable historical core" (White, 1). As White sees it, many of the Tishbite's most memorable moments in 1–2 Kings are modeled on earlier Scripture. Frequent allusion to the Moses narratives in the 1–2 Kings passages "is best explained as an attempt to identify Elijah as the prophet of his time…. To the extent that the Elijah of [biblical] legends is a second Moses, he is not the historical Elijah but a recreation of his predecessor, on whom he is modeled" (White, 11). White's documentary study encourages the conclusion that the prophet's authors (the individuals responsible for the accounts of Elijah that can be read now in 1–2 Kings) fabricated a description of a highly memorable figure from segments of prophetic tradition and from details of other historical lives.

It must be wondered, however, what is achieved by seeing the Elijah of 1–2 Kings as a patchwork of other texts, not as the literary record of an original individual. White's comparative method of study encourages the view that sacred history (the received text of the Bible) more relates to itself and comments on itself than it does on the lives of those it describes. Her careful matching of older and later segments of it leads her to believe that the Elijah of the drought legend is the only reliable historical core of all that is said about the prophet. However, groups that use oral transmission to keep their traditions alive—and this would include the oldest tellers of Elijah's tales—retain their memories in packets of speech. Bards and storytellers are able to remember and retell traditional stories by stringing together stylized story units for listeners. The stylization serves as a memory prompt as well as a part of the story. The Hebrew Bible displays many vestiges of oral traditions, and it is reasonable to believe that Elijah's life was rendered into writing from oral memory. That the narrative of Elijah in 1–2 Kings often obviously echoes earlier traditions of Moses or Jehu does not tell us how to account for the memory packets by which the historical man was memorialized. We can neither reconstruct (on our own present-day terms) nor deny the original existence of the man whom the Moses-like or Elihu-like passages describe.

The following offers a third explanation of why Elijah is such a powerful figure in 1–2 Kings. Like the first explanation, it is based on the premise that the Elijah narrative describes the lives of people, although admittedly in ancient ways. Elijah, Ahab, Jezebel, and the northern Israelites are all presumed to have lived. Its most important premise, however, is that the Elijah story is written to show God's impact on human lives. Regardless of which books one consults, the Bible always argues that God influences human beings. The explanation that follows plumbs the literary fact that all of Elijah's words and actions in 1–2 Kings dovetail with the words and actions of his Lord. In the books of the Kings, the prophet's personality demonstrates certain aspects of the one he served. Elijah is vivid because he is a sign of God to his people and to his readers.

The profile of God in 1–2 Kings is not he whose love endures forever or he who is sought but not found. Elijah's God is the God of Psalm 104, "who looks on the earth and it trembles, / who touches the mountains and they smoke." All of the prophet's words and actions and all of the actions and words of his God in 1–2 Kings, and for that matter, in the rest of the Hebrew Bible and the New Testament, demonstrate that no human or putatively divine power prevails against the Maker of the cosmos, who once again reclaims his own. "Would you invoke Baal and forsake the Most Gracious Creator?" asks Elijah in the Koran. "Allah is your Lord, and the Lord of your forefathers" (Surah 37:125). In the Elijah passages of 1–2 Kings, the outcome of each encounter demonstrates that this is true.

"Eli-jah," the prophet's name, asserts "My God is Yah[weh]." His actions mime those of his powerful Lord and at times merge with them, encouraging the reader to think of parallels and completions: as Elijah acts on earth, so God acts in heaven; as God acts in heaven, so his prophet does on earth. Deity and messenger cooperate in bringing on a drought and ending it. As God triumphs over Baal, so his servant triumphs over the Baalite prophets, King Ahab, and Queen Jezebel. The fact that Elijah's charisma symbolizes his Lord's manifest power has not been noted in scholarly literature. Other prophets in Scripture represent features of the divine nature as well. Hosea's marriage to a prostitute acts out God's faithful desire for his people in spite of their rejection of him, for example. In 1–2 Kings, Elijah's reckless, powerful, and solitary actions always point to specific facets of the God that the Hebrew Bible praises. The prophet's personality in his story especially represents God's peerless power, wielded to seize the heart of his people. Elijah's vivid actions and words in 1–2 Kings point to God's insistence on reclaiming those he chooses to be his followers. As above, so below. As Elijah acts, so does God act. When God acts, his prophet responds in the sphere of human life, in complementary or duplicate actions. Personal action that demonstrates something greater than itself is a key to understanding Elijah not only in 1–2 Kings but also in his legendary relations with different groups throughout the centuries that later chapters of this book will explore.

The thought that the distinctive scriptural "personality" of Elijah may lead readers to a particular perception of the nature of God provokes a second one. Given that Israelite prophets were mediators, serving, but also symbolizing, both God and their people, it must be asked, what if Elijah's vivid scriptural personality matched not only his God but also the lives of Israelites in the ninth century B.C.E. (and possibly also the sixth, in which the biblical stories were redacted and during which exiled Israelites were pondering the reasons for the loss of their kingdom)? Is it possible that in 1–2 Kings the zealous and at times violent prophet embodies not only ancient perceptions of God but also perceptions of a people?

This on the surface would not seem possible. Passages in 1–2 Kings often describe a Lord and people at odds. How could the Tishbite, who always is shown to have been fiercely Yahwist, symbolize his people as well as his God in Scripture? Here are several thoughts. First, despite their differences, in 1–2 Kings Elijah's expressions of personality (his characteristic words and actions) often complete contact between his people and their God. Second, the prophet's swift, vigorous movements resemble the gestures of the other two parties. For example, his massacre of Baalite prophets was a type of cleansing that Scripture says that God and the Israelites had both used at other times. Third, the three parties sometimes act out of common understanding. The books of Kings record that Yahweh, Elijah, and the northern Israelites all knew that the issue at stake among them was fidelity and that something had to be done about it. "How long will you go limping with two different opinions?" the prophet badgered the populace assembled at Mt. Carmel. "If Yahweh is God, follow him; but if Baal, then follow him" (1 Kings 18:21). Elijah's challenge was the meeting point where the issue of fidelity between the other two parties would be resolved.

Regardless of whether the words recorded in 1–2 Kings describe the vivid life of a man of God or describe other biblical figures, Elijah's entire life in 1–2 Kings acts out the "personalities" of his Lord and people. Publicly and privately, symbolically and interpersonally, Elijah in 1–2 Kings participates in a drama that demonstrates recapture of heart. Yahweh, the faithful possessor, powerfully insists that his prophet

and people return to him. Most important to the discussion that follows, the Tishbite's biblical story dramatizes the peerless power of
his God, the fierce, unruly character of his people, and God's impact
on their crisis of faith. In 1–2 Kings, Elijah moves in an intricate
double pairing. Those who kept other legends of him alive throughout the centuries also often continued to think of him in a double
relationship, symbolizing God and the people that God claimed all
the while he delivered his messages from above.

Elijah and His People

Elijah's people need further exploration. Who were they in Scripture, and why does it matter to the present book, which principally
will be concerned with other peoples in other times and places, to see
what Scripture says about his relation with them? The Koran and the
Hebrew Bible say that the Tishbite was sent to call followers away
from Baalite worship. Islamic scripture, which urges all humans to
cleave to Allah alone, comments on Elijah's people to generalize about
all human beings. Surah 2:37 connects Elijah's northern Israelite
"people" to Judgment Day, when all the inhabitants of the earth will
stand before Allah. Those who refused Elijah's message in ancient
Israel repeated what had happened before in history and would happen again. Israelites who worshiped Baal exemplify in the Koran the
many humans before and after them who turn away from the truth and
who will be punished for their unbelief at the end of time.

Although it, like the Koran, affirms that God rules all peoples, the
Hebrew Bible often explicitly preoccupies itself with the Hebrews
who entered into covenant with God at Mt. Sinai, followed by their
Israelite descendants. It often identifies God in ways familiar to that
group. In the 1–2 Kings passages Elijah preoccupies himself with the
people existing in northern Israel who were bound by Yahweh's local
demands. The whole of the book of 1 Kings makes this local attention
to theIsraelites in covenant with Yahweh clear. It relates that Elijah

was called because apostasy had compounded within the remnant of the kingdom created to be a dwelling place of God. According to the Bible, the Israelite King Solomon's worship of regional gods a century earlier had repeated itself in the actions of nearly all the northern Israelite kings before Ahab came to power. The public honor that Ahab gave to Canaanite gods was the worst Israelite offense against God yet in a chain of religious errors in Israel's history.

Preparing for the contest between Baal and Yahweh on the top of Mt. Carmel, Elijah "took twelve stones, according to the number of the tribes of the sons of Jacob, to whom the word of Yahweh came, saying 'Israel shall be your name'; and with the stones he built an altar in the name of Yahweh" (1 Kings 18:31–32a), then called on his Lord by the name "God of Abraham, Isaac, and Israel." The divine fire that fell on Elijah's sacrifice was a dramatic public demonstration of God's power meant to abort a train of Israelite apostasies. Elijah's slaughter of his prophetic competitors—also in the eyesight of all—was part of the demonstration. Yahweh and Elijah were working together to stop a local disaster in relationship with the divine. Shock tactics on Mt. Carmel were needed because sin was deeply embedded in a people under a particular covenant with God to be holy. No matter what additional meaning the passages offer later readers, 1–2 Kings originally described a particular ancient group with its own history and its own problem with the divine.

Scripture declares that the northern kingdom was in spiritual decline during Elijah's lifetime. Extrabiblical records of battles and trade relationships seem to confirm this. The kingdom suffered internal and external difficulties. When David's kingdom split into unequal halves upon the death of Solomon in 922/924 B.C.E. (some fifty years before Elijah began to prophesy), tiny northern Israel, which never attained an area of 150 square miles, embarked on a tangled history of efforts to survive among neighboring groups that worshiped different gods. Sometimes more peaceable external relations were established by marriage, as happened when Ahab united with Jezebel, princess of

Tyre. At other times the northern kingdom survived by paying tribute or through military coalitions. Its relationships with Syria, Edom, Ammon, and Phoenicia changed repeatedly after Solomon died. Northern Israel also sustained a string of bloody internal coups, as different leaders fought to establish themselves in the vacuum left by rejection of Davidic rule. Baasha was murdered by Zimri, who in turn was deposed by Omri, Ahab's father. Scripture and other documentary sources indicate that by Elijah's time, the kingdom was far removed from the ideal political state promoted by the Bible, in which all Israelite relationships depended on allegiance to God.

Religious sin was embedded in the north. Details gathered from major and minor prophetic books, from biblical psalms, and from the historical books of the Bible suggest that Canaanite fertility practices such as temple prostitution and child immolation were being carried out and that coworship of Yahweh alongside gods such as Baal, lord of storms, or Asherah, his consort, occurred. The writer of 2 Kings 17 listed the sins considered directly responsible for the Assyrian destruction of northern Israel a century and a half after Elijah's lifetime:

> In the ninth year of Hoshea the king of Assyria captured Samaria, and he carried the Israelites away to Assyria.... And this was so, because the people of Israel had sinned against Yahweh their God.... [They] had feared other gods and walked in the customs of the nations whom Yahweh drove out before the people of Israel.... And [they] did secretly against Yahweh their God things that were not right. They built for themselves high places at all their towns...; they set up for themselves pillars and Asherim.... They went after false idols, and became false, and they followed the nations that were round about them.... And they burned their sons and their daughters as offerings, and used divination and sorcery, and sold themselves to do evil in the sight of Yahweh, provoking him to anger. Therefore Yahweh was very angry with Israel, and removed them out of his sight. (17:6–18)

Applying present-day anthropological thinking about prophecy to Elijah's stories in 1–2 Kings, Robert Wilson concludes from King

Ahab and Queen Jezebel's pattern of behavior in Scripture that Baal worship was central and Yahweh worship was peripheral in the northern kingdom during the period in which Elijah began to prophesy.

Moral practices necessary for covenantal purity also seem to have broken down in the kingdom. The Book of Amos records that on the eve of the Assyrian invasion, the Israelites had allowed their courts to be corrupted, and profit was being gained by cheating the poor. Given that Scripture tends to record collective virtues and vices in descriptions of its leaders, Ahab's sin of marrying outside the Israelite tribal system perhaps points to that habit among his subjects. As the Bible reports it, his foreign queen confirmed the worst fears of the disruptions that could be produced by marrying outside the covenant group. In Elijah's story, Jezebel is sly, violently intent on requiring worship of Baal (imported from her native Tyre), and scornful of her husband's obligations to his people.

Simply named "the people," northern Israel is characterized in 1–2 Kings in ways reminiscent of the Exodus narrative, where "the people," who then were constituted by the Egyptian-born descendants of the sons of Jacob and their households, with a seemingly collective will wandered in the desert, complained of thirst, feared for their lives, and sometimes trusted in Yahweh. There are no tales of stragglers or subgroups in either the Exodus or the Elijan narratives. Both parts of the Hebrew Bible mean to treat Yahweh's followers as a whole. In 1–2 Kings the few individuals other than Elijah who are given names, such as Obadiah the majordomo or the widow of Zarephath, are meant to contrast with "the people" that Yahweh wanted to reclaim. As in Exodus, in 1–2 Kings "the people" gathered to witness God's power. Elijah branded them all with the sin of mixing Baal worship with worship of Yahweh. As their ancestors did in the Exodus narrative, the assembled northern Israelites collectively humbled themselves, speaking with one voice. When the fire of Yahweh consumed Elijah's offering, the people "fell on their faces; and they said, 'Yahweh, he is God; Yahweh he is God'" (1 Kings 18:39) just as their covenantal forebears said with one voice at Mt. Sinai, "All that Yahweh has spoken we will do, and we will be obedient" (Exod. 24:7).

These early Israelites were not like later readers of this book. Their ancient lifestyle, education, language, geography, political affiliation, and religion differed. Even infidelity, the core problem that the biblical Elijah forced northern Israelites to confront, cannot be easily translated to later repudiations of belief or modern waverings in faith. Elijah's people carried out its relationship to God, whom it especially knew as Yahweh the warrior and provider, in a perilously small kingdom located in a part of the world that needed rains and crops if its inhabitants were to survive. Loyalty to whatever was a source of life was necessary for survival in that region and time. The problem of finding and adhering to the source of life was more than a philosophical or a personal dilemma for northern Israelites; a misstep in fidelity cut away their means for life—in all its dimensions—in a very concrete way.

As a result, Yahweh's demands that the northern Israelites cling to his material support were steeper than what can be easily imagined now, and the way he enforced his will and communicated those demands have an ancient logic that fits their original situation but doesn't fit the lives of later readers. Societies and circumstances change. Cultural dissonances between the prophet's times and the present are great enough that readers must decide how, or even whether Elijah's story can be meaningful to their lives. If they are to be affected by the details of Elijah's life recorded in Scripture, present-day readers must notice how they are similar to and different from his people, or for that matter, similar to or different from the prophet himself. The Elijah of 1–2 Kings is not easily reconciled to the twentieth century. The final sections of this discussion will begin to suggest why this is so.

Elijah and His God

As will be seen, Muslim, Jewish, and Christian storytellers eventually substituted other groups for the people Elijah assembled on Mt.

Carmel. As they did this, they omitted some details of ancient Israelite life that matter in 1–2 Kings. The substitution of one people for
another was accomplished through shifts in explaining Elijah's relationship with God. His detachment from ordinary contact with the
people that he served and his special adherence to God attracted later
groups with similar detachments and bonds. Members of Christian
religious orders, Islamic Sufis, Jewish Kabbalists, and messianic and
apocalyptic groups in the three religions adopted the solitary prophet
as a model for their own lives. In time, these groups, as well as the
faithful in general, began to tell stories in which they themselves—or
people like them—replaced the northern Israelites. Elijah's relation
with God partially shifted in the later stories as well, but the ancient
issue, adherence to God alone, continued to animate later stories. It is
the core preoccupation of all of Elijah's legends.

The Kings passages suggest that the prophet spent much of his
time away from human contact. No one seems to have been able to
keep track of the Tishbite's whereabouts except his God. Only his
Lord could influence his coming and going. Several times servants of
the king were startled by his sudden appearance, it seems, out of nowhere (1 Kings 18:7–12; 2 Kings 1:6–8). While prophetic fraternities
of the time lived near shrines, God sent Elijah to the desert of the
Transjordan (1 Kings 17:2–4) and then sent him to a neighboring
country to stay with a widow, increasing the prophet's separation from
Israel for awhile (17:8–9). After the conflagration on Mt. Carmel,
Elijah fled deep into the desert south of Beersheba and then was divinely compelled to go even farther into it. He finally lodged in a
cave at Mt. Horeb, the sacred mountain that the Hebrews were constrained from touching, lest God's power break out against them (1
Kings 19 and Exodus 19:24). The prophet's physical separation from
others was at its maximum in the Mt. Horeb episode but continues to
be mentioned in later passages. Second Kings 1 remarks that Elijah
was found sitting on the top of a hill, apparently alone (1:9; see also 1
Kings 21:18). (Elisha, who inherited his prophetic spirit, was also
found on a mountaintop in 2 Kings 4:27).

Elijah was a solitary figure. The Bible usually mentions the ancestors or occupation of prophets before their calling. Although later legends supplied him a family history, he is simply "Elijah the Tishbite, of Tishbe in Gilead" in 1 Kings. His story says that he provided help to people around him—the widow, Obadiah the majordomo, and the assembled northern Israelites received the benefit of his efforts—but he received no aid from human beings. Even the food the widow gave him was provided by God. He operated alone until Elisha, his prophetic inheritor, became his disciple toward the end of his career.

In the end, even Elisha was left behind. Second Kings 2 says that the disciple and other prophets in the region were aware that the elder prophet's earthly existence was about to end. As Elijah moved from shrine to shrine, zigzagging toward the Jordan, Elisha went too, refusing his demands to leave him alone. The prophet repeatedly tried to separate himself from his disciple, but his "son" clung to him, insisting, "I will not leave you." At Jericho, a large number of prophets joined them, although they "stood at some distance" (2 Kings 2:7). Prophetic father and son crossed the Jordan (which, like the River Styx in classical mythology, separated life from afterlife in the prophet's story), and then Elijah was bodily taken away even from Elisha by a chariot of fire. His ascension severed his contact with other human beings (at least for a time, later legends say). There could be no more powerful demonstration of Elijah's adherence to God alone than the miracle that ended his story in 2 Kings.

As remarked earlier, Elijah's striking actions and separations from other people invite readers to think about the absolute autonomy of his God. Yahweh has no competitor in the story. Elijah's solitude echoes the unparalleled nature of his Lord. While Baal was unable to control the rains, did not manifest himself, and had nothing to say to his devotees, Yahweh spectacularly moved both the natural and supernatural realms, spoke through his prophet, and most certainly manifested his will. A fainter but important earthly sign of the supernatural drama being acted "above his head," Elijah triumphed over all his opposition. He destroyed hundreds of prophets, Ahab was slain in battle, and Jezebel the Baalite died in public shame. The prophet's ability to act without human aid and his triumphs over human opposition urge the reader to think about God's independent greatness.

The theme of detachment from all but God surfaces in several parts of the story. Just as Ezekiel's pantomime demonstrated to onlookers what they would do in the future, Elijah's independence from other human beings enacts the lengths to which the northern Israelites were to go in clinging to God alone. In addition to being a sign of his solitary Lord, Elijah's solitary dependence also reminded the Israelites of an old lesson, passed down to them from their Hebrew ancestors, that they were to be "a people holy to Yahweh"—that is, set aside from others—to serve and love God (Deut. 7:6 and 14:1–2). Holiness was perfectly realized in God alone, but nevertheless God had called the Israelites to strive for holiness in all they did. Elijah's solitude pointed to the integrated, exclusive state that could not be achieved without commitment to God alone.

His detachment is also connected to his public drive to purge Israel of apostasy. Ancient Middle-Eastern relationships were founded on an ideal of exclusive commitment. One could not serve two masters. Loyalty was not to be divided. Ancient extrabiblical treaty documents show that overlords demanded strict fidelity from their vassals in exchange for their protection. Preferring oneself (in any modern, individualist way) over the lord to whom one had pledged loyalty also damaged the ancient bond. The Bible describes the terms that Yahweh set for his followers in a loyalty language whose dynamic was well known to ancient Israelites. Northern Israelites knew, because their ancestors had long known, the first commandment of the treaty with which God cemented his relationship with the Israelites at Horeb. Like an overlord, the Creator laid exclusive claim to the fidelity of those who agreed to be his followers: "I am Yahweh your God, who brought you out of the land of Egypt, out of the house of bondage. You shall have no other gods before me.... I Yahweh your God am a jealous God" (Exod. 20:2–3, 5). Northern Israelite worship of Baal scandalously spurned a relationship that depended on single-minded fidelity.

The Bible suggests that stress on a bond between two parties could be relieved in two ways. Families and friends used separation to safeguard relationship with each other whenever potential conflict arose. Abraham and his kinsman Lot separated from each other to avoid family discord over grazing land, for example. Assignment of territory to each of the Israelite tribes also maintained loyalty bonds through dispersal. The second method of safeguarding loyalty was to destroy whatever polluted it. Present-day readers are disturbed by biblical accounts of God and his followers slaughtering other groups, but the other groups and the gods they worshiped did the same. In the purging, the issues were human-to-human loyalty bonds and worship of the tribal god. The Bible presents the case of Canaanites and Amorites who worshiped other deities. From an Israelite point of view, these people needed to be scoured from Yahweh's land. This, of course, was the same concern being addressed at the foot of Mt. Horeb when the Levites massacred anyone among the Hebrews who did not worship Yahweh alone.

These cultural facts clarify some details of Elijah's relation with his God in 1–2 Kings. His personal distance from other people exemplifies the first method of ensuring loyalty: by means of his psychic and physical seclusion from others, he ensured his own loyalty bond with God. His bloody purge of Baalite prophets was the second method of ensuring fidelity. It was a cleansing—literally, a bloodbath—meant to empty the spirit of his countrymen of what had crept in to weaken and divide it. As Baalite prophets fell under his sword, he was decimating the Baalite cult in northern Israel. As the Levites purged the Hebrew camp of worshipers of the golden calf, so Elijah purged northern Israel from within. Thus in many ways his story in 1–2 Kings showed ancient readers that they should separate themselves from all but God. The prophet's isolation was a sign that showed them that they should do this.

Later storytellers change or omit some of these details. They strip the old meanings from Elijah's detachments and fill them with new meanings. The prophet's bloody assassination of his God's competitors, so theologically and culturally necessary to his tale in the Bible, is infrequently mentioned in later legends. It is perhaps not a surprise that Christians in particular omit this part of the biblical story in their legends of Elijah. They lift his desert sojourn by the Wadi Cherith and his encounter with God at Horeb out of the story of God's recapture of an ancient people. When they do this, the issue of God's success in repossessing the hearts of the northern Israelites disappears in later tellings, and the prophet's desert experiences no longer symbolize anything about his nation. Among Christians, Elijah's encounters with God become events in a process of personal salvation. It is certainly true that no later groups ever adopt Elijah's biblical tale without changing it.

Knowing that to be the case, it is appropriate to pause to see what relation Elijah has with his Lord in the oldest tales. What, originally, was the nature of that bond between the two? Surah 6:85 of the Koran describes Elijah and God in a reciprocal relationship: "Zacharias, John, Jesus and Elias (all were upright men); and Ishmael, Elisha, Jonah and Lot. All these we exalted above Our creatures…we chose them and guided them to a straight path…. On those men we bestowed the scriptures' wisdom and prophethood." As the Koran presents it, the reciprocity between Allah and men like Elijah was divine recompense for a life of righteousness. The considerably longer 1–2 Kings text also highlights the reciprocity between Yahweh and Elijah.

Elijah is first caught in 1 Kings saying something that shows that he expected that his Lord would respond to him. He boldly said to Ahab's face: "I have not troubled Israel; but you have…because you have forsaken the commandments of Yahweh" (1 Kings 18:18). The prophet assembled the people, then publicly challenged his God: "O Yahweh, God of Abraham, Isaac, and Israel, let it be known this day that thou art God in Israel, and that I am thy servant, and that I have done all these things at thy word. Answer me, O Yahweh, answer me, that this people may know that thou, O Yahweh, art God, and that thou hast turned their hearts back" (18:36–37). "Let it be known this day that thou art God in Israel, and that I am thy servant." Uttering these words, Elijah put his total reliance on what God would do next. False prophets, that is, ones whose words did not come true, were to be stoned. If his God did not respond to his daring demand, Elijah would not survive. Scripture records that the response was instantaneous. Fire immediately came down from heaven, confirming indeed that God was God in Israel and that Elijah was his servant. God reciprocated his prophet.

Elijah's subsequent massacre of the Baalite prophets—which Wilson points out was such an assault on the national status quo that Ahab and Jezebel had to counteract it if they were to maintain their power—brought such a furious attempt to destroy him that he fled the kingdom. What happened thereafter suggests many things about his relation with God. Elijah's faith seems to have collapsed as he was pushed into physical separation from his people, first by his fear and then by his own God. His crisis recalls those of other scriptural prophets who suffered because of their fidelity to their mission. Before Jeremiah began to prophesy to the people, his Lord promised him, "Be not afraid of them, for I am with you to deliver you" (Jer. 1:8). The Judean prophet was greatly disillusioned when the prophecies he delivered caused him to be beaten and put in stocks: "O Yahweh, thou hast deceived me, and I was deceived; thou art stronger than I, and thou hast prevailed. I have become a laughingstock all the day; every one mocks me" (20:7). Pursued for his violent challenge to the king and queen, Elijah similarly told his Lord: "It is enough; now, O Yahweh, take away my life; for I am no better than my fathers" (1 Kings 19:4).

The prophet retreated, but his Lord pushed him toward action and reintegration. When he asked to die, Yahweh responded with the provision of food and a command to eat in order to be strengthened. When he lost heart—saying the "people of Israel have forsaken thy covenant, thrown down thy altars, and slain thy prophets with the sword; and I, even I only, am left; and they seek my life" (19:10 and 19:14)—God responded in 1 Kings with two commands: Elijah was to stand up, resuming the physical position of manhood and service, and to return to northern Israel, where he was to abort Ahab's rule by anointing new leaders for the region. God's counterpoint to Elijah's gestures of collapse did not accommodate the prophet's human needs for rest and reassurance, but they did make up for the prophet's human weakness.

Elijah's fear is visible in his physical gestures of fleeing, lying down, and retreating into a cave. Nevertheless, his bond with God held firm. Despite his timorousness, when God gave him commands, he obeyed them as quickly as his Lord had complied with the prophet's demands on Mt. Carmel, thus showing, as Scripture says that Jeremiah also eventually showed, that even as they suffered personally, those divinely called were bound to serve God. There was no other possibility for Elijah—or for his nation—in the story. In both cases, Yahweh, Lord of Creation, reclaimed those with whom he was in relationship. In both cases he obliged a response when his human followers failed him. Embedded in a story of God, Elijah's collapse of faith symbolizes his people's collapse. The prophet's obedience despite his objection echoes and foretells theirs.

The Bible and the Koran teach that God is beyond human understanding, not to be seen directly nor reduced to any particular manifestation. Nevertheless, Scripture occasionally describes moments in which a solitary individual has a close encounter with God. The Horeb (Sinai) and Temple theophanies, events witnessed by great assemblies, are important exceptions to this pattern. More often individuals are called through unusual, private revelations. Abraham's Egyptian slave Hagar was in the wilderness when she was told by Yahweh that she would be the mother of generations blessed by God (Gen. 16:7–14). Jacob, the future father of twelve tribes, wrestled alone with "a man" that he came to understand was "God face to face" (Gen. 32:30). Moses, the greatest of the prophets in the Hebrew Bible, encountered

God most intimately while alone on Mt. Sinai. Refreshed by the angel, Elijah had pressed on into the southern desert toward the solitary place where God would meet him.

As White and others have shown, Elijah's encounter recalls other biblical theophanies. Parallels with Moses' story are intended to be noticed. Elijah travels forty days, which reminds readers of the Hebrews' forty years of wandering under Moses' leadership, to Mt. Horeb, the earlier place of Hebrew contact with God, and finds a cave in which to lodge, which recalls the cleft from which Moses witnessed his Lord's passing. From that point forward, however, Yahweh's dealings with Elijah reverse the expectations of those familiar with earlier stories in sacred history. While Moses was required to hide and watch as God passed by, 1 Kings says that Yahweh required Elijah to come out of the cave and catechized him throughout the theophany.

His God began by asking him why he was there, a startling question since Elijah was so obviously at the mount because his God had obliged him to be there. Ignoring the obvious, Elijah responded according to his personal concerns: he was on Mt. Horeb because he was hiding for his life. Far from offering the prophet the bodily protection he sought, God demanded that the prophet come out of his cave to "stand upon the mount before Yahweh" to see his passing, which produced cyclonic winds, an earthquake, fire, and finally a "still, small voice," also translated as a "sound of thin silence." The sound reversed another expectation, being physically insignificant compared to other manifestations of God that the Bible records: the burning bush, the thunder on Mt. Horeb that the assembled Israelites heard, a pillar of fire, the glory that so powerfully filled the Jerusalem Temple that no one could enter it, or for that matter, the winds and earthquake that Elijah had just experienced. Nevertheless, the small sound revealed God most truly to the prophet, who the Bible says instinctively covered his face when he heard it, a universal response to sudden contact with power or knowledge.

It is consistent with the Bible's emphasis that God can never be known completely, that information about what happened between

Elijah and God is not fully given in the passage. The description of what happened at the mouth of the cave allows readers to see that the prophet was given insight by the theophany but little more. After the sound—or perhaps during it—1 Kings relates that Yahweh repeated his previous question: What was Elijah doing there? and Elijah also repeated his earlier answer: he was where he was because he had fled for his life. Lost to readers is the connection that the Tishbite drew between the theophanic sound and the insistent question: Why are you here? The effect of the epiphany is not hidden from readers, however. As such brushes with God are reported to have done for Moses, Job, and Mary, Elijah was moved to act on behalf of the divine. The Gospel of Luke says that Gabriel's message to Mary moved her to praise God and to prophesy. On seeing the burning bush and hearing God's name, Moses plunged into his mission to save the Hebrews from Pharaoh. After hearing the odd little sound and speaking with his Lord, Elijah zealously resumed prophetic service. It appears that the theophany—Elijah's perception of the sound—was a pivot in his relation with God.

Although Elijah was especially free of personal ties with humans in 1–2 Kings, he was not free of God. His life rotated around his bond. His Lord moved him about like a pawn: he was sent to live by a dried-up wadi, was sent away to another country, and then was sent to speak to King Ahab. He later was sent into the Judean desert and obliged to return to the north. Ahab's servant Obadiah believed that the Tishbite could be bodily transported anywhere by God's will, and when Elijah was taken to heaven by a supernatural chariot (something observable only to readers and Elisha), the prophets standing nearby thought that perhaps "the Spirit of Yahweh" had moved him to a mountaintop or valley. Even when Elijah lost heart, his Lord's commands produced his immediate obedience. His intense connection with the divine will was the center of his being in 1–2 Kings. All of his actions sprang from that connection. People in his story reacted to God's will when they reacted to him. The core of the prophet's identity, his bond with God's will, is always described in actions, in relating, in which divine and human parties were both agents.

What is most interesting about Elijah is that he was far from being a puppet dancing to the fingers of a puppeteer, despite the fact that he was, indeed, moved by God's will. His life originated in the will of his Lord, but it was characteristically expressed in a mutual relationship. This must be clearly said: While elsewhere in the Bible humans are reported in complementary relations with God—they are clay and he is the potter; they are limited and he is limitless—Elijah's tale explores the possibility that the Creator and a human being may interact mutually in counterbalances, exchanges, and shared action. In 1–2 Kings, Elijah and his God made demands on and responded to each other. The nearly nonexistent lag time between divine demand and human response, or human call and divine response, underscores the reciprocity.

It is very noteworthy that in 1–2 Kings, Elijah's Lord seemed so bonded on his servant, so willing to respond to the prophet's desires. There is really no equivalent to this in the Hebrew Bible. The Song of Solomon needs to be read allegorically before it can be understood as an expression of mutual love between God and his people. Only certain of Jesus' speeches in the New Testament suggest a reciprocal relation between Father and Son. In the books of Kings, Yahweh responded immediately to Elijah's demand on the top of Mt. Carmel. Grammatical symmetries in the text ask readers to believe that the divine responses matched the human demands. In 1 Kings 17:21–22, Elijah prayed "O Yahweh my God let this child's soul come into him again. And Yahweh hearkened to the voice of Elijah; and the soul of the child came into him again, and he revived." In 2 Kings 1:9–10, when messengers of Ahab's successors approached him saying "O man of God, the king says, 'Come down.'" Elijah answered, "'If I am a man of God, let fire come down from heaven and consume you and your fifty,'" after which "fire came down from heaven, and consumed him and his fifty." Although the prophet was swept up in the divine will, God and Elijah seem to have been in a thunderous dance with each other, changing leads moment by moment.

God is indeed the Lord of Creation in 1–2 Kings. He had as much power over his creature Elijah—body, heart, mind, and soul—as he did over the rains or fire. The God whom Elijah knew also pursued the heart of his Israelite people relentlessly, yet for whatever reason—perhaps Elijah's will and Yahweh's were truly one—1–2 Kings say that Yahweh bent, at times, to the will of his human servant. Elijah's courageous demands of his Lord make it clear that something other than the familiar difference in power between lord and servant is being modeled in the 1–2 Kings story. The symmetry, the passing back and forth of call and response between Elijah and Yahweh, models reciprocity and mutuality between Creator and creature, not the complementarity that one expects on reading other passages of the Bible. More will be said later concerning this unusual feature of the prophet's biblical relation with God.

Elijah's Scriptural Challenges

In the next chapter, Elijah's "personality," his characteristic words, actions, and relations with God and his peoples, will be traced in his developing traditions. New messianic stories about him developed before what came to be the Hebrew canon was complete. Among Muslims, the prophet became a witness to advanced mystical knowledge received by human beings and a participant in the eschaton. Among Jews, he became a scholar, a surprising helper, an angel, a divine representative at circumcisions, and the forerunner to the Messiah. He acts in this latter profile in the New Testament as well. Among some Christians, he became a praiseworthy hermit. Future chapters will particularly inquire into this last identity and will watch his personality unfold even further as one of his later "peoples," members of the Carmelite Order, took him as their patron during their transition from the slopes of Mt. Carmel in Palestine to urban life in medieval Europe. Before these inquiries into Elijah's expanding traditions are undertaken, the balance of this chapter will remark on several differences between his oldest story and the life of many readers in the present. The exotic features of any ancient work always provoke thought.

Present-day readers may pause to think about the dramatic biblical demonstrations of Elijah's attachment to God's will, which was so great in the story that Obadiah worried that the prophet would be physically swept away. John Craghan advises modern Christian pastors, "The manner of the prophetic minister is, first and foremost, to let the Word saturate his/her very being" (Craghan, 95). Israelite prophets did not have this option, for they did not choose to give themselves to God's service. Michael Fishbane remarks that ancient prophets' lives belonged to God because God had seized them: "In the end, therefore, any revolt against one's prophetic destiny, against the divine *davar* (word) infused in one's mouth, was futile" (Fishbane, vol. 1, 67). Elijah must be seen as impelled to do and say what he did since that is what his story often shows.

Conscription by God does not fit a belief prevalent in the West that loyalties can be chosen by the individual, can be parceled out, and can be withdrawn. If they are to compare Elijah's narrated life with their own, present-day readers—especially readers whose private dwellings and financial resources encourage them to think that they can spend their life as they choose—must discover a circumstance in which, like Elijah, they are moved by a power that preempts personal choices. The Tishbite did not choose God or his people for prophetic relation. God chose him. In Elijah's situation, the power that took over his will was not a group of laws or a totalitarian leader. It was the unknowable, unthinkable divine.

Elijah also interacted with God as God's partner. This role in relation to the divine is perhaps especially disturbing. As mentioned, the Bible and religious life modeled on it tend to assign humans a subordinate relation to their Creator. The Christian monastic *Rule of St.*

Benedict, for example, promotes belief that relationship to God resembles the relation a child has with a father. Its first words emphasize docility of will:

> Listen, my son, and with your heart hear the principles
> of your Master. Readily accept and faithfully follow the
> advice of a loving Father, so that through the labor of obe-
> dience you may return to Him from whom you have with-
> drawn because of the laziness of disobedience. My words
> are meant for you, whoever you are, who laying aside your
> own will, take up the all-powerful and righteous arms
> of obedience to fight under the true King, the Lord Jesus
> Christ. (Prologue)

The *Rule of St. Albert* that governs the Carmelite lives that will be of concern throughout the second half of this book begins in similar fashion. Albert of Avogadro's first words address "his beloved sons in Christ, B. and the other hermits under obedience to him" who are called to "live a life of allegiance to Jesus Christ and serve him faithfully with a pure heart and good conscience" (Prologue).[2]

The dominant and subordinate roles for God and human follower are deeply embedded in monotheistic faith life. The dyad of the governing father and obedient son are a preferred metaphor for the hierarchical, complementary relation between God and his people that the Bible generally describes. The metaphoric pairs of lord and servant or husband and wife are used in the Bible (and often in later religious tradition) to reinforce the perception that the ordinary relation between God and his followers is complementary. Humans fit to and are molded to the will of God. The obligation to act with God as a child obeys a father has existed for millennia.

The monastic "child's" obedience of his or her "father" is meant to school the personal will. The paternal-filial model in which

---

2. All quotations from St. Albert's *Rule* are taken from the English translation included in *Albert's Way*, edited by Michael Mulhall.

the spiritual child obeys the fatherly abbess or abbot, or obeys peers as if they were fathers, provides the individual under monastic obedience an opportunity to relearn a child's trust and dependence on God, as these are biblically articulated. This kind of relation, in which the child's actions complement, or fill out, the intentions of a dominant parent, requires that those acting in the role of the father do so with continuous good will and wisdom, since there is no place in the dynamic for the child to obtain relief from injury at the hands of the parent. Benedict was highly aware of this as he wrote the *Rule*. He urged readers to understand that the parent, that is, the abbot or abbess, bears full responsibility for the success of the father-child relationship, in which the child ideally matures by becoming more and more like the parent: "The abbot must always remember what he is and be mindful of his calling; he should know that the greater his trust, the greater his responsibility.... He must prepare himself to account for the souls in his care; for on Judgment Day he will have to account for all his monks' souls, as well as his own, no matter how many" (*Rule of St. Benedict*, chap. 2).

A child's obedience of his or her father is not the relationship of will that Elijah's stories model. Even as he was moved by God's will— and, it should be reiterated, the 1–2 Kings passages make it clear that this was not only true but that his Lord's will was the source of his larger-than-life personality—there was something in the prophet, some certain knowledge of himself in relation to God that he trusted so well, that he could demand great things of his Master. The biblical Elijah differs from the monks modeled by the Benedictine *Rule*. While he was swept up in the divine will and had no ability to avoid it even when he feared for his life, the prophet's extraordinary contacts with God in biblical pages show that, with the exception of his actions in the southern desert before mystical contact with God renewed his will, Elijah leaned into and used the divine will instead of pulling away from it.

Modern readers who explore Elijah's biblical life in their imagination must accomplish a difficult feat in the end. They must imagine their wishes preempted, but more, if they respond to his biblical story, they must imagine themselves not cowed by the tremendous force that sweeps them up. Instead, if they would be like Elijah, they would lean into the power that moves them, calling to it, making demands of it, and sustaining the shock of divine compliance. Elijah's daring demands of his Creator encourage his readers to imagine a spiritual relationship in which initiatives and responses come from both parties. God's seizure of Elijah obliges the prophet's response, but Elijah, too, confidently seizes his God, and God responds.

Another notable feature of Elijah's story in 1–2 Kings is his lack of physical privacy. Surroundings and possessions are the physical workshop in which lives are constructed. People think differently when in different surroundings. Certain possessions, or their lack, can affect relationships. For example, outsiders often question monastic enclosure. Some wonder if monks and nuns hide themselves away from a fearful world or reject other people. St. John of the Cross remarks, however, that "the lowliness of our condition of life" leads us to "think that others are as we are, and we judge the rest as we are, judgment beginning in ourselves and not outside of us" (*The Living Flame of Love*, 4:8). Walls and possessions may be instruments of growth or of defense for anyone.

Regardless of one's motive for protecting one's tranquil space, Elijah's abnormal rootlessness and poverty can be unsettling to those who notice it. In 1–2 Kings he not only lacked an ego that he could call his own in any present-day sense but also lacked the most rudimentary human possessions. Even the destitute construct roofs of scrap lumber or cardboard to cover their heads. In Scripture, Elijah seems to have had neither a home nor a monastic cell nor, apparently, a hovel. He came from somewhere—Tishbe—but apparently had no functioning ties with kin, which is noteworthy, given that family relations governed Israelite society. He often lacked food and water. With the exception of Elisha, he had no companion. Most later legends about Elijah leave him this footloose, although they rarely emphasize his destitution as strongly as the Bible does. One of his storytelling groups, the medieval Carmelites whose Elijah legends will receive comment, in fact created a secluded, stable life for the prophet on the top of Mt. Carmel and gathered disciples around him, but in his biblical anecdotes, he was obliged to set out alone, time and again.

Elijah's lack of a corner to which he could retire challenges the uses of privacy. Members of monastic communities know the sanity that is possible in certain separations from larger society. They are quite aware that in joining a monastic community and way of life, they relinquished more physical possessions than they gained, but they believe that seclusion from one's brothers and sisters and from society at large is a necessary condition for life with God. Vows, monastery walls, cells, and the full monastic habit with its hood can all be used as necessary barriers behind which one may live with God more fully. A passage in the *Rule of St. Albert* imposes the eremitical obligation on each Carmelite brother or sister to "remain in his [or her] cell, or near it, meditating day and night on the law of the Lord and keeping vigil in prayer" (*1287 Rule*, ch. 7). Here, the cell functions to separate from other people, but it also stands as a sign of intimacy with God.

The lack of protective boundaries in Elijah's life in 1–2 Kings should disturb anyone who interprets section 7 of the Carmelite *Rule* to mean that full-hearted life with God is an affair from which other humans must be distanced. While he certainly preached separation from Baal, the prophet is not shown to have had any way to keep his own people or his own God away from him, despite all the solitudes he achieved. Elijah was not a private man. He did not belong to himself. He had no cell to "teach him everything." And he certainly was not God's possession to be kept away from others. God stole his prophets from their Israelite society out of divine concern for it, not for them as individuals, and he stole them only to send them back to their people. Elijah's full pattern of physical movement in 1–2 Kings is not away from other humans but back and forth, at the behest of his God, between solitude—which for him was not a "corner of defense" since it was nowhere in particular but so full of God and God's concerns for his people—and prophetic contact with the Israelites. Unprotected by even a roof over his head, he was obliged to exist in a supremely social spiritual zone between the God who chose him and the people about whom God cared. He apparently owned nothing to buffer himself in that paradoxical position. His unbuffered, homeless, public life directly questions stereotypes of monastic seclusion or, for that matter, of secular privacy.

Elijah's profound poverty asks those who pass much of their life in seclusions—created by lawns, by the workplace, by answering machines, or by the door of a monastic cell—what the separation truly promotes within the home or community. His lack of seclusion also questions the intended use of psychic buffers that humans so nimbly devise. Explanations frequently given for why people own or protect what they do on first examination do not resemble Elijah's lack of everything normal except a relation with the divine. Surface differences between one's own boundaries and the prophet's many biblical destitutions of all but God encourage further thought.

Possibly most strange and challenging to present readers encountering Elijah in 1–2 Kings or the briefer passage in Surah 37 in the Koran is the fact that the true protagonists of these narratives are God and "the people." Striking as their actions are in Scripture, Ahab, Jezebel, and Elijah are secondary characters in the biblical tale of a deity who refused to leave his people alone. Repudiation, hollow worship, fear, self-interested rulers—the Bible reports that nothing stopped Yahweh over the years from seizing, and then seizing again, the whole heart of an entire nation. The long sacred history that contains Elijah's anecdotes in 1–2 Kings is often not a logical tale, as God's repeated disruptions and suspensions of his own covenantal system of benefits and losses show. The scriptural narrative of humanity's relation with God is a moving, occasionally horrifying, sometimes breathtaking tale told in proportions that are very hard to reimagine in modern terms, of a relentless God who claimed an irrevocable bond with a people. Both ancient protagonists are hard to imagine now.

How are present-day readers to imagine in their own terms, not in archaic ones, the God whom Israelites could imagine and describe? Yahweh in 1–2 Kings controls fire, the breath of life, and the weather—all of the cosmos, in other words. If present-day readers are to think of God in the magnitude with which Elijah and the Israelites thought of him in 1–2 Kings, they must think beyond what the Bible says. If they don't do this, the sure present knowledge that other universes exist will make biblical hymns to God's exclusive preoccupation with the earth—'adhamah, inhabited by humans, also 'adham—seem puny; and the consumption of the holocaust on Mt. Carmel before the eyes of the Israelites, a casual bit of fireworks. After all, present-day readers now know that stars explode and that other galaxies exist. They must amplify their view of God's power over visible and invisible worlds if they are to sense the terror that invaded the Israelites when they saw fire falling from the sky on Mt. Carmel.

The present-day mind must also warm, at least, to the complexities of making any analogies between a present society and the northern Israelites of Elijah's oldest tale. There is no simple equation possible between that group and any group now. Now, after centuries in the West in which, among other things, God has been declared dead, declared alive but uninterested, declared to be a male face projected onto the unknown, and declared to be the consciousness that knits together all things, no nation on the face of the earth can be as confident as the Israelite writers of Scripture were that they knew what God was like. Some smaller groups in modern societies may feel secure that they know who God is, but Elijah's story aims to challenge the whole of a nation that had known him collectively in the past and could collectively remember how he was. There is no nation on the face of the earth with that consistent knowledge now, and the world now sees itself as made of many nations. Not only have the potential faces for the One God multiplied for believers, but also his believers themselves have become varied. Belief in the God of the Bible and the Koran has spread far beyond the patch of Canaanite land on which David established his kingdom and far beyond the Middle East. Perception of God has diversified (or statements of perception have). Crucial questions that present-day readers must address if they are to use Elijah's stories in their lives are these: Where is the best current equivalent to Elijah's "people," and how should that "people" relate to the other peoples around it? How much of the ancient Israelite response to Yahweh should the modern Elijan people adopt?

And finally, there is Elijah. Vivid as he is in 1–2 Kings, the prophet slips between our fingers if we try to give him a modern Western psyche or try to pin him down in modern historical ways. We find that if we invest him with a modern inner life, he mirrors us. We cannot then think that we have named the prophet as he was. Nor can his lived existence be ours to grasp. What he is most, in his oldest story, is a mediator between God and his people, a sign of the One he serves, and a surprising invitation to mutual interaction with the divine. For centuries readers have remembered and retold the most dramatic parts of his old story, such as the holocaust on Mt. Carmel or Elijah's ascension into heaven. However, in his oldest tale found in 1–2 Kings, what matters most about Elijah are the results of such powerful experiences, not the spectacular events themselves. These and everything else in that story knit his people to God.

For Further Reading

Bright, John. *A History of Israel.* 3rd ed. Philadelphia: Westminster, 1981.

Fishbane, Michael. "Biblical Prophecy as a Religious Phenomenon." In *Jewish Spirituality from the Bible Through the Middle Ages*, edited by Arthur Green, 62–81. New York: Crossroad, 1988.

Mulhall, Michael, O. Carm., ed. *Albert's Way: The First North American Congress on the Carmelite Rule.* Rome: Institutum Carmelitanum; Barrington, Ill.: Province of the Most Pure Heart of Mary, 1989. See especially the Carmelite *Rule* and Bruno Secondin, "What is the Heart of the Rule?" on pp. 93–132.

The Rule of St. Benedict. Translated by A. C. Meisel and M. L. del Mastro. New York: Image, 1975.

Wilson, Robert R. *Prophecy and Society in Ancient Israel.* Philadelphia: Fortress, 1980.

Chapter 2
The Prophet in Later Legends

Most people learned about Amelia Erhart and Huck Finn by hearing stories of their deeds. Newspaper reports gave the world the tale of Amelia Erhart's adventures. Huck Finn, a fictional character, became known through Mark Twain's novel. The aviatrix and the adventuresome boy are tied to their original stories. This is often the way with figures who claim the public imagination. Napoleon Bonaparte, to take another historical example, and Paul Bunyan, to take another fictional one, are remembered in terms of certain events. On the other hand, there are public figures who are not so tied to specific happenings. A small group of famous women and men are remembered for what they did in the stories told about them, but they also seem able to inhabit new tales as well. Something in this second group of figures inspires invention.

Jesus of Nazareth is considerably more than a story character to Christians, but in terms of his stories, he is just this kind of attractive, generative figure. People often first learn about Jesus by reading one of the New Testament Gospels or perhaps by hearing a story of him composed from Gospel details. These oldest written stories of Jesus matter a lot to Christians, whose relationship with God hinges on what the Gospels say. They believe that they must imitate their Savior's actions and attitudes as the Gospels describe them. Christians have also told countless new stories of Jesus, in which features of the Gospels are included and in which they themselves have often figured. Jesus sometimes says or does something new in these later stories.

In later Christian stories about Jesus, setting, agents, and events all can change.

Don Quixote matters less to the world than Jesus does, and he never lived in the flesh, but like Jesus, he is remembered in an original situation and in later variations on it. In the novel by Miguel de Cervantes that introduced him to the world, Don Quixote put a cardboard helmet on a head crammed with fantasies of chivalry then went looking for them in real life. The old knight instantly charmed his readers. Cervantes' first installment of the novel was so popular that spin-off novels of Don Quixote's life began to be written. He began to do so many new things in plots invented by other writers that Cervantes, who needed the income from his writing, decided to regain control of his attractive character by having Don Quixote comment on how awful the writing in the spin-offs was, by having him do different things than these authors had reported him doing and by having him die in bed. The knight escaped his planned demise, living on in other authors' later stories—and more recently in musicals, movies, and pictorial art—that only partially resemble Cervantes' novel. To a lesser degree than Jesus, Don Quixote inspires flesh-and-blood admirers.

Elijah joins these special heroes who have certainly not left behind their original stories but have lived in new accounts. The prophet has had a particularly strong hold on the collective imagination. Stories of Don Quixote inspire people to pursue their dreams with courage. Jesus of Nazareth challenges those who hear his stories to live the same relationship with God and fellow human beings that his stories say he did. Christians believe that Jesus is the Christ because he made it possible for people to do this. As will be seen, Elijah became different things to different groups but always seems to have been inspiring as a human being. None of his tales treat him as a fictional character living in a dream, and even though some legends give him powers equal to those of the Messiah, none treat him as a more than human savior. No matter what he does, whether it is calling down fire from heaven in 1 Kings, praying to God to restore a child's life in the same story, or patting the Messiah's head to soothe him in a later Jewish legend, people inside Elijah's stories tend to react to him as a human person. He can be complained to, as Obadiah discovered in 1 Kings; importuned, as the widow of Zarephath found out; or scared out of his wits, as he himself discovered when Jezebel tried to kill him. He was so carried away by his own zeal that God needed to restrain him, one Talmudic tale says, reminding audiences of the well-known human tendency to overdo.

His oldest story provides glimpses of his humanity. First Kings says that when he despaired, he lay down on the ground, for example. Later tales answer questions about his human ways, explaining what physical gestures he used when he prayed and how he was affected by his extraordinary flight into heaven. Others relate how he looked or what he wore when he reappeared. Some Christian and Jewish legends say he will be martyred in the last days, in a heroic and certainly human death. If there is any general lesson that can be drawn from the legends that were invented about him, it may be that people can accomplish godly deeds while remaining human. No matter what he does for what group in which story, his storytellers seem to have appreciated him as a human being caught up in relation with God. People worldwide have cared about Elijah as one able to help others because he served God with all his heart.

In *Nello spirito e nella virtù di Elia* (*In the Spirit and Power of Elijah*), Emanuele Boaga presents a theory about how the many stories told about Elijah over the centuries were created. Boaga believes that the new Elijan stories surfacing among Jews, Christians, and Muslims all can be traced back to the 1–2 Kings passages. He conjectures that new stories of Elijah were created as were the Jewish *haggadot*, as didactic retellings of Scripture that imaginatively fill in gaps in the original narrative or embellish one or another feature of it. *Haggadot* thus insert new plots, new motives, and new characters in a tale that is already well known to hearers. If legends were spun out from the passages of 1–2 Kings as Boaga says, it would explain why later recountings of the prophet's legends diverge remarkably from each other, while older ones resemble each other more closely.

Boaga was particularly interested in a group of Elijah legends retold by his religious order. Important collections of stories of the prophet also appear in the fifth- and sixth-century Jewish Talmud, in the writings of the early Christian Fathers, and in the stories that provide context for Muslim *hadith*. Stories of the prophet with new features continued to appear in the Middle Ages, the era in which Boaga's Carmelite forebears began to think about themselves and Elijah. The Carmelite scholar's surmise appears to be correct. No matter how late or how unusual the legend, there is always something in it that links it to the oldest written life story of Elijah that we possess, the text of 1–2 Kings that appears in the Hebrew Bible.

The prophet has been a phenomenally attractive figure. Although his oldest story continued to be read widely, he moved beyond its boundaries and beyond the local concerns of his original faith community. No group or religion owns him. Stories told of him in one part of the world have reappeared, sometimes almost exactly, but sometimes also partly or greatly modified, elsewhere in the world. Beginning in stories told about him around the Mediterranean, but then moving as his storytellers traveled throughout Europe, the Middle East, India, and North Africa, he has managed to reappear in multiple places.

The previous chapter suggested that the prophet's personality in 1–2 Kings really cannot be separated from the nature of his God or the characteristics of the northern Israelite people. In 1–2 Kings, whatever makes Elijah's actions memorable turns out to have more to do with his God and his people than it does with him as an individual. This phenomenon, that Elijah embodies other human beings or embodies something that points to God, continues in later stories about him. As the groups retelling his legends began to multiply, they began to tell stories of the prophet that reflected their own lives and their own perceptions of the Creator.

Messianic prophets and their followers are one people of Elijah who continued to be influenced by the old stories in 1–2 Kings but also began to tell new ones about themselves and the prophet. Their new legends helped them live in times of stress. The Bible and the Koran declare that in the final days of the world, God will put an end to human struggles, establishing his dominion once and for all. Messianic believers have often thought that Elijah will appear to help bring about the end. A fifth-century B.C.E. Judean prophecy affected this eschatological belief profoundly. Countless Jews, but also very many Christians and Muslims awaiting the end, have focused upon the events involving God and Elijah described in the book of Malachi.

As groups developed separate identities, their traditions concerning Elijah developed distinctive features. The Gospels, written in the first century, record that the first ones to believe that Jesus of Nazareth was the Messiah were Jews living in Israel who shared expectations about the end of time with their neighbors. Malachi's prophecy that Elijah would reappear at the end of time was widely believed. However, when Jesus' followers were joined by a large number of Gentiles living around the Mediterranean, Christian stories about Elijah began to shift. As their group identities slowly diverged, the prophet became one thing to Christians and another to post-Temple Jews. Among Christians, attention to the prophet waned and his prophesied activity was absorbed into belief about Christ.

Jews gave the prophet a higher and higher profile. The Roman destruction of the Second Temple in 70 C.E. probably helped bring this about. When the Temple no longer existed and when they were banished from its vicinity, Jews, who were by then scattered around the Mediterranean, lost the means to turn to God in the ritual space their Scriptures commanded. The spiritual dilemma, how to perform God's cult as God required when his divinely regulated Temple no longer existed, was solved by a shift in mentality. The Torah came to replace the Temple as the primary location of religious life for the Jewish faithful. After the first century, Jewish worship of God increasingly involved sacred response to the Divine Word and inquiry into its meaning.

Rabbis, whose lives were dedicated to Torah study and moral conformity to its precepts, replaced earlier Israelite priests and prophets as spiritual models for their communities. When the belief arose in some Jewish groups that God had given Moses interpretations and applications of the Torah at the same time that he gave him the written covenant on tablets of stone—in other words, that he gave Moses an oral Torah when he gave him the written Torah now recorded in the Hebrew Bible—the spiritual stock of rabbis rose even higher, for it was they who especially safeguarded the long accumulation of the oral Torah for their groups. For those rabbis and the Jewish faithful who came to believe that the Messiah would not come until all Jews were returned to Torah righteousness, the Talmudic scholar became a messianic figure. Many believed that a wise rabbi's study, interpretation, and application of the Torah to the lives of Jewish faithful would hasten the long-awaited end. Rabbinic traditions began to appear in which Elijah helped scholars in their labors. For rabbis and those who revered them, the Tishbite became a provider of revelations concerning Torah life. Many of these stories have been preserved in the Talmud itself.

Elijah's later legends often depict him interacting with leaders. His most important contact of this kind is with the Messiah, God's anointed king and military champion. Traditional stories also describe him helping prophets, preachers, and the already mentioned rabbis to guide their flocks. It would, however, be inaccurate to say that Elijah became the legendary companion of the leadership class alone. He appears in many stories involving plain folk. The New Testament Gospels provide glimpses of what ordinary Jews believed about the prophet and themselves in first-century Israel. The Talmud, compiled in the fifth and sixth centuries, contains more tales of the Tishbite's involvement in ordinary lives. Muslims have also preserved stories of his domestic involvement. Elijah's humble storytellers seem to have been especially inclined to swap anecdotes about the prophet across religious lines, since similar tales in which he is found helping common folk reappear in so many places. Throughout the centuries, the audacious prophet continued to appeal to the popular mind, as iconography of him in tombs, on church walls, and in oral recounting attests.

Finally, those dedicating themselves to a life of prayer have claimed the prophet in special ways and so can be fairly called an "Elijan people." The Carmelites, other Christian religious orders, Muslim Sufi fraternities, and Jewish mystical circles have always cherished the help that the prophet in legends has given them. Stories of him told by monks, nuns, Kabbalists, and Sufis display similarities, despite some obvious differences in the religious adherence of the storytellers. This chapter will discuss the legends of early Christians; of later rabbinical communities; and of Muslim, Jewish, and Christian common folk. Stories of him belonging to spiritual groups will be addressed in the next chapter.

Elijah as a Sign and Promoter of Insight

God sent biblical prophets to address crises in Israel. Elijah zealously fulfills this role in the books of 1–2 Kings. By word and action, he demonstrates Yahweh's fierce insistence that the northern Israelites turn back to the God they once knew and obeyed. The books of Kings tell us that the prophet and his Lord reclaimed the former followers. When fire fell from heaven, the assembled northern Israelites "fell on their faces; and they said, 'Yahweh, he is God, Yahweh, he is God'" (1 Kings 18:39). Later legends also show the prophet promoting insights that, in one way or another, produce a shift in relationship with God.

He sometimes delivers his conversional messages by speaking. At other times, his movements trigger insight. Perhaps he performs a miracle or suddenly appears or disappears. His miraculous rescues and protections are never in themselves the point of the story. They are bids to change the awareness of the people to whom he comes. In his legends, Elijah brings unfortunate individuals hope, helps Torah scholars grasp the real meaning of what they study, and signals the beginning of a new era. Groups dedicated to prayer tell stories in which, in one way or another, he promotes insight into the nature of God. Whatever he does he can be seen at work fulfilling his original call to strengthen the bond between God and his followers through shifting their perceptions.

The biblical book of Malachi says that Elijah will foster important recognitions at the end of time. Malachi (meaning "my prophet") is a group of prophecies delivered to Jews living in the southern kingdom of Judah around 500–450 B.C.E. God announces in Malachi 4:5–6:

> Behold, I will send you Elijah the prophet before the great and terrible day of Yahweh comes. And he will turn the hearts of fathers to their children and the hearts of children to their fathers, lest I come and smite the land with a curse.

First, Elijah's reappearance will be a sign of "the great and terrible day of Yahweh." Second, he will turn the "hearts of fathers to their children and the hearts of children to their fathers," and they will recapture the harmony that they once knew.

Other passages in the book of Malachi mention a return of the heart. They suggest that Elijah's reconciliation predicted in Malachi 4:5–6 will involve more than putting things right in human families. In Malachi, God worries that his followers are not committed to him: "'I have loved you,' says Yahweh. But you say, 'How hast thou loved us?'" (1:2). "A son honors his father, and a servant his master. If then I am a father, where is my honor?" (1:6). He pleads with the Judeans to turn back to him: "From the days of your fathers you have turned aside from my statutes and have not kept them. Return to me, and I will return to you" (3:7). The prophecy of Malachi 4:6, in which Elijah will reconcile the hearts of fathers and children, speaks of a return to God, the greatest father, and, most hearteningly, of God's return to his covenant "children." The book of Malachi suggests that God so desires his followers that he will be willing to use a mediator, Elijah, to ensure the bond.

Malachi 4:5–6, in which Elijah will reappear before the Day of Yahweh, comments on prior tradition, adds something new to it, and connects the prophet to the era in which Malachi's prophecy was written down. In 1–2 Kings Elijah recaptured the hearts of the northern Israelites for God by triumphing over the local deity Baal. Malachi suggests that neither that triumph on behalf of God nor any subsequent one cemented the loyal love that God wanted from his followers. What he says about Elijah presumes that no matter whose hearts are set aright along the way, at the end of time there still will be those who need to return to right relationship with God and with other human beings. Malachi was as concerned about the core problem of full-hearted fidelity to God as were the writers of the books of Kings.

The statement in 2 Kings 2:11 that "a chariot of fire and horses separated the two of them and Elijah ascended in a whirlwind into heaven" until Elisha could no longer see him gives the impression that the elder prophet's earthly life ended in the event. God's words recorded in Malachi 4:5, "Behold, I will send you Elijah the prophet before the great and terrible day of Yahweh comes" extends the prophet's earthly existence to the Last Days and opens wide the door to legendary speculation concerning what the prophet might be doing between his ascension and the end. As Don Quixote eluded the demise that Cervantes planned for him, so the Tishbite escaped the ending apparently given to his mortal existence in 2 Kings.

The news that Elijah would return was delivered to hearers around 450 B.C.E., long after his contest with Ahab in northern Israel and after the Babylonian destruction of Solomon's Temple in Jerusalem in 587 B.C.E. By the time the prophecy had been uttered, the Persians had conquered the Jews in southern Israel, and their ancestors had been deported. The remaining Israelites rebuilt Solomon's Temple, but the reduced numbers scratching out a living in their homeland were demoralized. God's apparent neglect of Israel seems to have deeply troubled the Judeans. Why had their Lord abandoned them? Why did he not protect the land he had said was his holy possession? When would God return to save his chosen people, as so many earlier Israelite prophets had said would happen?

The prophecy about Elijah was delivered in a time and place that especially needed to hear Malachi's message. It has ever since provided hope in times of trouble. On Malachi's authority, many have expected that when they see the prophet reappear (something that many, following what Scripture says, have believed will happen soon), they will be able to relax. Their relation with their Creator and fellow human beings will finally be settled. Malachi brought the relieving news that Elijah will set hearts right before the stroke of judgment falls. Believers are given all this hope through Malachi's modification of Elijah's life story.

The comforting prophecy about the Tishbite has been repeated throughout the centuries, although not always exactly as Malachi details. This usually happens to a story retold over a long period of time. Legends are generally adapted to the circumstances of those who pass them on, and storytelling tends to appeal by combining the well-known with the new. Malachi's prophecy of what Elijah will do in the final days added a new feature to his lifetime described in 1–2 Kings. *The Lessons in Wisdom and Knowledge* by Jesus Sirach (also known by the title, *Wisdom of Ben Sirach,* and as Ecclesiasticus among Christians) in its turn added something new to Malachi. The work was written about 180 B.C.E., several centuries after the prophecies of Malachi were collected. Although Jews did not include it in their canon, and some Christians removed it from theirs, the *Wisdom of Ben Sirach* was influential. Fragments of it have been found among the remains of the apocalyptic communities at Qumran and Masada.

Sirach mentions Elijah's contact with Ahab, his interaction with Yahweh at Horeb, and his ascension—all events described in 1–2 Kings. In Sirach 48:10–12, he addresses the prophet as if he were present:

> Scripture records that you are to come at the appointed
> time to allay the divine wrath before it erupts in fury, to
> reconcile father and son, and to restore the tribes of Jacob.
> Happy are those who see you, happy those who have
> fallen asleep in love!

What Sirach says here repeats Malachi's prediction that Elijah will "turn the hearts of fathers to their children and the hearts of children to their fathers" but adds a significant new phrase. Where Malachi's prophecy adds a future return and reconciliation to Elijah's life, Sirach adds the detail that he will "restore the tribes of Jacob" in the final days.

The Hebrew Bible repeatedly says that the Lord of the universe will finally restore the tribes of Israel: "For behold, days are coming, says Yahweh, when I will restore the fortunes of my people, Israel and Judah, says Yahweh, and I will bring them back to the land which I gave to their fathers, and they shall take possession of it" (Jer. 30:3). The assertion of Sirach that Elijah will "restore the tribes of Jacob" during the final age of the world gives him powers greater than the ones he displayed in 1–2 Kings. As the word is used in the Bible, "restoration" involves more than conversion of heart. It is a complete repair that involves putting society and the cosmos right. The biblical view is that only God can bring about such universal healing. Sirach, then, is saying a lot when he declares that Elijah will "restore the tribes of Jacob." The belief that Elijah would bring restoration in the eschaton continued to circulate. Matthew and Mark report that Jesus told the crowds that Elijah had returned "to restore all things" (Matt. 17:11; Mark 9:12).

The Jewish *Lives of the Prophets* was written in the first century C.E., near the time that the Gospels of Matthew and Mark were produced, some 250 years after Sirach and some 500 years after Malachi appeared. It expands Elijah's powers in another direction and adds a different set of new details to his life story. Christians and Jews thereafter repeated the changes when they told stories of the prophet. First

Kings says nothing about Elijah's life before his prophetic career began, but *Lives of the Prophets* says that before he was born, an angel told his father that his future son's "dwelling will be light, and his word revelation, and he will judge Israel with sword and with fire" (Torrey, 47). Once again, a task that Scripture obviously assigns to God is given to Elijah. According to the Bible and the Koran, the Creator will assess each person when the Book of Life is opened (Malachi declares this in 3:5, for example: "Then I will draw near to you for judgment; I will be a swift witness against the sorcerers, against the adulterers, against those who swear falsely,...says Yahweh of hosts.") In *Lives of the Prophets,* Elijah performs this important eschatological function.

Jewish belief in Elijah's powers grew when their communities suffered. During the Middle Ages, Jewish neighborhoods in European towns and cities were repeatedly destroyed. In *The Messiah Texts*, Raphael Patai notes that thirteenth- and fourteenth-century Jewish legends claim that in the final days, which Jews saw as their time of release, Elijah will force Israel to repent, stand atop the montains of Israel to announce the Redeemer, slaughter "the celestial prince of Edom (Rome), become the spokesman of Moses," settle disputes, and "plead Israel's case before God." Elijah will provide "miraculous sources of sustenance." He will achieve the rank of a Redeemer" (Patai, 132). Still other medieval tales say that in the last days Elijah will wake the dead and record the deeds of individuals in the Book of Life.

Elijah's story lines continued to develop new features until legendary claims about him were far from what was said of him in 1–2 Kings. In his oldest tale he is a human prophet who speaks and acts as others prophets do. He is charismatic, poor, and solitary. He is like other classical prophets, who did not depend on any institution for what they did. When his original story is remembered, Elijah is portrayed wearing a rough coat of skins, a sign of his residence in desert places.

The scene painted on a twelfth-century Spanish Seder document changes his identity and garments. Passover, the annual Jewish feast that commemorates Yahweh's breaking of Pharaoh's power over the tribes of Jacob and protecting them from the Angel of Death, came to symbolize the eschatological Passover in which God would finally break the hold of evil on human beings. A cup prepared for Elijah the forerunner sits in a prominent place on each traditional Seder table at Passover, reminding those gathered of Malachi's prophecy that Elijah will reappear in the Last Days. The place made for the prophet among worshipers signifies their faith in future divine redemption.

The twelfth-century Passover manuscript includes and illumina- ✓ tion of Elijah arriving at the doors of a city. While other legends say that it will not be easy to recognize the prophet when he reappears, this scene suggests that the recognition will be easy. A line of onlookers peers at Elijah from the ramparts of the city. He comes blowing a *shofar* (ram's horn) sounded at Mt. Sinai to announce the Lord's presence and, Jewish tradition says, to be blown by the prophet on the Day of Redemption. Patai reports that the tenth-century *Ma'aseh Daniel* declares that in the eschaton "Messiah ben David, Elijah, and Zerubbabel...will ascend the Mount of Olives and Messiah will command Elijah to blow the shofar" (Patai, 143). Elijah's blasts will make the dead rise, announce the *Shekinah* (the Presence of God), and turn mountains into plains. Those hearing the tremendous sound of the shofar will know that Elijah has arrived.

In the illumination the arriving prophet also wears the Messiah's crown and approaches the city riding on an ass. These details will remind Christians of Jesus' entry into Jerusalem at Passover narrated in the Gospels. Jews, for whom the picture was painted, will be reminded of the earlier Zechariah 9:9–10 prophecy that the anointed Messiah of Peace will appear mounted on a humble beast at the time of the final redemption:

> Rejoice greatly, O daughter of Zion! Shout aloud, O daughter of Jerusalem! Lo, your king comes to you; triumphant and victorious is he, humble and riding on an ass,

> on the colt the foal of an ass. I will cut off the chariot from
> Ephraim and the war horse from Jerusalem; and the battle
> bow shall be cut off, and he shall command peace to the
> nations; his dominion shall be from sea to sea, and from
> the River to the ends of the earth.

Joseph Gutmann, editor of the collection in which the illumination appears, remarks that similar composite Elijah-Messiah figures can be seen in about a dozen surviving fifteenth-century Ashkenazi *Haggadah* illuminations from Germany. In the Middle Ages, at least some European Jews were merging the identities of Elijah and the Messiah in their traditional storytelling. Merged with the Anointed of God, the prophet far surpasses what he accomplishes in 1–2 Kings as a lone, often unwelcomed messenger of God. As God's final king, he has powers to conquer and rule. Anyone thinking of the figure as Elijah-Messiah surely believed that his restorative powers would be great indeed. The zealous old prophet who slaughtered Baalite prophets in this instance became a sign of peace.

Other contemporary legends portray Elijah doing and saying very different things at the end of time. During the same period in which the *Haggadah* illuminations collected by Gutmann indicate that Jews were awaiting an Elijah merged with the Messiah, some European Christians were also awaiting Elijah, although they could not combine him with Christ, for reasons given later. The Calabrian abbot Joachim of Fiore's teaching that human history fell into three eras drew the attention of many. The abbot believed that the third era, which was the final age of the world, began in his own lifetime at the end of the twelfth century. Joachim used but revised Malachi's prophecy. Like many Christians before him, the abbot believed that Elijah, John the Baptist, and one of the two martyred prophets mentioned in the book of Revelation were one and the same.

What resulted was complex, at least as Elijah was concerned. Possibly influenced by Luke's conclusions that John the Baptist was filled with the spirit of Elijah and that the early Church was guided and protected by the Holy Spirit, Joachim declared that in the third age (which he thought was then beginning), Elijah's spirit would help the faithful to restore the world. He prophesied in his *Exposition on the Apocalypse* that preachers "in the spirit of Elijah" and "in the spirit of Moses" would "preach the faith and defend it until the consummation of the world" (ff. 175v–176r, translated and cited by McGinn, *Visions of the End*, 136–137). Christian contemplatives, who in the abbot's view included both community monks and solitary hermits, would in the final days "be like a blazing fire...the former order [of preachers] will be milder and more pleasant in order to gather in the crop of God's elect in the spirit of Moses. This order [of contemplative monks and hermits] will be more courageous and fiery to gather in the harvest of the evil in the spirit of Elijah" (ibid.). These extreme differences in medieval legends of Elijah transmitted by Jews and by Christians prove that the prophet has been a sign to which many meanings may be attached. The tendency of his storytellers to align or merge Elijah with other figures is noteworthy. Once Malachi provided the opportunity to think about his actions in a definite but un-dated future, the prophet became the focus of a constantly expanding set of expectations.

Elijah is Difficult to Discover

Trusting Malachi's prophecy, many have believed that when they see Elijah, they will soon see the Messiah. Christians have commonly believed that the earliest of their ranks encountered both when they met John the Baptist and Jesus of Nazareth. Jews have never had that certainty and from time to time have had to look for Elijah to evaluate the claims of messianic candidates who have appeared among them. (Christians have also occasionally had to evaluate those claiming to be the Christ of the Parousia.) Memories of Elijah have never been far from Jews hoping that the Messiah had finally come. In seven-teenth-century Turkey, when many began to think that the long-awaited Chosen of God had appeared in the person of Rabbi Shabbetai Zevi, sightings of the prophet also began to be reported. Those who said they had seen Elijah were faithful to their Scripture and to their tradition. Seventeenth-century Turkish Jews, who wondered if Rabbi Shabbetai were the Messiah, knew that Malachi's prophecy, "Behold I send my messenger to prepare the way before me, 'and the Lord whom you seek will suddenly come to his temple; the messenger of the covenant in whom you delight, behold he is coming, says Yahweh of the hosts," needed fulfillment. Elijah was a necessary herald who would help believers confirm Rabbi Shabbetai's identity.

The Gospels of Matthew, Mark, and Luke, recording events that occurred some fifteen centuries before Shabbetai Zevi's appearance, suggest that those who crowded around Jesus as he preached acted like the Turkish Jews. Elijah's name crops up when the Gospels describe onlookers puzzling over Jesus' identity. They say that disciples and passers-by guessed that John the Baptist and Jesus of Nazareth were Elijah, the messenger whose reappearance would signal the final days (Matt. 16:14; Mark 6:15 and 8:28; Luke 9:8 and 9:19). Given what else the Gospels say about Jesus and John the Baptist, the guess seems to have been a good one. Both preached repentance and the coming Last Days. Both labored to accomplish the return of the heart to the Lord combined with reconciliation with fellow humans that Malachi prophesied that Elijah would perform near the end of time.

The Synoptic Gospels and later Muslim, Christian, and Jewish comments about the prophet suggest that although many have wanted to see Elijah, he has rarely been easy to find. This is paradoxical, considering how widespread the certainty has been over the centuries that the Tishbite will reappear as Malachi says, as a sign recognizable to all, and considering how necessary his traditional stories say that recognition of his reappearance will be. The Gospels suggest that onlookers and even Jesus' followers were confused about how Elijah and Jesus were related. As a matter of fact, these early works raise more questions than they answer concerning what the earliest Christians believed about Elijah's return, and given his return during Jesus' lifetime, how the old prophet had made his reappearance.

Luke

To take the narratives one by one, in the Gospel of Luke, an angel is said to have declared to Zechariah that his wife Elizabeth would bear a son who would fulfill Malachi's prophecy. He would go before the Lord, filled with "the spirit and power of Elijah, to turn the hearts of the fathers to the children" (Luke 1:13–17). Early Christian readers or hearers of the Gospel would not have missed the fact that Luke was telling them that Malachi's prophecy was fulfilled during Jesus' lifetime. The writer thought that John the Baptist was moved by Elijah's spirit during an era, which he thought was the final one, in which the Holy Spirit was very influential. For Luke, the Spirit of God was a powerful agent with its own particular work. It taught all things. It confirmed God's acceptance of those baptized. It enabled healing, preaching, and speaking in tongues. It was, then, no small thing for Luke to write that John the Baptist was filled with the "spirit of Elijah." Malachi's prophecy was at hand. Luke shows that Jesus himself was moved by the Spirit of God and could command it.

John

The Gospel of John understands Elijah, Jesus, and the eschaton differently. It promotes the belief that the Kingdom of God came once and for all when Jesus appeared. Because the writer John believed that the moment of Elijah's reconciliation had passed, that the Lord had already come and that the Kingdom had come, he treated the Tishbite very differently from Luke. John's Gospel reports John the Baptist publicly denying being either Elijah or the Messiah:

> And this is the testimony of John, when the Jews sent priests and Levites from Jerusalem to ask him, "Who are you?" He confessed, he did not deny, but confessed, "I am not the Christ." And they asked him, "What then? Are you Elijah?" He said, "I am not." (1:19–21)

At that point John's Gospel says that the Baptist told his listeners they were not asking him the truly important question. There was indeed a critical recognition they needed to perform but they were off the track. The hour had advanced; Elijah's appearance was not at issue. The question really had to do with Jesus' spiritual identity, not John the Baptist's or, for that matter, Elijah's: "among you," said the Baptist, "stands one whom you do not know...the thong of whose sandal I am not worthy to untie" (John 1:26–28; Luke 3:15–17).

Recognition of the divine is of critical importance. Jewish, Islamic, and Christian scriptures explicitly challenge their readers to see, recognize, admit, and believe in signs that often require strenuous effort and a purified mind to grasp. This perhaps begins to explain why Elijah's legends have shown him to be so elusive. The divine world itself is hard to discover. Those who seek God must struggle to find the real under illusionary appearances. Not only are Elijah and Jesus difficult to identify but so also are the Jewish Messiah, his Muslim counterpart, the Mahdi, and the Mahdi's eschatological helper Ilyas-Khidr, figures who will be introduced later in the discussion. The mental state needed to make such identifications is rare and difficult to achieve.

In the Gospel of John, the Baptist reoriented the questions that members of the crowd were asking him. He drew his listeners' attention away from the problem Malachi had given them of recognizing the forerunner Elijah and away from wondering who he himself was ("Are you Elijah?" He said, "I am not"). Neither he nor Elijah matter as much in the Gospel of John as they do in Matthew, Mark, and Luke. Instead, in the story told in the Gospel of John, the prophet's questioners were pressed to recognize the meeting of heaven and earth in Jesus. In John's Gospel, Elijah's traditional powers to reconcile believers with God are not mentioned, and the figure's role as herald of the final era is not emphasized. Restoration and judgment on the Lord's Day, which the *Wisdom of Ben Sirach* and the *Lives of the Prophets* indicate were already being assigned to Elijah by the Gospel writer's lifetime, are assigned to Jesus (see, for example, John 1:29 and 5:19–23).

The forerunner is played down in the Gospel but not entirely ignored. In John's first chapter, the Baptist declared that he must "bear witness," then pointed to Jesus among passers-by, seemingly fulfilling Malachi's prophecy with a gesture of his hand. The balance of the

Gospel, however, is filled with incidents in which individuals need no Elijah to find the Christ. In Jesus' encounter with the Samaritans, a woman said to Jesus:

> "I know that Messiah is coming...when he comes, he will show us all things." Jesus said to her, "I who speak to you am he." ...So the woman left her water jar, and went away into the city, and said to the people, "Come, see a man who told me all that I ever did. Can this be the Christ?" ...Many Samaritans from that city believed in him because of the woman's testimony, "He told me all that I ever did." ...And many more believed because of his word. They said to the woman, "It is no longer because of your words that we believe, for we have heard for ourselves, and we know that this is indeed the Savior of the world." (4:25–42)

In this passage of the Gospel, those surrounding Jesus recognized that he was the Messiah, using everything but a supernaturally sent forerunner. Some in the town were able to recognize that Jesus was the Messiah because of the testimony of a public sinner who was never seen as anything else than that. Others in the John 4:25–42 passage recognized the Messiah when they heard Jesus speak ("It is no longer because of your words that we believe," some said to the Samaritan woman, "for we have heard for ourselves, and we know that this is indeed the Savior of the world"). Although John the Baptist pointed Jesus out when the two were near each other, this Gospel makes it clear on several occasions that no one really needed the Baptist (or Elijah) to discover who their Savior was. That is accomplished in the heart when Jesus' word is received, the writer John believes. Elijah is inconsequential in this story of Jesus.

The Gospels of Matthew and Mark, on the other hand (and Luke in a later passage), pointedly suggest that John the Baptist was Elijah, the prophet of God described in 1–2 Kings about whom Malachi prophesied. Mark promotes this idea by opening his story with a conflation of the sentence from Malachi 3 with the Isaiah 40:3 announcement of a voice crying in the wilderness, "Prepare the way of the Lord." Mark leaves it up to his readers to conclude that John the Baptist was the messenger predicted in Malachi and Isaiah but makes it easy to come to that conclusion. He says that the Baptist preached repentance, was clothed in a coat of camel's hair, wore a leather girdle around his waist, and ate locusts and wild honey (Mark 1:6), inviting his audience to remember the Elijah of Malachi and 1 Kings, who also preached and will preach repentance, and the Elijah of 2 Kings, who was immediately recognizable to king Ahaziah by his "garment of hair cloth, with a girdle of leather about his loins" (2 Kings 1:7–8).

Elijah's physical appearance is often an issue in his stories. Sometimes his garments identify him, and sometimes they hide him. The Christian Fathers write that hermits occupying the deserts of Syria, Israel, and Egypt wore the animal skins and long hair of Elijah and John the Baptist as reminders of the deep commitment to the Lord's service for which the two prophets are known. His mantle and coat of skins have generally symbolized ideal moral and spiritual life. However, in some legends, Elijah deliberately fools expectations by wearing unusual garments that test his onlookers' ability to figure out who he is. The crowds described in the Gospels puzzled over who Jesus and John the Baptist were, apparently matching the actions of the two against their appearance. In later stories, the herald of the final redemption at times wears harlot's silks, the dress of an Arab, the armor of a Roman soldier, or beggar's rags—that is, the clothing of those whom many Jews especially despised or ignored.

The Gospel of Matthew completely bypasses the problem that Malachi gave to believers of identifying Elijah. Matthew reports that Jesus proclaimed to the crowds that John the Baptist was the prophet whose return was predicted by Malachi. The crowds have the task of finding Elijah performed for them:

> This is he of whom it is written, "Behold, I send my messenger before thy face, who shall prepare thy way before thee." ...For all the prophets and the law prophesied until John; and if you are willing to accept it, he is Elijah who

is to come. He who has ears to hear let him hear. (Matt. 11:10–15; Luke 7:24–28 repeats part of Matthew, although he omits Jesus' emphatic reiteration "if you are willing to accept it, he is Elijah who is to come.")

By declaring to them that John, whom onlookers have seen baptizing and preaching repentance, "is Elijah who is to come" and by citing Malachi 3:1, Jesus was announcing that Malachi's words were being fulfilled then and there. Matthew couldn't have been more dramatic. Those hearing Jesus and believing their ears would have received the double shock of recognizing the forerunner Elijah and the Lord (whether God or his appointed regent, the Messiah) in the same instant. In Matthew's report, Christ identified his forerunner, not the other way around, as Malachi said it would happen. Matthew's inversion of the events in a widely known prediction powerfully increased Jesus' stature in the divine plan.

Elijah, John the Baptist, and Typology

Christian works written after the first century usually connect the Tishbite with John the Baptist. The Gospels say that John was Elijah or was not Elijah or was filled with Elijah's spirit. Later writers often handle these differing scriptural claims by asserting that John the Baptist and Elijah related to each other as type and fulfillment. Those who did this were using an interpretive strategy that the New Testament taught them, which was generally in use among Jews and Christians. New Testament writers often handle the Hebrew Bible as a partially enigmatic description of events and figures of Jesus' lifetime, or in some cases (following Luke's historical schema) of the period of history beginning in Jesus' lifetime and stretching until the end of the world. The Apostle Paul, for example, treats Adam, the first human being, as a type (that is, as a prefigure) of Jesus, whom he calls the New Adam, and explains that Christians are the true spiritual descendants of Abraham, suggesting by this that Abraham's faith in

God foreshadowed the faith of Christians. For Christians, sacred history, including the record of Elijah's ninth-century B.C.E. lifetime, was full of signs of greater events and figures to come.

Detecting a typological relationship between two lives or two events requires the finding of parallels. The thirteenth-century compiler of Christian legends Jacobus of Voragine pondered the meaningful relation of Elijah and John the Baptist by comparing features of their lives. He uncovered many symmetries: "John is called Elijah by reason of place, because both lived in the desert; by reason of what they ate, because both ate little; by reason of their external appearance, because both cared little about what they wore; by reason of their office, since they were both forerunners, though Elijah was forerunner to the Judge and John to the Savior; and by reason of zeal, because their words burned like torches" (Voragine, vol. 1, 329).

The relation of the type (or prefigure), in this case Elijah, to the antitype (or fulfillment), John, is usually discovered on a deeper level than what Jacobus indicates. Typology works by dovetailing the person or event seen as secondary with the figure or event deemed most important. Christians have often understood that Elijah began something that was completed in John the Baptist's first-century mission. The ninth-century man of God was the type and John the Baptist the antitype. On this view, the full importance of Elijah's actions recorded in 1–2 Kings could only be grasped by thinking backward in sacred history from the person of Christ and the people and events described in the Gospels. "In many and various ways God spoke of old to our fathers by the prophets," the letter to the Hebrews begins, "but in these last days he has spoken to us by a Son, whom he appointed the heir of all things" (Heb. 1:1–2). According to Christian thinking, Elijah was undeniably a prophet in his own right, but his ninth-century prophetic mission could not be fully understood for all of its implications for sacred history until that mission was fulfilled by John the Baptist, the antitype.

Christians thus often saw Elijah and John in a lesser-to-greater relationship: Elijah was a prophet, but John was all he was and greater.

"Which of the prophets, by being a prophet, could make someone else a prophet?" says John Chrysostom, patriarch of Constantinople (d. 407 C.E.) in a passage that Jacobus of Voragine included in his *Golden Legend,* "Elijah, indeed, anointed Elisha as a prophet, but did not confer on him the grace of prophesying. John on the other hand, while still in his mother's womb, bestowed knowledge of the coming of God into her house upon his mother, and opened her mouth to the word of confession of faith, so that she recognized the dignity of the one whom she did not see in person, saying, 'Why is this granted me, that the mother of my Lord should come to me?'" (Voragine, vol. 1, 333). For Chrysostom, John was the greater figure, the fulfillment of Elijah, the type.

Typology is a flexible instrument. Justin Martyr, a Christian convert living several centuries before John Chrysostom, understood the meaningful relation of Elijah and John the Baptist not by looking backward from John's day to the ninth century B.C.E., the more usual movement for Christians, but forward to Judgment Day, the interpretive direction encouraged by Malachi and Sirach. Justin saw the eschatological Elijah as the greater and John the Baptist as the lesser. In his *Dialogue with Trypho,* in which he makes a case for Christianity's superiority over Judaism, Justin has the character Trypho, a learned Jew with whom his Christian narrator debates, ask some pointed questions about discrepancies about Elijah found in the Gospels. Concerning the variety said about the prophet in Matthew, Mark, Luke, and John, Trypho remarks that it is hard to grasp that the Spirit of God that moved the prophet in the ninth century was the same Spirit that was in John the Baptist and to think at the same time that Elijah would return in person in the final days, as Malachi predicted. How many times could Elijah reappear?

"As many as God chooses," responds Justin's Christian narrator. If Christ came and will come again, then Elijah, who was certainly lesser than Christ, could appear more than once as well:

> Even so, God was able to cause [the spirit of] Elijah
> to come upon John; in order that, as Christ at his first

> coming appeared inglorious, even so the first coming of
> the spirit, which remained always pure in Elijah like that
> of Christ, might be perceived to be inglorious…. You can
> perceive that the concealed power of God was in Christ
> the crucified, before whom demons, and all the principali-
> ties and powers of the earth trembled. (Justin Martyr, 220)

The beliefs underlying the above remarks that God's spirit repeatedly
breaks into human history and that the old prophecy from Malachi
would be fulfilled literally end up rearranging the poles of the typology. Here John the Baptist is Elijah's type, not the reverse, as John
Chrysostom understood the pair. For Justin, John the Baptist is the
earlier "inglorious" occasion for the activity of the Spirit that will
find its fuller manifestation in Elijah's later appearance in the Last
Days about which Malachi prophesied.

Justin obviously believed, as have many since, that Christ first
came in humility to be crucified but later would return in triumph. He
also believed, probably following Luke, that all of human history was
arranged according to the pattern of Christ's life. It thus was reasonable for Justin to deduce that John the Baptist's life was an introduction to the greater actions Elijah would perform in the Last Days.
Justin Martyr joins Joachim of Fiore but also many Jewish, Islamic,
and Christian writers whose works have not received comment here,
who found it easy to think that Elijah could surface in history in more
than one era and even in more than one form. Typology is another
means by which the Israelite spiritual warrior slipped out of the boundaries of his oldest plot in 1–2 Kings into a variety of new ones.

Details in their Gospels suggest that Matthew, Mark, and Luke
knew that Elijah's traditions circulating among the people could produce confusion among potential converts to Christianity. The three
writers (but not the Gospel writer John, who, as explained earlier,
seems to have believed that the world had passed beyond needing
Elijah, since the Messiah and his Kingdom had already come) address some of those potential confusions in their report of the miraculous event of the Transfiguration. All three Synoptic Gospels say that

a small group of Jesus' disciples beheld Moses and Elijah speaking with their master, who stood between them, and that the disciples then heard a heavenly voice declare concerning Jesus, "this is my beloved Son; listen to him." (See Matt. 17:1–13; Mark 9:2–13 and Luke 9:28–36 for the whole episode.)

The passage addresses questions about the relationship of Jesus, Elijah, and Moses that the Gospels in other places do not answer. Elijah, representing the prophets of Hebrew Scripture, and Moses, representing the Torah, are here visibly distinct from the person of Jesus. There is no possibility in the report of Matthew, Mark, or Luke of merging the identity of the forerunner Elijah with that of the Messiah, as we have seen happen in later Jewish legend or as we will see the Gospel writers (excluding John) do elsewhere in their narratives of Jesus. The physical separation of the three in the Transfiguration demonstrates that neither Elijah nor Moses is the Messiah, although their grouping together says that the three men and what they represent are related. Jesus' central position and the divine voice communicate that he is the greatest of the three. The heavenly voice declaring "listen to him" indicates that Jesus' word should be accepted along with the teachings of the Law and the Prophets. His central position suggests that his teaching relates to, but supersedes, the Torah and Prophets.

As has been shown, the issues of identifying Elijah correctly and grasping his significance in relation to the Messiah crop up in many different legends. Those inside the legends must tackle more than detecting who he is in spite of his unusual garments or actions. In the Christian Gospels and in Jewish tales from the early centuries, discovering Elijah always also involves discovering the object of his mission and taking a stand concerning it. Different stories say that he comes as a prophet denouncing worship of foreign gods, as a preacher of personal repentance, or as a public sign of the Savior who is about to appear. In the following chapter, it will also be shown that he at times comes to people as an invisible spiritual companion or as an angel. For those humans who interact with him inside his traditional stories, discovering the presence of the prophet means, more than anything else, having an opportunity to discover something about God.

Elijah and the Eschaton

Along with traditional Judaism and Christianity, traditional Islam expects that a final king will govern the nations of the world. Some Muslim traditions say that a descendant of Muhammad, the Mahdi, will fill the earth with peace and justice during a seven-year respite from chaos. Shi'ite legends claim that the Mahdi was revealed in the person of the twelfth *imam,* Muhammad Abu l'Qasim, was hidden, and will return, while Sunnis, in the other major division of Islam, believe that the Mahdi has yet to appear. For some Shi'ites, the Mahdi will be the last *imam* or spiritual leader and intercessor, who on his return will conquer all religions and take vengeance on the wicked. Legends declare that after the seven-year reign of the Mahdi, the Antichrist will appear, and Jesus, son of Mary, will destroy the Antichrist. Some believe that Khidr, a figure whom some legends connect with Elijah, will serve as the Mahdi's aide in the final days. Khidr and the Mahdi will do less in the eschaton than what Jews and Christians believe that Elijah and the Messiah will accomplish. The Koran teaches that Allah will perform the mighty acts of judgment that complete the eschatological drama.

Whether the king who rules in the Last Days is called the Christ, the Messiah, or the Mahdi, and whether Elijah or Khidr lends him aid, adherents of all three traditions have been interested in the mortality of the figures. Muslim legends say that the Mahdi, of known human descent, will be slain by the Antichrist. Khidr's mortality is a complex issue (as the next chapter will discuss, he is often thought to have escaped usual bodily limitations), but he still matters to Muslims, regardless of their differences over him, as someone who was at least originally mortal.

Some Jewish and Christian legends say that the prophet will be killed and raised from the dead in the last days. Revelation 11:1–13 declares, for example, that when foreign nations "trample over the holy city," two "witnesses" will be martyred for their testimony then brought back to life by God. The puzzling passage begins in the future tense, shifts to the present, and then ends its narrative in the past. It ends:

> After the three and a half days a breath of life from God entered them, and they stood up on their feet, and great fear fell on those who saw them. Then they heard a loud voice from heaven saying to them, "Come up hither!" And in the sight of their foes they went up to heaven in a cloud. And at that hour there was a great earthquake, and a tenth of the city fell. (Rev. 11:11–13)

Some Jewish apocalyptic legends report a very similar event. Christians and Jews have said that one of two martyrs would be Elijah. The second has usually been identified as Enoch or Moses.

Jewish and Christian disagreements over the death of the Messiah are well known. The two groups have not agreed about the claim, founded on the promise God made to King David in 2 Samuel 7:16: "Your house and your kingdom shall be made sure forever before me; your throne shall be established forever," that the Messiah is, or will be, a descendent of the Israelite king. They have disagreed over the end of the Messiah's human life. Christians have often appealed to the Suffering Servant passages in Isaiah and to one or two documents outside the New Testament to explain the messianic significance of Jesus' death, but overall the Hebrew Bible provides little support for the conclusion that the Messiah died a human death in the first century. For many Jews, Jesus' first-century execution cannot be reconciled with messianic prophecies, which say that God's chosen will conquer foes and rule God's final kingdom. Agreeing on the Messiah's Davidic ancestry, early Jews and Christians divide concerning his mortality.

Basing themselves on traditions that they traced to eyewitness reports, Christians asserted that Jesus was and is the Messiah, that he died for others in obedience to his Father's will, that he rose from the grave, that he reappeared to his disciples, that he ascended to heaven, and that he will return in the eschaton to conquer and rule God's Kingdom, fulfilling biblical prophecy. One group of Talmudic legends suggests that at least some Jews in the first centuries of the common era were thinking over the importance Christians gave to Jesus' death. These legends say that God will send two Messiahs, not one, at the end of time. The first, Messiah ben Joseph (Messiah, son of Joseph, a figure not named in the Hebrew Bible, but obviously connected to Jesus, whom the Gospels say was Joseph's son), is destined to suffer and die for Israel in the final days (not in the first century) and then be replaced by Messiah ben David, who will conquer and rule God's kingdom.

Beliefs regarding the Messiah and Elijah have always helped people confront dangerous crises. It mattered to what must have been a minority of Jews at the time to think that Messiah ben Joseph would be martyred on behalf of Israel in the final chaotic age of the world. For those who believed his legends, Messiah ben Joseph was a final figure in a pantheon of spiritual heroes to whom the Jews had always turned for encouragement in difficult times. Other martyrs willing to die for their faith, such as the Maccabees, were graven in Jewish memory, as were, in time, the memories of other children of Israel who were killed because they were Jews. All these mortal figures taught the lesson that one must be faithful to one's relationship with God even in the face of death. Belief that Elijah or Messiah ben Joseph would be martyred for God in the last days gave Jews and Christians encouragement, and Jesus' death provided the same help to Christians. The two figures' manner of life, their death, and their resurrection gave followers a model in the worst of times. To be martyred as Christ or as the lesser figure Elijah was martyred in the service of God gave Christians firm hope of eternal life. Both ascended to heaven.

Elijah and his Muslim associate Khidr stand in the background when God's Anointed is discussed, except in Jewish stories where the prophet is always a large, wonderful figure. By the Middle Ages, Elijah had unfolded into something like a second eschatological Messiah among Jews. Some late Jewish legends say that both will announce the eschaton. One or the other will slay the ultimate challengers to God's power. As mentioned above, some Jewish legends say that both will be martyred. Other Jewish stories say that both will be honored with a place in the paradisal kingdom of God. According to Louis Ginzberg in *The Legends of the Jews*, the Talmud places Elijah in a cabinet of princes advising the Messiah in the final kingdom. Both are involved in the judgment of souls. Legend says that sometimes Elijah makes the assignments to heaven or hell, that sometimes that task belongs to the Messiah, and that sometimes judgment remains in the hands of God. Other tales say that Elijah will be a notetaker for the Holy One and his Anointed, jotting down people's good deeds in the Book of Life.

Elijah in the eschaton is a helper or a double or, rarely, merged with the Messiah. He comes and goes by himself in stories set before the Last Days. In these he often helps individuals as a sort of a humble, domestic savior. The personal aid he provides sometimes resembles the individual miracles he performs in 1–2 Kings. Common folk have especially loved to tell this kind of tale. Ginzberg remarks: "Elijah's removal from the earth [in a chariot of fire], so far from being an interruption to his relations with men, rather marks the beginning of his real activity as a helper in time of need, as a teacher and as a guide" (Ginzberg, 202). Legends say that he gave miraculous powers to a casket of earth, flew a long distance to catch a rabbi who had thrown himself from a loft, took the place of a poor man in slavery, cured poisonings and toothaches, and reestablished peace between husband and wife. Muslims tell similar stories of Khidr protecting infants or resolving domestic squabbles. Kees Waaijman comments that "people expect closeness, comfort and help" from Elijah. "He is on their side—the side of the ordinary people" (Waaijman in Chandler, *A Journey with Elijah*, 75).

The prophet's bold accusations of Ahab and the northern Israelites may have inspired later stories in which he encourages people to come to the new realizations they must make if they are to improve. By bringing good fortune, he has shown the pious how they stand in God's eyes. He has shown others that their riches or public respectability are a veneer for moral depravity. In stories set before the end of time, Elijah has been a redeemer well fitted to the difficulties of ordinary human life. He has given food to the starving, lessons in humility to the self-satisfied, and, always, tangible proof of the existence of the divine.

How different Elijah's role has been in Christian storytelling about the end of time or about the time that passes before it arrives. His feats in Jewish legend, such as feeding the hungry or teaching the conceited a lesson, tend to be assigned to other Christian saints, and his activities in the Great Redemption—his announcement of the eschaton, judgment of souls, and restoration of life—are almost completely taken over by the Son of God. Belief that Jesus was God's Son probably caused the lowering of Elijah's stock among Christians. What could the Tishbite do to help people relate to God that Jesus in his divine and human nature could not do better? Trusting Jesus' ability to ensure their relationship with God, Christians have often not thought too much about Elijah. They remember the prophet's 1–2 Kings stories, the Gospel references to him, or the Malachi prophecy, but he is usually a minor moon in their planetary system, a praiseworthy example of zeal among many others, much as the Koranic Ilyas is to Muslims. Followers of Jesus tend not to mention Elijah when asked about the end of their own life or about the eschaton.

Their silence about the prophet indicates how thoroughly the supernatural saving actions performed by Elijah in Jewish traditional stories have been absorbed into Christian beliefs about Jesus Christ and how much the teaching in John's Gospel that the Messiah can be found without recourse to Elijah his herald has been generalized in

Christian belief. As Malachi prophesied that Elijah the forerunner would do in the latter days, Jesus the Messiah, Christians believe, is continually inviting the turning of children's hearts to their Father in a critical age. Because they believe him to be the Son of God, divine as his Father is divine, Jesus often is experienced not only as the promoter but also as the object of the repentant turn of heart.

Christians furthermore expect that Jesus the Savior and Lord, instead of Elijah the forerunner, will be the definitive sign of the coming Kingdom of God. They are encouraged in this by passages in the Gospels. Matthew, Mark, and Luke say that after he and his disciples arrived in Jerusalem for Passover, Jesus prophesied that earthquakes and chaos would soon signal the beginning of the eschaton. Modifying Malachi's influential prophecy, "Behold I will send you Elijah the prophet before the great and terrible day of Yahweh comes" (4:5), Jesus instead told his disciples that his own reappearance would signal the Day of the Lord. Mark 13:24 says: "But in those days, after that tribulation…then they will see the Son of man coming in clouds with great power and glory." Matthew 24:29–31 repeats the passage of Mark just cited, as does Luke, who in 21:28 adds Jesus' words: "Now when these things begin to take place, look up and raise your heads, because your redemption is drawing near."

Jesus' prediction of his own return to inaugurate the Last Days adds a link to the chain of events that began with Elijah's ascension to heaven. Second Kings gives the impression that the prophet's earthly life ended when he disappeared into heaven in a chariot of fire. Elisha's inheritance of Elijah's mantle seems to corroborate that the Tishbite's work on earth was concluded. As has been seen, Malachi stretched Elijah's lifetime and mission until the end of the world and gave him important new tasks in that age. Elsewhere in what they write, Matthew, Mark, and Luke strongly suggest that what Malachi prophesied came to pass in the activity of John the Baptist.

However, when Jesus announces his own return to signal the beginning of the eschaton in Mark 13, Matthew 24, and Luke 21, a new and highly interesting link is soldered onto the chain of events that we may call Elijah's lifetime. Perhaps the writers of the Synoptic Gospels thought that God's final Kingdom would be inaugurated in two phases. John the Baptist, who preached repentance and pointed out Jesus as the Messiah, seems to have fulfilled Malachi's prophecy in their eyes. Perhaps that was the first phase. But they also report that Jesus himself said that his visible return would be the telling sign of the end. Passages in the Acts of the Apostles, Paul's epistles, and the Book of Revelation demonstrate that early Christians believed this. Those faithful to Scripture who thought that Jesus' Parousia would signal the eschaton most likely viewed Elijah/John the Baptist as the lesser manifestation in history, that is, as a type of what would happen more fully in the Second Coming. For those who wait for his return, Jesus has replaced Elijah as herald of the critical hour.

Many Christians today also believe that Christ is, and will be, the only true reconciler of hearts. They give Elijah little thought in the matter, if they mention the prophet at all. Much of Elijah's 1–2 Kings identity (that is, his distinguishing characteristics, such as his zeal or his violence) does not seem to have been absorbed into Christ's identity. It would be more accurate to say that Christian Scripture and subsequent Christian legends assigned the prophet's great eschatological actions to Christ. Where among Jews the Israelite prophet came to have greater and greater God-given powers to help people and to accomplish the eschaton, Christians reverted those powers to God by reassigning them to his divine and human Son.

The Bodies of Elijah and the Messiah in Heaven

Claims that Elijah and Jesus will be able to restore others to life have ample footing in Scripture. First Kings says that the prophet prayed to God to return a boy's soul to his body, "Yahweh harkened to the voice of Elijah; and the soul of the child came into him again, and he revived" (1 Kings 17:22). His disciple Elisha performed a very similar miracle (2 Kings 4:11–37). Jesus returned the daughter of Jairus to life and raised his friend Lazarus from the dead (Matt. 9:18–26 and John 10:40–11:54). After Jesus' ascension to heaven, Peter restored the disciple Dorcas to life (Acts 9:36–42).

Similarities between the Elijah/Elisha and Jesus/Peter sets of stories suggest that the first Christians used earlier Scripture to think about Jesus' power over death and the ability of his disciples to inherit that power. What matters here is that although the resuscitations teach about spiritual relationship with God, the lessons are being taught by means of the body. Where 1 Kings reports that Elijah had to stretch his body over the dead child and pray to God with all his might, Jesus is said to have performed his miracles by extending a hand or speaking, his slighter bodily gesture suggesting his greater supernatural power. With God's help, Elijah returned the breath of life to the body of the child. Many New Testament passages say that Jesus rose from the dead bodily. It should be remembered that when the claim of Jesus' power over his own death was first voiced, Christians as a group had yet to arrive at the conclusion that Jesus was God. The first-century Gospel assertions that the Savior returned himself to life were staggering. Not yet having developed a doctrine of his divinity, followers in the first century saw Jesus as much more than a powerful prophet. From the beginning, Elijah (and all other prophets, including the great Moses) stood in Jesus' shade among Christians.

Elijah cast a lengthening shadow as a restorer of life among Jews, however. The Talmud, compiled in the fifth and sixth centuries, contains a variety of stories in which Elijah saves people from death. One says that the prophet was able to thwart the Angel of Death by hurrying ahead to urge those marked for an exit to do certain good deeds before the angel arrived. Another says that during the eschaton, the prophet will busy himself reuniting people with their dearly departed (a modification on Malachi's prophecy that answers the question, "how can one reconcile with one's relatives in the last days if they are dead by then?"). As Ginzberg reports the legend, after Elijah raises the dead, the Messiah will appear to the crowd of onlookers and newly

revived relatives. Both tasks that Malachi assigns Elijah will thus handily be accomplished: the prophet will unite fathers and children by
restoring life. By reviving the dead, he will also prepare the people to
recognize their Messiah.

Tales such as these, or of Elijah's or the Messiah's martyrdom and
resurrection, have helped the faithful foray into a part of their life that
they have yet to experience. Legends in which the two figures deal
with bodily death offer encouragement, and often comfort, to those
wanting to know what may happen when they reach their mortal limits. Like a telephoto lens, some legends even track the bodies of the
two figures passing into heaven. This latter group of stories about
heaven often mentions features of a physical world that no one now
believes exist. From prebiblical times until the late Middle Ages, Jews,
Christians, and Muslims thought that God had created the world in
layers. The bottom layer was the underworld, where the dead went.
The middle layer was the earth, which God created as the domain of
human existence. The third created layer was the vault of heaven.
Genesis says the stars, sun, and moon were hung in this vault. Heaven
matters most to Scripture because God's dwelling place was believed
to be beyond, or above, the vault. Scripture often says that God looks
down on earth from heaven and that his messengers come from there.

The belief that layers of cosmos were stacked one on top of each
other persisted until the end of the sixteenth century, although after a
while the image of the whole was changed from a kind of a layer cake
into the nesting spheres of an onion. Those in later centuries who
thought about creation as spheres within spheres placed the earth at
the core of the so-called onion. Spheres were eventually added between earth and heaven. And God's abode was thought to be outside
the outermost layer of the created world. Copernicus in time proved
to the West that this arrangement didn't really exist in the physical
world, but the image of the "onion-layered," earth-centered arrangement of the cosmos that included heaven as a special place continued
to explain God's orderly creation for a long time.

For ancient and medieval people who trusted that the physical world was arranged either as a layer cake or as an onion, it was one thing to believe that mortal life could be restored on earth, the abode of human beings, as 1 Kings says Elijah restored the widow's son, and as the Gospels say Jesus reappeared to his disciples after death. Such miraculous restorations were conceptually possible to ancient people, for earth was the abode of human life. Relying on the words of Genesis, those who held the "layer" or "onion" myth understood that the earth was the natural, God-given place to which humans were assigned to carry out their existence. God's preoccupation with humans on earth, as they carried out their lives on the middle layer, is repeatedly described throughout the Bible and the Koran. However, it was quite another thing for those same believers to wrestle with claims that a human being from the earthly plane could go or be taken to heaven (as 2 Kings says happened to Elijah, and as the New Testament says happened to Jesus). All things were possible of God, of course, but bodily ascensions to heaven strained biblical categories.

Stories in which Elijah, Jesus, Enoch, or anyone else entering into heaven while alive in the flesh narrated a great disturbance (or departure) from God's original distribution of life in the cosmos. Visitors from one sphere to the other were rare exceptions that proved the rule that humans were to remain on earth. Anything originating in the material world, which was earth, was long believed to be by its nature an intrusion in heaven. In the ancient view, God made earth-things for the earth and heaven-things for heaven. Nevertheless, there always has been human pressure to hope for bodily entry into heaven. All three religions possess legends in which the question is explored, "What happens to human beings that bodily ascend into heaven?" These legends often rely on the bodies of Elijah and the Messiah, as they provide an answer.

One medieval Jewish folktale declares that after the chariot transported him to heaven, Elijah won a personal struggle with the Angel of Death. The tale appears in the *Sefer ha-Zohar,* the late

thirteenth-century masterpiece of Jewish Kabbalah by the Spanish
Rabbi Moses of León. As Rabbi Moses tells the story, when Elijah
was taken from earth to heaven in a chariot of fire, the Angel of Death
attempted to block his entrance into the celestial realm, saying that
only the dead could enter there.

We can be sure that what concerned the angel was Elijah's body,
not his soul. Jewish tradition taught that the souls of the just could
enter heaven, and Elijah was always thought to be extremely righteous. Instead, the prophet had showed up at heaven's gate with body
and soul intact. Rabbi Moses says that God waved away the angel's
objection that only the dead—presumably, those having left their bodies below—could enter heaven. God said, "Elijah is not like other
men. He is able to banish thee from the world, only thou dost not
recognize his strength" (Ginzberg, vol. 4, 201). Elijah then wrestled
with the angel, won the match, and entered heaven, triumphantly and
bodily alive. This late legend demonstrating Elijah's power to preserve his own bodily life showed Jews the extraordinary benefits available to the righteous. It should be noted that in the legend Elijah, not
God, performs the acts that get him over the threshold into the divine
abode. God is an approving bystander in the tale. In this tale, at least,
Elijah's personal powers equal those Christians claimed for Jesus.

Christ is, of course, the principal Christian model of righteous
behavior sufficient to merit bodily salvation, but a few Christian
stories have survived that discuss Elijah's entry into heaven. The
second-century Christian *Apocalypse of Peter* says that Elijah, Moses,
and Jesus ascended to heaven after the apostles saw them on Mt. Ta-
bor. (Readers will remember that in the Gospels, disciples see the
three figures and hear a heavenly voice commanding them to listen to
Jesus, but that Jesus rejoins the disciples, and they descend the mountain.) Just about every new feature of the amplified Transfiguration
story told in the *Apocalypse of Peter* has to do with human bodies.
The Gospel story mentions the dazzling light streaming from Jesus
but does not describe the appearance of the other two figures on the

mountain, other than saying that they are to the left and right of Jesus. In the *Apocalypse of Peter,* Elijah and Moses' faces and garments shine and are said to be astonishingly beautiful. Jesus' physical splendor is said to be greater than that of the other two. All three are crowned with spikenard. While in the Gospels, Peter, James, and John recognize Elijah and Moses standing with their master, in the *Apocalypse*, Peter must ask who the two figures are, to which Jesus replies, "your righteous brethren whose form you did desire to see" (Barnestone, 535–536). Then Jesus, Elijah, and Moses are caught up in a cloud to heaven, where Peter, on looking up, sees "men in the flesh" coming to greet them.

References in the *Apocalypse of Peter* to bodily beauty and bodily ascension encourage readers to come to some of the same conclusions promoted by Rabbi Moses' later tale of Elijah wrestling with the Angel of Death at heaven's gate. Both narratives demonstrate that righteousness is necessary for bodily entry into heaven (a theme to which the following chapter will return). The story in the *Zohar* sets an extremely high standard for intact entry into heaven: one needs to be as virtuous as Elijah. The *Apocalypse of Peter,* written a millennium earlier, allows readers at least some room to hope that such an experience may not be so rare, since in it not only Jesus, Moses, and Elijah ascend to heaven in bodily perfection but "men in the flesh" come to heaven's door to welcome the three when they arrive. In many later traditions Elijah's ascent to heaven in a chariot of fire becomes an emblem of virtue. Syrian Christians in particular treat virtuous Elijah as a sign of eternal life.

Challenges

Certain profoundly human issues begin to emerge from Elijah's fund of stories worldwide. It is noteworthy that so many legends have been passed down in which people have difficulty finding the prophet. The problem is not trivial. The stories say that if people around the prophet overlook him, either because he doesn't look like what is expected or because the story inhabitants are too dull to see who stands before them, much can be lost. Messages may not be delivered, critical signs may be overlooked, and miracles will not be performed. Tales often do turn out well, but in others, Elijah is not discovered and those being tested miss their chance. Stories in which people need to discover the prophet in order to find the Messiah are the most anxious. The crowds flocking around John the Baptist and Jesus repeatedly asked, "Are you the Messiah? Are you Elijah?" First-century Jews in Israel certainly have not been the only ones to ask this urgent pair of questions. Overlooking Elijah is often due to inattentiveness, self-absorption, or an overly conventional mind. Much depends on one's ability to see things as they are.

The previous chapter of this book commented on Elijah's lack of shelter and resources in 1–2 Kings. The rabbinic, early Christian, and messianic tales gathered here spend little time describing his unprotected state or his risky, brave dependence on God. In the legends recounted in this chapter, the prophet is neither an ordinary man with boredoms and chilblains, nor on the point of giving up, as 1 Kings says he once was, nor is he a supernatural being. He is a challenging human model because, while being neither an angel (except to spiritual people, as we shall see in the next chapter) nor the divine Son of God, he is able to accomplish extraordinary deeds. He doesn't easily let hearers of his stories excuse their weaknesses.

People who believe that they live unlegendary lives cannot find it easy to compare themselves with this later Elijah who is outfitted by God to succeed in everything he does. Regular people know that they cannot perform miracles and know that they have limits. It makes sense to them that an angel, or Jesus Christ, or some other powerful entity should tackle huge problems. "Let these superpowers take care of the worst cases and God bless them," the thinking may run, "they are better suited for the task than I am." As a persistent counterweight to this excusable, reasonable attitude, Elijah in these stories stands on the human side of the border between the supernatural and the natural. Groups worldwide have continued to retell stories of a man who was always only a human being, but who participated in greater events than humans usually do. They have kept before their eyes the figure of a human who tackled huge problems and did well. Elijah has shown his audiences that human beings can, indeed, do great things with the help of God.

Stories collected in this chapter also mull over the important question of how people can carry on in dark times, with few confirmations of underlying order or well-being. According to the Bible, Israel in the centuries before the common era was still a place in which one could see evidence of God's existence. Storms, droughts and miracles proved Yahweh's power and his intentions to the Israelites. Confirmations in those days could be observed in the sky or felt inwardly. King Saul's divine election was confirmed by a prophetic ecstasy. An attendant touched the ark of the covenant to steady it and was struck dead. The whole people of northern Israel were reported to have seen fire fall from heaven to consume Elijah's sacrifice on Mt. Carmel.

In high contrast to the biblical stories in which God's involvement in human lives is visible, later legends say that Elijah appears among people when God's presence is not easily detected. People who first heard these legends were usually in a difficult spot where a sign or a hand from God was desperately needed. This was true of Malachi's hearers, as it was true of the crowds thronging around Jesus in first-century Israel. It was true of Christians harassed and martyred in Rome who awaited the end of the world. It was true of Jews fearing death at Christian hands in medieval Europe. Finally, it was true, if only in the facts of the stories, in all the legends in which Elijah intervened to set one or another person's moral life right, to feed the hungry, or to protect a woman in childbirth. The prophet's legends meditate on what will happen to human beings and on how they should perform during the most critical moments of their existence, moments for which they do not expect themselves to be prepared.

When Elijah suddenly appears to them, story characters respond to the prophet as onlookers do to a firecracker exploding in a hot summer night. Waiting for fireworks to begin to explode plays at half believing, half doubting that any light will appear in the dark sky. The absence of help, goodness, or order that people in Elijah's legends experience before he arrives is no such game. The skies have often been dark in the eras in which his peoples have comforted themselves with Elijah's stories. His sudden, often miraculous visitations provide brief flashes of insight and power that allow people inside his stories to see that there is more to the dark times than they thought. His legends say that help can come in a time of crisis. Elijah gives those who can see him a sign that God is present and will be revealed.

In sum, Elijah's traditions retold in this chapter, regardless of what group they involve, revolve around the profound human desire to be fully alive. The prophet is a restorer of harmonious relations, a blesser of households, and a teacher of true knowledge. The last group of his legends discussed above briefly probe the greatest hope of believers, that they may continue to live after their mortal extinction.

For Further Reading

Arberry, A.J., trans. *The Koran Interpreted*. 1955 Unwin; New York: Simon and Schuster, 1996.

Barnestone, Willis, ed. *The Other Bible*. New York: Harper Collins, 1984.

Ginzberg, Louis. *The Legends of the Jews*. 7 vols. Philadelphia: JPS, 1938.

Patai, Raphael. *The Messiah Texts*. Detroit: Wayne State University Press, 1979.

Scholem, Gershom. *Kabbalah*. New York: New American Library, 1974.

Smith, Jane Idelman and Yvonne Yazbeck Haddad. *The Islamic Understanding of Death and Resurrection*. Albany, N.Y.: SUNY, 1981.

Voragine, Jacobus de. *The Golden Legend. Readings on the Saints*. 2 vols. Translated by W. G. Ryan. Princeton, N.J.: Princeton, 1993.

Chapter 3
Elijah and the Spiritual Life

In his introduction to *Creative Imagination in the Sufism of Ibn 'Arabi,* Islamic historian Henry Corbin remarks that despite what separates them, Muslim Sufis and Protestant Christian mystics such as Jacob Boehme and Emanuel Swedenborg belong to a "community of the *ta'wil* (attainment of true meaning)" whose members are "vertically" united with each other. Each travels a path of perception that converges on the one God (Corbin, 92). This is also true of the spiritual people whose legends of Elijah are described in this chapter. The Christian desert fathers and mothers and their heirs, Jewish Merkavah and Heikhalot mystics, and their Kabbalist and Sufi confraternities unite in seeking to approach God.

There are important differences in the subgroups in Elijah's "community of the *ta'wil.*" They are Christians, Muslims, or Jews. Some have been gnostics and others ascetics, while others have emphasized contemplation. Some, due to their experiences, can be called mystics, as the term is now used to refer to individuals who have intense personal experiences of God. For others, encounter with God has been collective or transpersonal.

The subgroups have lived long distances from each other. The earliest whose writings we now possess were second-century Jewish mystics and fourth-century Christian hermits living in the Middle East. By the thirteenth century, spiritual groups from the three religions had spread around the Mediterranean, as far north as Ireland and east into India. Despite physical separations and differences in religion, the spiritual groups have shared an attachment to the figure of Elijah.

Wherever they turned, there was the face of God, but God has been beyond their grasp. No Sufi or Christian holy woman has believed that she could see the face of the Creator and live; no monk or Kabbalist thought he could feel the weight of the divine hand without annihilation. God has no face or hand, no final name for Elijah's multifaceted spiritual community. The subgroups in it insisted (and insist, for each tradition has present-day inheritors) that, though near, even immanent, God is infinite, transcendent, and absolute. As a result, their inner progress toward him, what Corbin terms the "vertical ascent" of their perception, has been like an elevator rising in a building with no roof. For Sufis, Christian holy women and men, and Kabbalists, to arrive in God, to "see" him or "touch" her, is to cease to be human: no one can see the face of God and live. Regardless of any human effort, despite God's gracious gifts, God is always beyond their grasp, within or, one might say, without, always more and always a mystery. For them, God contains creation and moves it but is not equal to it. Members of Elijah's spiritual groups have believed that they will never reach the unmediated Divine while remaining themselves.

Aware of the tension in which they live, these groups also have been committed to the second term of a paradox. On the evidence of their experience or the experience of those who preceded them, they have believed that human beings can know and love God in extraordinary ways. God is, and will always be, beyond them. God is also relatively accessible. It is impossible and possible to hope to be drawn into the process of divine love. One cannot, in any ultimate way and yet can in infinite lesser ways, participate in the transforming activity of divine intellection. God will never be reached but is always the goal of Christian monastic, Sufi, and Kabbalist aspiration. God can be known and loved more nearly as the individual develops in heart and mind toward the Infinite. God's creative names can be known, and human lives can be changed by their nearer impact. In their legends of him, Elijah very often helps spiritual brothers and sisters move up the shaft of inner life toward God. Stories of him have helped seekers remove obstacles or cross chasms in the ascent.

In his legends worldview, the prophet is very often a mediator who cements bonds between two other parties. In some legends he carries messages between heaven and earth. In others he reconciles family members or calls an individual back to God. Some of his mediations recounted here resemble those mentioned elsewhere. This chapter will begin with a look at the rare and highly prized "revelations of Elijah" that Jewish mystical tradition says the prophet has delivered as he brings other kinds of messages from heaven. However, he more characteristically aids his "spiritual peoples" through his own person and his spiritual life. Stories told elsewhere stress the miraculous, often visibly spectacular actions of the prophet. The group of beliefs and legends discussed in this chapter describe him as a spiritual companion or mentor. He still mediates in spiritual legends but does so as a human model. Legendary Elijah demonstrates that intimate relation with God is possible.

Taking him as an example of the kind of life they lead, some of his spiritual people wear his clothing. Christian hermits, for instance, adopted the coat of skins that he and John the Baptist were supposed to have worn, and their medieval Carmelite descendants wore a mantle recalling the garment that Elijah and Elisha used to part the waters of the Jordan. Some groups (such as, again, the Carmelites, who originally occupied Mt. Carmel, or any one of a number of eastern and western eremitical groups lodging by the Jordan) established their communities in places where the prophet was thought to have resided. Elijah's spiritual people has scrutinized him closely. Sufi, Merkavah, Kabbalist, and Christian legends comment on his habits of prayer, the content of his visions, his conversations with God, his ascetic practices, and his achievements in virtue. His journey to heaven in a chariot of fire has drawn particular interest. All the groups have believed that the prophet's spirit could foster their inner advancement. He has been a powerful figure able to help them approach God because they have believed that he excelled as a spiritual man.

Elijah and Jewish Mystical Attainment

The Talmud contains many tales in which Elijah teaches the pious something about the Torah. Sometimes the *haggadot* that were found there say that he brings knowledge about it from heaven. In other stories, he himself is the sage who delivers the Torah consultation. Elijah is generally revered by Jews for his knowledge of Scripture, as his cognate Khidr is similarly revered among Muslims. A well-known Jewish proverb declares that Elijah will answer all unresolved Torah questions at the end of time.

Kabbalists and Merkavah mystics have also cared about conformity to Torah rules of life that preoccupy Elijah in many Talmudic stories. Their most avid desire, however, has been to plumb the inner meaning of the divine word. Such an inquiry requires the engagement of one's full mental being. For Kabbalists and their Merkavah and Heikhalot ancestors, to uncover the deep secrets of the Torah has meant more than learning about God. By participating in the meanings, the relationships, and the potentialities of the words of the Torah, Jewish mystics enter into the activity of the divine mind. They accomplish such an extraordinary undertaking by studying and performing the Torah (for example, in recitation) in special ways handed down privately from master to disciple.

Revelations of Elijah

Elijah has provided them much legendary aid. Some stories say that he has brought inner knowledge about God and creation to Jewish mystics. What especially distinguishes these heavenly messages from those he bears to other groups in other legends is their mysteriousness. The reader will remember that the prophet's messages recorded in the scriptural books of Kings and Malachi were, or, if cast into the future, are expected to be, quite public. The whole of the kingdom of northern Israel heard the prophet's challenge and saw God's power on Mt. Carmel. Malachi suggests that the nations of the world will be affected by the messenger in the Last Days. The Gospels indicate that the crowds around John the Baptist and Jesus expected Elijah to make a public appearance. Many beliefs and legends point to the expectation that the prophet will communicate with whole groups, even all the nations of the world, at the end of time.

Talmudic legends tend to report the prophet delivering his messages somewhat more privately. Sometimes he relays Torah knowledge from God or from a heavenly academy to an earthly recipient in a one-on-one conversation. Those who receive Torah messages are usually pious rabbis, a select group. In some cases the Tishbite increases the privacy of the exchange by making his delivery of scriptural knowledge while wearing a disguise or while invisible to others. The content of such messages, nevertheless, can be expected to have come out in public in one way or another. Given their social function, any wisdom Elijah conveyed to Talmudic sages would have been put to use in raising the level of exoteric Torah righteousness of the community.

"Revelations of Elijah," prized by Jewish mystics over the centuries, have been even more privately delivered and more mysterious in content. Documents suggest that such revelations have occurred very infrequently. Many Kabbalists and earlier mystics were rabbis, but since not all rabbis have been inclined to such specialized pursuits, Jewish mystics have not been numerous. Of this highly secluded, small group, apparently only a few of the most spiritually advanced have received "revelations of Elijah," and only at certain times. According to Gershom Scholem in *Origins of the Kabbalah*, Elijah's special revelations of inner knowledge have been reported when widespread, profound shifts in religious understanding were occurring.

Prayer and Ascent

The prophet has given more general help to Kabbalists and their mystical ancestors by modeling important features of their way of life. In *Kabbalah: New Perspectives*, Moshe Idel relates that

Elijah's drought-breaking prayer described in 1 Kings is often used to explain what may happen to a virtuous individual who achieves *devekuth*—the cleaving of thought to the divine qualities—for the welfare of others. Ancient mystical lore says that the prophet, Enoch, and Moses were the only three human beings righteous enough to achieve permanent *devekuth*. The lesson that mystics drew from Elijah's effective prayer was that if they hoped to attain *devekuth*, even as a fleeting experience, they needed to strive for the extraordinarily high level of righteousness that he had attained.

The prayer stance that the Bible says Elijah used to end the drought has also been an aid to mystical endeavor. In Scripture, the prophet "bowed himself down upon the earth, and put his face between his knees" (1 Kings 18:42). According to Idel, the Talmud, Heikhalot literature, and the twelfth-century Kabbalist masterpiece, the *Sefer ha-Zohar,* describe individuals adopting the same posture. Tradition says the technique was effective. Jewish mystics praying like Elijah, with their head between their knees, are reported to have obtained blissful death, visions of heavenly palaces, and secrets of the Torah. By imitating Elijah's prayer stance, the Jewish mystic hoped to increase his possibility of attaining advanced experience.

Descriptions of mystics' inner ascents to heaven parallel Elijah's biblically recorded journey to heaven in some ways. References to Jewish mystical ascents, in which the seeker interiorly departs from the earthly realm to enter heaven seeking knowledge, are very ancient. Given how spectacular the "chariot of fire," "horses of fire," and "whirlwind" must have been to Elisha standing below and how vividly the scene remained in general memory, it is perhaps a surprise to find that Kabbalist and Merkavah descriptions of mystical ascents do not really dwell on the chariot or the celestial details of the journey.

In the detailed chariot descriptions that do appear in Jewish mystical lore, the chariot is God's, not Elijah's, the base scriptural passage is found in Ezekiel, not 2 Kings, and the topic usually under discussion is the meaning of the chariot, not the experience of the human ascent into heaven. While sitting on a river bank in Babylon, Ezekiel saw God's chariot composed of "four living creatures" with "four faces, and each of them had four wings" and wheels "upon the earth beside the living creatures," all of which moved "wherever the spirit would go." The creatures and their wheels supported "a throne, in appearance like sapphire; and seated above the likeness of the throne was a likeness as it were of a human form.... Such was the appearance of the likeness of glory of Yahweh" (Ezekiel 1:5–6, 15, 20, 26, 28). Ezekiel's vision has supplied vocabulary for speculation about the divine presence and has helped mystics report the content of their own visions of the near presence of God.

The second book of Kings says that Elijah and his disciple Elisha crossed the Jordan to its east side. "And as they still went on and talked, behold, a chariot of fire and horses of fire separated the two of them. And Elijah went up by a whirlwind into heaven," disappearing from Elisha's view (2 Kings 2:11–12). Ithamar Gruenwald notes that while Jewish apocalyptic and Merkavah writers sometimes describe ascents accomplished by means of something resembling Elijah's whirlwind, they also say the ascents were made with ladders or with the help of angels. The prophet's journey to heaven was not the only tradition they used to prepare themselves for the interior experience. For whatever reason, reports of actual mystical ascents—that is, the process of transit from the earthly to the heavenly realm—seem to have been brief (the descriptions of what the mystic finds in heaven are lengthy). Gruenwald notes that the protagonist of 1 Enoch was taken "aloft on the chariots of wind" and "in a whirlwind," that the *Peskita Rabbati* describes Moses carried to heaven in a cloud, and that the *Heikhalot Rabbati* describes an ascent by means of a whirlwind and a wagon (Gruenwald, 119–121).

What Jewish mystics have said happened to the prophet's body (and to the patriarch Enoch's body, although the latter figure will not be discussed here) once it entered heaven generally parallels what they expect will happen to their own when arriving into that realm. Christians have viewed entry into heaven as a release from tribulation. This belief has taken a variety of forms, one group of present-day Christians concluding, based on a meshing of 1 Thessalonians 4:16–17 with tribulation passages in the Book of Revelation, for example, that although the present world will end in conflict, and the vast number of its inhabitants will suffer wretchedly, they will be "caught up together with them in the clouds to meet the Lord in the air," (4:16–17). The apostle Paul's following remark to the Thessalonians that "God has not destined us for wrath" (1 Thess. 5:9) has been interpreted by some in this group to mean that those "caught up" would be exempted from a horrendous cataclysm going on below. Whether they adhered to this particular literalist reading of juxtaposed Scripture or not, Christians have always understood that passage to heaven will bring removal from suffering. The glide upward is expected to be smooth.

Jewish mystics have hoped to make such a journey before they die and before the world ends. They expect ascents to heaven to involve great dangers only avoided through rigorous virtue, extreme spiritual wariness, magical techniques, and aid from inhabitants of heaven. Merkavah mystics expected to be rewarded not by entry into heaven per se but by the content of secret revelations they believed that they would receive if they survived the arduous journey. However, early Jewish mystical traditions agree with more general expectations concerning the Day of Judgment (whether Jewish, Christian, or Muslim) on the issue of righteousness. Whether the person entering heaven was rewarded at life's end or whether the individual arrived there on an inner journey such as a Jewish mystic hoped to make, fidelity to God and moral perfection were required for entry. Elijah's ascension to heaven narrated in 2 Kings was often mentioned to support this belief.

Reports vary in saying what happened to the body of the mystic or the body of Elijah once heaven was entered. Some stories divorce the mystic's soul from his body and separate Elijah's soul from his "human form." Perhaps these sunderings were influenced by the old belief, sketched in the previous chapter, that heaven and earth were two entirely different realms, each with its own appropriate content. Idel notes, for example, that medieval Kabbalist documents report that the souls of mystics ascended to heaven while their bodies slept, proving the point that one's earthly form could not make the journey. Sometimes the family or disciples were said to have observed the mystic's immobile body, then watched him rouse himself to describe his ascent.

Sometimes Elijah is also described leaving his human body below on earth. At other times it is transformed. The story retold in the previous chapter in which the prophet triumphantly enters heaven, body and soul intact, after besting the Angel of Death in a wrestling match, although famous, is rare for medieval Kabbalist writing. More frequently Elijah, Enoch, and a few other figures are described receiving a celestial form once they enter the heavenly abode. From this, it is clear that Kabbalists believed that divine power readjusted the limits of ordinary human life for the advanced in spirit.

Mystics have not said that their counterparts became angels, as their lore says happened to Elijah and Enoch, but older Merkavah accounts do say that ascenders either shed their human body, leaving it below asleep as later Kabbalist works report, or slipped on a heavenly form or garment when they arrive. Like a fireman's coat, the celestial body or garment protected the humanity of mystics from the power of heaven or perhaps from the power of the secrets they received there.

Once in the realm and clad in their celestial form (or, some legends say, garment), Merkavah mystics resemble Elijah. Their reasons for being in heaven and their subsequent return to earth generally resemble his as well. Just as Elijah in many mystical and nonmystical legends is reported to have carried special knowledge down to earth for the benefit of humankind, the mystic who accomplishes a successful ascent receives special, secret knowledge in heaven not for his own power or edification but with the obligation to carry it to earth for the benefit of others, even if, in this case, the others are limited to spiritual specialists pursuing inner knowledge of God. When they descend to earth, Elijah and the mystics resume human bodies to complete the constructive mission. Such obvious similarities in the states of the body of the prophet and that of the mystics experiencing an ascent must have groomed the expectations of Merkavah and Kabbalist initiates who hoped to undertake the daring excursion in search of knowledge of God. The legendary insistence that even Elijah and Enoch, who were extraordinarily righteous, needed a transformed body to enter heaven makes the point that other human beings—such as the mystics who wrote the works—should expect something to happen to their bodies before they attain special knowledge. That such humans needed to be extremely virtuous is also obvious from the legends of the great figures.

Elijah has been a forerunner for Jewish mystics over the centuries. He has not appeared to them as a sign of the coming Day of Judgment, as Malachi so influentially predicts that he will do for later eras, nor has he performed for them the reconciliations that different traditions say that Jesus and Elijah will accomplish on behalf of those who will stand before their Maker. The prophet most often has been a forerunner for Jewish mystics because they have believed that he underwent what they expect to experience. His legendary ascent to heaven and commission there to bring beneficial knowledge down to earth have provided mystics, especially early practitioners of Merkavah techniques and later Kabbalists hoping to ascend or to attain *devekuth,* a mirror of what they themselves might accomplish in their own lives. Elijah illuminates the mental ascensional journey that Jewish mystics pursue. Legends of his effective prayer, his virtue, his successful entry into heaven, and his bodily transformation have also been of use. Jewish mystics have hoped for such high accomplishments themselves.

Ilyas, Khidr, and Sufi Knowledge

Elijah's tendency to parallel or merge with other figures is one of the more striking features of his legends worldwide. An instance of this has just been discussed. In Jewish mystical legends, what happens to Elijah's body in heaven resembles what is believed to happen to an individual who experiences an inner ascent. The prophet has also been absorbed into the figures of John the Baptist and the fiercely zealous Phinehas whose actions are recorded in the biblical Book of Numbers. He often shadows the actions of the Jewish Messiah as his near double. Christian tradition absorbed Elijah's great saving actions into its teachings about Christ. While some groups adopt his coat of skins or mantle, legends also say that the prophet merges, in appearance and sympathy at least, with the poor, the alien, and the shamed.

He is an even more quicksilver figure in Muslim legend. Corbin points out that some Islamic legends report Ilyas (Elijah) interacting with Khidr, a figure especially important to Sufis, while other Muslim legends merge the two and still others describe Khidr (or Ilyas-Khidr) participating intimately in the consciousness of spiritually advanced Sufis. Commentators who set out to explain who Khidr is and how he relates to Ilyas usually begin by remarking on the complexity of Muslim belief about the figures. The best way into the thicket may be to retell the details about Ilyas and Khidr found in the Koran.

The two passages that mention Ilyas, or Elijah, by name present him as an exemplar of faithfulness to God. Surah 6:82–85 lists three sets of leaders whom God chose to guide and exalt. The first set includes patriarchs, prophets, and kings: Noah, Isaac, Jacob, Joseph, Job, Moses, Aaron, David, and Solomon (6:84). Elijah appears in the second set, related to the birth and mission of Jesus: "Zechariah and John, Jesus, and Elias; each was of the righteous" (6:85). The third group, beginning with Ishmael, was chosen by God and guided to a straight path (6:87). Surah 37 explains Elijah's righteousness by taking up the Mt. Carmel story at the moment in which the prophet hurled his challenge to the northern Israelites to choose between God and Baal. "They cried him lies; so they will be among the arraigned, except for God's sincere servants." Elijah's faith is highly praised: "Even so We recompense the good-doers; he was among Our believing servants" (37:131–132).

The History of Prophets and Kings (whose title in William Brinner's recent translation is *The History of Al-Tabari*) by Abu Ja'far Muhammad ben Jarir al-Tabari (839–923 C.E.) assembles scriptural, legendary, and factual accounts into a universal history of the ancient nations. Al-Tabari decided that Elijah and Khidr were two separate figures. He located Elijah in history. He was a servant of God who prophesied to the northern Israelites. The legends of Elijah that al-Tabari mentions all expand on details of Surah 37. They dramatize the prophet's zeal, his intimacy with God, and the wavering faith of the Israelites, who appeal to the prophet for help when they suffer drought, but, in the Koran account, turn their backs on God ungratefully when the drought is lifted.

The Bible does not say that Elijah requested being taken to heaven, nor does it comment on how the fiery ascent affected his body, but it does show that the prophet was aware that his career on earth was about to end. The Koran does not mention the ascension. However, al-Tabari recounts a legend that says that the prophet, on seeing the stubborn ingratitude of the Israelites, "prayed to his Lord to take him to Himself and to give him a rest from them." God agreed to this, telling the prophet to go to a certain place. "A steed of fire approached, until it stopped in front of him. He jumped on it, and it took off with him." The legend said that Elijah's body began to change: "God covered him with feathers," al-Tabari says, "clothed him with fire; and stopped for him the pleasure of food and drink." The prophet did not entirely lose his humanity on entering heaven: "He flew with the angels, becoming human-angelic, earthly-heavenly" (al-Tabari, 125). This resembles what Jewish mystical tradition says happened to the prophet's body on entering heaven, although the Muslim legend al-Tabari recounts emphasizes the prophet's hybrid form once in heaven, while Jewish legends, perhaps reflecting Jewish abhorrence of mixtures, say that the prophet inhabited an angelic body, not a composite of the two.

Muslim myths of Elijah unspool from Koranic details as Jewish and Christian legends develop from the Bible. Sources for Khidr's legends are more difficult to trace, in part because Khidr is not explicitly mentioned in the Koran as Elijah is in Surahs 6 and 37. Early Muslim commentators decided that an unnamed figure in a story in Surah 18 was Khidr, but the reason for this decision is not known. Literary sources for the passage, which include the epic of Gilgamesh, the romance of Alexander, and a Jewish legend of Elijah and Rabbi Joshua ben Levi, do not help explain how Khidr in particular became so firmly associated with Surah 18. Perhaps Khidr existed in collective memory before the Koran was written and commentators matched his features with those of the figure in Surah 18, but there are other possibilities as well. Surah 18 may have been intentionally composed to encourage its readers to think that the nameless servant of God was Khidr. The Koran repeatedly urges believers to develop the ability to read the created world as a sign of God, a point that the story in Surah 18 presses heavily. Khidr's identity may be one of the discoveries that readers of Surah 18 are encouraged to make. Once traditions connected Khidr explicitly to the Koran, features of the Surah 18 story began to unfold into Khidr traditions in the usual haggadic way, and some Khidr legends merged Muslim traditions of Elijah.

Moses' Guide

In the Koran, Moses journeys in search of "the meeting of the two seas." He and his page achieve this first goal, "going past" or "passing over" the confluence of the two bodies of water. On discovering that they left behind a fish that was to be their breakfast, they turn back, encountering "one of Our servants," the figure whom tradition says is Khidr, "unto whom We had given mercy from Us, and We had taught him knowledge proceeding from Us." Moses and the servant of God continue their travels together.

Surah 18 gives its readers many opportunities to connect the un-named figure with wisdom. The servant of God has been taught "knowledge proceeding from Us" (18:65). Moses is aware of this and also knows that the content of the Khidr-figure's special knowledge is *rushd,* the "right judgments" (18:66) one makes after attaining one's full powers. The prophet asks to be taught this knowledge, but the servant of God declares that Moses will not be able to tolerate what he "never encompassed in [his] knowledge" (18:68). Nevertheless, he accepts Moses as a disciple, instructing him, "Then if thou followest me, question me not on anything until I myself introduce the mention of it to thee" (18:70). As the pair travel, the man does things that Moses finds so shocking to decency and the Law of God that he is driven to ask questions. The servant parts from Moses, but before he leaves, he explains the lifesaving motives of his strange actions.

The servant is obviously a teacher of inner knowledge, as Khidr certainly has been in post-Koranic tradition. Moses fails three times to place a puzzling action in its right interpretive context. The unnamed guide has to provide the keys, which among other things, involve events that he, not Moses, could foresee. (The guide also correctly foretold that Moses, the sage of exoteric Law, would not be able to tolerate puzzles.) Al-Tabari reports that Ibn 'Abbas, one of his sources, paraphrases the guide's question in the Koran, "How can you bear what you cannot encompass in knowledge?" as "You know only what is obvious about justice, but you have not encompassed the esoteric knowledge that I know" (al-Tabari, 14). The servant's puzzling behavior and explanations are reminiscent of Elijah's sur-prising movements and deep mastery of the Torah among Jews. In Surah 18, the servant teaches Moses that he needs advanced under-standing of hidden qualities if he hopes to discern the real meanings of God's Law.

Al-Tabari recounts the belief that Muhammad had remarked that Khidr was the one man wiser than Moses, along with its variants that said that the angel Gabriel informed Moses of this fact and that God himself said that Khidr was his wisest servant, "to whose knowledge the people's knowledge aspires, so that it might attain a word that will lead one to guidance or turn one away from evil" (al-Tabari, 11). Al-Tabari also includes an anecdote that extends the Surah 18 story. In the legendary addition, Moses and the servant of God eventually reach the meeting place of the two seas, "than which no place on earth has more water." The pair watch a swallow drinking from the boundless ocean. Khidr comments, "O Moses! My knowledge and your knowledge are to God's knowledge like the quantity of this water that this swallow drinks" (al-Tabari, 13). No man or woman of knowledge, not even Khidr, ever even begins to grasp the deep things of God. Not even the confluence of esoteric and exoteric knowledge, the meeting of the two seas that Moses seeks, begins to show a human being God's wisdom. As will be seen below, Khidr's role as a guide to special knowledge expanded among Sufis, who developed inner teachings of Islam.

Moses' Mental Quest

In the story found in Surah 18 of the Koran, Moses is on a difficult journey. The narrative is begun in medias res, the prophet caught in the act of telling his page, "I will not give up until I reach the meeting of the two seas, though I go on for many years." In later quests involving Khidr, great distances are crossed and perils are surmounted. Several features distinguish the Surah 18 journey from later quest legends. In the latter, travelers certainly encounter difficulties, but they do not veer from their trajectory and they reach their goal. They often find a surprise at the end of their quest, usually involving identity. Perhaps, with Khidr's help, they find someone, a relative, or perhaps themselves. In contrast, Moses' discoveries come along the way, and have to do with inner knowledge. His path constantly zigzags. He does not reach the end of his journey.

The Koran says that the prophet originally sets out to find the confluence of two seas. Some commentators deduce that he arrived at the juncture, didn't recognize it, and passed on still in search of it. Once the prophet finds that he has lost something (the fish), he reverses his steps when his page announces what he forgot, which is that the fish "took its way into the sea in a manner marvelous." Ironies abound at this point: the fish, at least, made it to the destination toward which Moses was originally aiming (the great sea), but Moses, on hearing about the fish, exclaims, "This is what we were seeking!" and reverses direction, going to the spot where the fish was left (but is there no more, since it swam away).

What converges at the spot the second time around are the "two seas" of the mind of Moses, filled with the knowledge of God's Law and the mind of the servant given knowledge of *rushd* by God. However, the meeting of the mind seas is not, as it turns out, the important destination of Moses' journey, for the page disappears from the story and the new pair sets off again, traveling toward an unnamed destination while the man of God begins to tutor Moses. Moses' journey really has no end in the Surah, although it develops an intention. When the prophet muffs his lessons (each time failing to accomplish a connection between obvious and implicit meaning—failing again to recognize confluences), he and the servant of God part. Moses is left to journey on alone, but with a final gift, the guide's explanatory remapping of all that happened to the pair in the past. At this point, the story breaks off. Moses is left still in medias res. If he can detect inner meaning in outer evidence from here forward, he will be able to "cross the gap" or ford the "convergence of two seas" in knowledge. He will become an adept in inner knowledge.

Later legends tying Khidr to quests cast him as a teacher, but his pupils in popular legends are not called on to exert such mental muscle in twists and turns in learning as Moses is in the Koran story. In tales collected by Ananda Coomaraswamy, a Hindu princess seeks the water of life to heal her father and in the process encounters Khidr who requires that she show her human form (she has been invisible) in exchange for the water. In a Muslim Indian folktale, a prince of Persia travels to India to find his slain father, whom Khwaja Khizr helps restore to life. Although these later legendary journeys take their travelers very long distances, even into the caverns of the earth, the Moses of the Koran tale would have found the mental challenges of such journeys easy.

Water, the Fish, and Immortality

Surah 18 inspired many later legends that connect Khidr with water, a fish, and immortality. The fish seemed to be a secondary part of the Koranic story—it was to have been breakfast and was left behind—until it "took its way into the sea in a manner marvelous." Folktales suggest that many Muslims reading Surah 18 thought that the fish had been dead before it swam away (it was, after all, left behind on a rock). Coomaraswamy reports many variants concerning the miraculous fish and Khidr. In one legend Ilyas and Khizr, not Moses, are the journeyers. They stop to have a meal of dried fish, let it fall into a fountain, and are astonished to see it revive, a signal that they have come to the Fountain of Life, "from which they both drink" (Coomaraswamy, 161). In another legend, the fish pulls Noah's Ark through the waters of the Flood. Khwaja Khizr is said to travel on a fish. Coomaraswamy even traces Khidr and the fish back to Ea, son of Enki, the Sumerian lord of the waters, who is shown in iconography holding a fish and a vase that is the source of immortality. In all the variants the fish is involved with the power to gain immortal life.

The relation of Khidr to immortality is most complex. As Christians and Jews did for Elijah, Muslims created a historical birth and ancestry for Khidr, although Corbin notes that the whole body of his legends shows that Khidr—like Elijah among Christians and

Jews—is not confined to a single life story. Some legends say he was a son of Adam who buried his father's body when Adam died after the Flood. Others give Khidr an Egyptian or Persian ancestry. He was said to have been a companion of Abraham, Moses, and Alexander. He and Elijah are sometimes said to make a yearly pilgrimage to Mecca. Some say that he ordinarily resides in Jerusalem or meets Elijah there once a year. Coomaraswamy relates that in India, Muslims and Hindus honor Khidr, whom they alternatively see as a prophet, a deity, and a saint, as Khwaja Khizr. For them he is generally a sage and is often said to be elderly. He is often associated with the color green, which has multiple meanings. For this reason, his name is often spelled *el Khadir*—the green one who wears a green robe or perhaps sits on a green mat. As such, he entered Western iconography as the Green Man, whose verdant face often appears in the carvings on public buildings. While the color is universally associated with life, Muslims also connect it with surrender to God in response to God's revelation.

Some (not all) post-Koranic legends say that Khidr escaped the bonds of mortality. They say he did not do this by an ascension to heaven on a fiery steed or in a chariot of fire, Elijah's two modes of transport. Instead, Khidr usually is said to have made the change from a human into an "angel-human" by drinking from the Spring of Immortality. Like the Elijah of general Jewish belief, Khidr often restores or gives life. Some Muslim legends strongly associate him with the vegetable kingdom, and others with the sea, features that have no obvious equivalent in Elijah legends. According to one Muslim tale, on reaching the Spring of Life, the figure is told, "Thou art Khadir and where thy feet touch it, the earth will become green" (Wensinck, 905).

A group of stories that some think probably entered Islam from Christianity says that the unnamed guide of Surah 18 was once the mortal Prince Abul Abbas. Forced to marry by his father, Prince Abul persuaded his future bride to join him in a vow of perpetual chastity.

When the couple fled to an island to preserve the way of life they had chosen, the prince found the water of immortality, drank from it, and completed his transformation into Khidr. He thereafter could make himself invisible to fly to help those seeking spiritual attainment such as Moses was in Surah 18, or such as Sufis later would do. As happens so often in other of Elijah's legends worldwide, Abul Abbas' virtue—in this case, his bodily abstinence—is a precondition for receiving supernatural power.

It should be noted that the Koran has nothing to say about a physical transformation in the servant of God or in anyone else, except, perhaps, the fish, which swims away in a most marvelous fashion. Two of the Koranic guide's most puzzling actions are, in fact, on the surface "anti-immortal": he kills a boy and puts others in danger of death. To think about immortality while reading the Surah 18 story, one must focus not on bodily change but on the obligation to use one's mind often commented about in the Koran. Service of God with one's lips or by mechanical adherence to rules is not enough for Paradise. "And the Trumpet shall be blown; that is the Day of the Threat. And every soul shall come, and with it a driver and a witness. 'Thou wast heedless of this; therefore We have now removed from thee thy covering, and so thy sight today is piercing'" (Surah 50:20–22). "Know that God revives the earth after it was dead. We have indeed made clear for you the signs, that haply you will understand" (Surah 57:15–20). Surah 18 describes Moses, already a great teacher of cult and ethical life, discovering that he must look beyond the obvious to the heart of matters if he truly wants to know God's Law.

Guide to Inner Life

Spiritual traditions depend for their survival on lived interaction between master and disciple. A Zen master's words are only partially effective in written form. Not only has one to be present to receive the full impact of Zen *koans,* but one must also be under the master's obedience and must participate in the daily meditations and rituals. The necessity of a lived teaching relationship between guide and aspirant is also highly visible in Christian monastic life. One of the effects of the Benedictine vow of stability is that it obliges those who make it to undergo years of regular contact with a single community, which for Benedictines is one's teacher (the elder among the community and the abbot or abbess taking especially important roles). The desert fathers and mothers also used a system of formation in which neophytes lived with experienced hermits before living by themselves. Kabbalists depend on one-on-one conversations for teachings to be passed down. Most Sufis learn by formal submission to a *shaikh* who can trace his or her teaching ancestry along a line of transmitters stretching back to Muhammad.

The spiritual traditions also have a place for unusual individuals who pursue self-initiation. Occasional Sufis, such as Ibn 'Arabi, to whom Corbin devotes his study, learn from many human teachers, but never link themselves into a line of transmission through formal obedience to a human *shaikh*. Their tutelage instead is said to be supervised by Khidr. Corbin remarks that not all of what it meant to the Sufi who said that he or she was a "disciple of Khidr" can be gathered from documents. The ritual and inner details of the investiture with Khidr's mantle that Ibn Arabi reports was bestowed on him on three different occasions are not known, for example. Nevertheless, Corbin surmised that to be a "disciple of Khidr" meant to "become" Khidr, in some way acquiring the same mind or the same state of mind that the archetypal figure had (Corbin, 65).

The question, of course, is what the content of Khidr's mind was thought to be, or perhaps better said, what it was that a Sufi such as Ibn 'Arabi might be thought to have obtained when he reached the state in which he might say that he had "become" Khidr or become his disciple. A hint of an answer may lie in an anecdote that Corbin collected from Suhrawardi's autobiography, in which the latter reports an inner ascent of the cosmic Mount Qaf to reach the Spring of Life on its summit. An angel tells Suhrawardi that if he hopes to complete his climb, he must put on Khidr's sandals. Once the Sufi bathes in the spring, he will be "preserved forever from all taint" and will have "discovered the meaning of mystic Truth…. If you *are Khidr* [Corbin's emphasis], you too can ascent Mount Qaf without difficulty" (Corbin, 60).

Entering into a mental relationship with Khidr demonstrates a characteristic feature of Sufism. Among Sufis there is no one single way to pursue the path of knowledge and love of God, and subsequently there is no single authoritative teaching tradition (or for that matter, any exclusive interpretation of phenomena, whether they are literary, physical, or mental), even though there are particularly rich pathways and highly influential teachers. Khidr's tutelage embodies the freedom of Sufi inquiry, which honors individual differences in perception, all the while demanding extreme rigor in pursuit of them. Corbin remarks:

> Khidr's "guidance" does not consist in leading all his disciples uniformly to the same goal, to one theophany (that is, to one manifestation in the realms below the Absolute) identical for all, in the manner of a theologian propagating his dogma. He leads each disciple to his own theophany, the theophany of which [Khidr] personally is the witness, because that theophany corresponds to [the disciple's] "inner heaven," to the form of his own being, to his eternal individuality (*'ayn thabita*), in other words, to what Abu Yazid Bastami calls the "part allotted" to each of the Spirituals, and which, in Ibn 'Arabi's words, is that one of the divine Names which is invested in him, the name by which he knows his God and by which his God knows him; that is the interdependence between *rabb* and *marbub*, between the lord of love and his vassal. (Corbin, 61)

One can certainly find general analogies here with the Christian understanding of the "spirit of Elijah" as a particular manifestation of the Spirit of God, or the Holy Spirit, focused through a zealous follower, but it must be noted that Muslim tradition uses Khidr's inner state to describe different features of consciousness than Elijah's spirit describes for Christians. The latter do not speak of an inner landscape through which seekers ascend until they encounter a divinely allotted theophanic name of God. Nor among Christians does being filled with Elijah's spirit equate with gnostic interplay between seeker and sought, in a dynamic *coniunctio oppositorum* of knowledge. Among Christians Elijah's spirit is his zeal, the full-hearted force of his will, or love, bent on his Lord. Among Sufis, Khidr's spirit or being mediates and confirms gnosis of God.

Louis Massignon remarks that Khidr helps spiritually inclined Muslims gain access to suprahistorical life. He comments that the figure offers many things, including hope, the paragonic example of his own chastity (attached to him by the group of traditions that explain that he was formerly Prince Abul Abbas), and the inspiration to seek perfection: "As is true of Elijah's survival in Judaism, Khidr's existence and survival is important in Islam for maintaining messianic hope blended with the desire for abstinence and chastity [as the Sufi] pursues the perfect life" (cited in *Élie le prophète*, vol. 2, 275). Massignon perhaps places too much emphasis on chastity, now thought to be an imported feature, in his characterization of the Muslim response to Khidr, but the similarity he sees in the behavior of messianists, Sufis, Khidr, and Elijah is instructive. Wherever they are found in the world, those who live in preparation for the eschaton agree with those seeking spiritual attainment that mental and bodily disciplines are necessary preparation for encounter with God. That encounter may occur at the end of time, as the messianist expects; at the end of mortal life, as the pious generally believe; or before it, as various spiritual groups believe can happen. Through the example of his life and through his other mediations, Khidr leads seekers to their goal.

Elijah and Christian Perfection

Elijah has also helped dedicated Christians respond to the demands of perfection. In the Gospel of Matthew, Jesus' call to perfect life caps his teaching that hearers should obey Torah stipulations:

> Till heaven and earth pass away, not an iota, not a dot, will
> pass from the law until all is accomplished. Whoever then
> relaxes one of the least of these commandments and
> teaches men so, shall be called least in the kingdom of
> heaven, but he who does them and teaches them shall be
> called great in the kingdom of heaven. (Matt. 5:18–20)

One should fulfill both the letter and spirit of God's Law: "You have heard that it was said to the men of old, 'You shall not kill.... But I say to you that every one who is angry...whoever insults...whoever says, 'You fool!' shall be liable to the hell of fire" (5:21–22). Jesus tells the crowds that purity of intentions and purity of actions should be extreme in those wanting to enter God's kingdom: "You, therefore, must be perfect, as your heavenly Father is perfect" (5:48).

Christian beliefs about the how inner perfection relates to right action developed as the new religion began to take characteristic shape. Early Israelites had considered the heart to be the seat of the personality or mind. More than the source of feelings, it was the center of an Israelite's being. Purity of heart could not exist without action. "How long will you go limping with two different opinions?" Elijah asked the northern Israelites, "If Yahweh is God, follow him"; that is, actively serve God, to the exclusion of other gods, "but if Baal, then follow him" (1 Kings 18:20–21). To have a pure, unmixed heart, one had to bring offerings to Yahweh, obey him, destroy idols, purify one's ranks, and care for others. Early Scripture taught that inner life was completed by outer fidelity. Jesus reversed the terms, emphasizing that inner purity should move one's actions, but he did not sever the two. Clearly for Jesus, purity of intention was not enough for salvation.

A Model Martyr

Christians continued to believe that efforts at perfection required active, unmixed fidelity to God. Jesus' self-offering in obedience to God's will was the greatest example of purity of heart that they had. It was reinforced in their mind by the scriptural stories of Daniel in the lion's den, Jeremiah's suffering, and the slaughter of the Maccabees. Once his epistles began to circulate among the churches, the Apostle Paul's emphasis on willing suffering on behalf of the Gospel of salvation cemented the relation between Christian faith and acceptance of physical suffering. Stories of exemplary deaths circulated. Martyrdom constituted Christian perfection in the first age of the Church.

As was shown in the last chapter, although always eclipsed by the examples of Jesus and the Apostles, Elijah is occasionally praised in early Christian writings for the manner in which he died or would die. He was most often thought to be still alive in heaven, waiting to return to usher in the eschaton, as Malachi said. Christian writers did draw on the book of Revelation and quite possibly early oral tradition to declare that in the Last Days, Elijah would be slaughtered by forces of evil and be returned to life by God. The prophet's association with John the Baptist may have transferred to him the spiritual prestige of the latter's death at Herod's hands. Early legends of Elijah the martyr are scarce, however. Christians more easily saw him as a holy recluse dedicated to prayer.

The Desert Ascetic

The emperor Constantine's fourth-century decision to make Christianity the principal religion of the Roman Empire shifted the relationship between the Church and secular rule. Their religion now identified with the state, Christians could no longer define themselves in opposition to worldly power. Regretting the change, some followers began to withdraw from populated areas. The number of Egyptian or Syrian Christians living alone, in groups of two or three on the outskirts of towns or in larger communities separated from the world by walled compounds, was rising by the end of the century. Hermits and cenobitic (community) monks of both genders pursued silence, exterior discipline, interior scrutiny, dependence upon God, and prayer.

They redefined the Church's ideal of perfect life, and Elijah became a mirror for the kind of life they led.

According to Peter Brown in *Society and the Holy in Late Antiquity*, Christian desert ascetics understood perfection to have two axes. Occurring on the historical plane were the hermit's never-ending attempts to repent, pray, and perform ascetic acts that were so often mirrored in legends of Elijah, as will be seen. The vertical axis of the perfect life included life on earth but also connected the hermit with heavenly life, no matter what horizontal perfection in virtue or physical discipline the person had achieved. By no means thinking that they were morally or spiritually perfect (the reference point of perfection was, after all, God), Christian hermits did claim another elitism for themselves. They believed that when they left the corrupt and chaotic world of ordinary human interaction (which they also often called the "city" or "Babylon"), they entered an incorrupt state, which practices such as continence and fasting helped them maintain. Horizontally, in the plane of their historical efforts to conform to Christ, hermits were imperfect; vertically, they were in a state of perfection that was a true prelude to heaven. The desert authors refer to both axes of perfection when they praise eremitism as the Church's best model of Christian life.

Details of his scriptural life story encouraged the proponents of desert Christianity to conclude that Elijah was a hermit. Although it is apparent that he was called to a public mission (as all Israelite prophets were), anecdotes about him in 1–2 Kings suggest that Elijah was psychically isolated from human beings. His only real help came from Yahweh. Two biblical episodes and several scattered references also place him in the mountains and wastelands, types of locales favored by early hermits and monks. These details encouraged Christians who wanted to pursue the spiritual life in deserted places. Elijah's name vied with that of John the Baptist, Antony, Macarius, and Paul of Thebes as the originator of Christian desert life or, as the Church Fathers often said, monasticism, explaining that the hermit was *monos,* alone. Boaga notes that once Christians began saying that Elijah inaugurated hermit life, they soon gave him legendary followers. As the next chapter will show, thirteenth-century European Carmelites developed many Elijan legends from these beginnings.

The influential fifth-century hermit, monastic organizer, and spiritual writer John Cassian says that the prophet achieved eremitical perfection. Cassian advises the readers of his *Institutes* and *Conferences,* two classics that have shaped the lives of countless religious, of the need to perfect the ordinary virtues in a community of peers before attempting the more spiritually challenging life of a hermit. Many are best suited to community life, but some desire greater perfection. These go out to engage demons "in clear battle" in the "great hiding places of the desert." They "are surely the imitators of John the Baptist, who remained in the desert throughout the whole of his life. They do like Elias and Elisaeus, about whom the apostle [the author of the biblical book of Hebrews] had this to say: 'They wandered about dressed in the skins of sheep or goats. They were persecuted and poor—they of whom the world was unworthy. They went to live in lonely places, on mountains, in caves, in the hollows of the earth' (Heb. 11:37–38)" (Conference 18:6). Jerome, Gregory the Great, Ambrose, and many of the early Fathers join Cassian in seeing Elijah and John the Baptist as exemplars of Christian desert combat with personal weaknesses and with the persecuting forces of evil, that is, with the vigorously active pursuit of spiritual perfection on its horizontal axis.

According to some, the Tishbite decided to become a hermit. "Elijah was such a one who fled the tumult of human society and chose to live in the desert" says the fourth-century writer of the *Commentary on Isaiah* (Bardy in *Élie le prophète*, vol. 1, 142). Elijah's decision to turn his back on the distractions of town and city has no equivalent in Muslim and Jewish lore, nor does it have a good foothold in the Bible, since none of Elijah's desert sojourns described in 1–2 Kings came about because of his choice. The often-repeated remark of the Fathers (which we will see survived among Carmelites) that Elijah chose to live in the desert is yet another example of the tendency of his legends to shift in content until they are more familiar and so more meaningful to their later audiences. Christian monastic life has always required its members to take a vow (or several over a period of time), demonstrating freewill commitment to that way of life. It was only natural that Elijah became a sign to Christians of a cognizant choice of the spiritual life.

Benedictine historian of monasticism Jean Leclercq explains how the Church Fathers could have said something about the prophet that so flatly contradicts the letter of Scripture. In *The Perfect Life,* Leclercq discusses how cenobitic monks connected themselves to first-century followers of Christ by emphasizing certain scriptural features and downplaying others. Details of the life of the prophets, Jesus, and his apostles were fastened on as prefigurations. A distinction was drawn between "apostolic ministry," which was the preaching and pastoral work that Jesus called his followers to perform, and "apostolic life," which proponents of monasticism matched with the community life they knew. Examining passages such as Acts 4:32–35, early writers such as Basil and later proponents such as Peter Damian concluded that Jesus' earliest disciples had attained the "apostolic life" of charity, self-abandonment, prayer, common life, renunciation, and life in the presence of God that they themselves hoped to attain. It was only a small step more to say that Jesus' followers had founded Christian cenobitic life.

The same process was used to say that prophets such as Moses, Elijah, Jeremiah, and John the Baptist were founders of Christian eremitical life. Leclercq notes passages in which Jerome and his contemporaries affirm that "monks of the Old Testament," such as Elisha's "sons of the prophets" but also individual prophets such as Elijah, "instituted monastic [solitary] life" (Leclercq, 57). Arguments were based on details that could be gleaned from the Bible concerning the prophets' personal "state" or "way of life" (Leclercq, 58). The prophets were seen to embody the desert ideals of austerity, purity, eschatological orientation, spiritual enthusiasm, and celibacy. What the Fathers learned from Scripture, they added to from their own lives, then allowed Sacred Writ to mirror the new reflection back to them. Athanasius's remark that Antony "used to tell himself that from the career of the great Elijah, as from a mirror, the ascetic must always acquire knowledge of his own life" suggests that early Christian writers understood that what they said about Elijah was meant to reflect their own ideals (Athanasius, sec. 7, 37).

Anytime they mention Elijah as a precursor of ascetic life, early Christian writers can usually be found supplementing Scripture with one thing or another that allows them to align him with the model of life that they are promoting. The writer of the *Commentary on Isaiah* quoted earlier, who some think was the Eastern Father Basil, believed that fasting, vigil, and other disciplines were necessary for successful contemplation. The prophet modeled these: "Elijah was such a one who fled the tumult of human society and chose to live in the desert. If the saints are firmly resolved to search for the truth, isn't it absurd to wish to attain the fruits of innumerable labors without effort? Consider Elijah: After how many retreats, how many periods of quiet, how many fasts did he merit seeing God?" (Bardy in *Élie le prophète*, vol. 1, 142). Here the fourth-century writer deduces that the Israelite prophet must have engaged in retreats, silences, and fasts while living in the desert, since Scripture records that he had extraordinary spiritual experiences there.

The most important feature of Christian asceticism attributed to Elijah was virginity, which was seen as a spiritual as well as a physical state, part of the vertical axis of perfection mentioned earlier. The belief was bequeathed to the Fathers from Jewish lore. Jerome, Augustine, Gregory the Great, and John Cassian pause to mention the prophet's immaculate state, usually saying that he was firmly committed to it. Cassian comments in the sixth book of his *Institutes*: "For it is one thing to be abstinent…and another to be chaste and, to put it this way, to pass over into a disposition of integrity and incorruption.... This is a virtue that is bestowed in a very special manner only on those who remain virgins in both flesh and mind, as both Johns are known to have been in the New Testament, and also Elijah, Jeremiah, and Daniel in the Old" (Cassian, *Institutes*, 154). According to Cassian, Elijah's scripturally recorded life (which doesn't mention his sexual condition) demonstrates that virginity promotes spiritual life more easily than does mere sexual abstinence. Elijah's virginity manifested his "integrity and incorruption of the heart." In Elijah, Cassian finds a model of Christian perfection attained through careful maintenance of an original God-given state that encompasses body and soul.

Gregory of Nyssa's fourth-century description of the Tishbite's physical appearance, cited by Gustave Bardy in an article on legends of Elijah among the Greek Fathers, deftly evokes the ideal inner state for which the Christian hermit strove:

> Then [in the course of sacred history] God presents Elijah who possesses a power to heal equal to the size of human maladies, who scorns the needs of the body. He is a man with a gaunt visage hidden by a mane of hair. He is recognizable for his kind of life. He possesses a venerable, sad and mirthless demeanor. His eyes are fixed directly on their object, and he faces it fully. His body is covered only with a goatskin...without protection from cold and heat. (*Élie le prophète*, vol. 1, 144)

The medieval Kabbalist Moses of León tells a story in which Elijah was able to conquer death at heaven's gate because of his righteousness. Gregory here connects the prophet's virtuous abstinence from food, comfort, and human interaction to his inner achievement of detachment and his power to heal great illness.

Elijah's Interior Life

After they occupied Canaan around 1000 B.C.E., the Israelites built a society around worship of Yahweh and service to a king.

Biblical stories from this period added to what was needed for spiritual perfection, although fidelity to the one God remained the central requirement. Job's story, which scholars believe was written down in its present form sometime between 1000 and 800 B.C.E., supplements trust in God alone with harrowingly scrupulous self-examination that older parts of the Hebrew Bible do not mention. Much of the emotional tension of Job's tale springs from the dilemmas that Job partially trusts but also wishes to examine his God's purity of intention, and sometimes trusts but also anxiously scrutinizes his own. His scrutiny of himself and attempted scrutiny of God are part of his interior growth. The men of God who began to prophesy around the same time, in the ninth and eighth centuries B.C.E., also taught Israel that holiness amounted to more than exterior acts of obedience to the divine will. For those such as Hosea, holiness required a "circumcised heart." Thus, the later Hebrew Scriptures bequeathed to Christianity an attention to the inner condition of holiness that Jesus' teachings and Paul's epistles plumb still further. What the Hebrew Bible describes as an open, well-inclined heart has been highly desired in Christian spiritual life. In their caves and huts, Christian monks and hermits recited the Psalms that so often speak in the language of inner perfection: "My soul longs, yea, faints for the courts of Yahweh; my heart and flesh sing for joy to the living God" (Psalm 84:2). "Teach me thy way, O Yahweh, that I may walk in thy truth; unite my heart to fear thy name" (Psalm 86:11).

Early monks and hermits thought about Elijah's inner life as well as his physical achievements. In a highly influential work, Athanasius wrote that the Egyptian hermit Antony (another for whom the title of founder of Christian monasticism was claimed) often called to mind the Tishbite's bold declaration, "Yahweh the God of Israel lives, before whom I stand" (1 Kings 17:1), pondering what a man would have to do to be able to utter that sentence. Antony resolved to endeavor "each day to present himself as the sort of person ready to appear before God—that is, pure of heart and prepared to obey his will, and no other" (Athanasius, sec. 7, 37).

Elijah's declaration that he stood ready to serve Yahweh has affected many over the years. When Athanasius's *Life of Antony* was translated into Latin around 375 C.E., it became a staple of monastic teaching. Augustine of Hippo reports that when he read the story of Antony's heroic struggle to live up to Elijah's interior perfection, he was able to overcome a spiritual block and commit himself to a celibate, retired religious life. Centuries later, the Carmelite reformer Teresa of Avila said that Augustine's conversion story gave her courage to relinquish herself fully to God. What carries from one tale to the next is what the original anecdote from the book of Kings shows that Elijah originally had, an inner disposition of complete self-offering to God. By Teresa's day, Elijah's name had disappeared from the sequence of life-changing stories, but his generous spiritual gesture had not.

His name remained attached to mystical contact with God. The Fathers concluded that the prophet's audition of the "still, small voice" while standing in front of the cave on Mt. Horeb showed that he was a soul of very great attainment. While Jewish mystics told legends of Elijah's entry into heaven to help them think over what might happen to them in a similar experience, Christian hermits and members of cenobitic life retold Elijah's encounter with God at the mouth of the cave to help them meditate on what might happen in especially direct experiences of God during their lifetime.

Proponents of Christian desert and cenobitic life muse on Elijah's experience in various ways. Gregory of Nyssa argues that the best way to ensure rare encounters with God such as Elijah's at Horeb is to enter religious life at a young age. In *On Virginity* he writes, "From adolescence these two men [Elijah and Elisha] withdrew from human society...only with interior [and, Gregory says elsewhere, exterior] agitations discarded did they establish themselves in such a calm and tranquillity that they raised themselves to the height of divine things reported of each" (Bardy, cited in *Élie le prophète*, vol. 1, 145). Paul Chandler retrieved Gregory the Great's conclusion that the prophet's experience was one of paradoxical unknowing: "For we perceive, as it were, the whispering of a gentle breeze when in a sudden grace of contemplation we have subtle taste of unbounded truth—for it is true that we know something about God when we feel ourselves unable to know anything about him…. After the whispering of the gentle breeze, the prophet covers his face with his cloak, because in this most subtle contemplation of the truth, he knows by what a cloak of ignorance man is covered" (*Moralia* 5:26:66, cited in Chandler, *A Journey with Elijah*, 119).

While his experience at Mt. Horeb is treated as a very special moment of mystical encounter, the Fathers also sometimes seem to be saying that Elijah achieved a continuing state of contemplation. Cassian groups him and Elisha with Paul, Antony, and John the Baptist, as men of the desert who "in the quiet of their solitude…enjoy the closest union with God" (Conference 14:4). In his *Letter 8*, Ammonas presents the prophet to his monks as someone who spent a life in full-hearted pursuit of contemplation and action: "You will obtain this peace if you throw your souls into bodily work and the labor of the heart…. Lift your thoughts to heaven and day and night call on the Holy Spirit with your whole heart, and it will be given to you. This is how it was with Elijah" (Hayek, cited in *Élie le prophète*, vol. 1, 165).

Elijah and Attainment

The groups whose legends are discussed in this chapter sometimes borrow a two-phase pattern of movement from the Greek Neoplatonists to describe the whole scope of eternal life. They sometimes write that the life of all things began in an emanation, or unfolding, of God. They found support for this in the Koran and the Bible, which say that God indeed is the origin of all life in the cosmos. In the Neoplatonic paradigm, God is the first pole of a creative movement that reaches a destination in a second pole, then loops back to its source.

Once God "thought" or "breathed them forth" in creation, and creation reached its maximum of multiplicity, all creatures, from the most rudimentary and mute to the most complex, began to move back toward Absolute Unity in a second phase of activity. Every creature sought to return to its source, but humans were especially capable of making the return. Sufis, Christian holy men and women, and Jewish mystics saw that it was in the nature of things, that is, part of the great creative movement of life, that humans yearned to reunite with God. It was in the nature of things that they used their most distinctive attributes as humans—their body, heart, mind, and soul—to make the return. Or they could use them. Humans had the capability to seek closer and closer proximity to God; since they possessed free will, they could choose to apply their full powers to the ascent or not. Hermits, Sufis, and the other groups understood that what set them apart from other human beings was that they had chosen to try to make the ascent, to move along the trajectory of the loop from the second pole to the first.

The Neoplatonic two-phase model allowed spiritual people to study the human side of the divine/human dyad, considering what a human being could do, with God's help, to climb up in inner life to come closer to God. God ultimately was beyond study, but the approach to God was not. Elijah has been helpful to the inquiry. Although stories in which God moves him about ("whither I know not where," Obadiah complains in 1 Kings) or gives him something are important, a large number of his spiritual legends concentrate on the prophet's spiritual achievements. For early Christians, it was important to think that Elijah fasted, struggled with temptation, and withdrew from the corruption of cities. All the groups comment on the results of his dedicated actions. Jewish mystical traditions say that if one prays as Elijah prayed, with one's head between one's knees, and certainly with purity of intent, one can achieve a blissful death or special knowledge of the divine. If one trains one's mind to rise from realm to realm, perceiving the things of God, Khidr traditions suggest that one may drink from the well of immortality, read minds, and move invisibly from one place to another.

Legends of his involvement in the spiritual life were most varied
by the Middle Ages. It was then that he became a special inspiration
to the brothers and sisters of the Blessed Virgin Mary of Mt. Carmel.
As might be expected, some of the Carmelites' most cherished stories
of Elijah were variations on earlier Jewish and Muslim traditions or
came down in modified form from the great promoters of the Christian desert life. In their own eddy in the wide river of legendary stories about the prophet, Carmelites began meditating on special details
of the man Elijah that helped them forge their communal identity, and
Elijah, as he did for so many other groups, began to merge with them.
For this group, Elijah remains alive as a legend, even to this day.

For Further Reading

Arberry, A. J., trans. *The Koran Interpreted*. 1955 Unwin; New York:
Simon and Schuster, 1996.

Athanasius. *The Life of Antony and The Letter to Marcellinus*. Classics of Western Spirituality Series. Translated by Robert C. Gregg.
New York: Paulist, 1980.

Brown, Peter. *Society and the Holy in Late Antiquity*. Berkeley,
Calif.: California University Press, 1982.

Bynum, Carolyn Walker. *The Resurrection of the Body in Western
Christianity, 200–1336*. New York: Columbia University Press,
1995.

Cassian, John. *Conferences*. Classics of Western Spirituality Series.
Translated by Colin Luibheid. New York: Paulist, 1985.

Chandler, Paul, O. Carm. "A Journey with Elijah: *Princeps et exemplar Carmelitarum"* in *A Journey with Elijah.* Edited by Paul Chandler. Rome: Carmelitanum, 1991.

Coomaraswamy, Ananda K. "Khwaja Khadir and the Fountain of Life in the Tradition of Persian and Mughal Art" in *What is Civilization?* Pp. 157–167. Great Barrington, Mass.: Lindisfarne, 1989.

Corbin, Henry. *Creative Imagination in the Sufism of Ibn 'Arabi.* Translated by R. Manheim. Princeton, N.J.: Princeton, 1969.

Ginzberg, Louis. *The Legends of the Jews.* 7 vols. Philadelphia: Jewish Publication Society, 1938.

Gruenwald, Ithamar. *Apocalyptic and Merkavah Mysticism.* Leiden, Holland: Brill, 1980.

Idel, Moshe. *Kabbalah: New Perspectives.* New Haven, Conn.: Yale, 1988.

Scholem, Gershom. *Kabbalah.* New York: New American Library, 1974.

al-Tabari, Abu Ja'far Muhammad b. Jarir. *The Children of Israel.* Vol. 3 of *The History of Al-Tabari.* Translated by W. Brinner. Albany, N.Y.: SUNY, 1991.

Chapter 4
The Prophet in Early Carmelite Documents

Citizens of the United States have lost some of the role models of past generations. Americans no longer learn by imitation as much as they did. This has partly been caused by migrations from place to place within the country. Family and community ties are often loosened when a new job is taken in a distant state or when a student leaves the nest for college. When this happens, chances to watch a resourceful aunt solve a problem or see a grandfather's courageous response to a difficult situation are often lost. When contact is broken with the daily lives of admired relatives or friends, the opportunity is often lost to apprentice oneself to noble human beings.

Present inhabitants of the United States also seem less inclined to pattern themselves on public figures than in times past. Nowadays citizens are reluctant to imitate someone who may not turn out to be a very good model after all. Public figures, whether politicians, athletes, teachers, physicians, lawyers, or pastors, are often suspected from the outset of having an identity that probably does not conform to what is presented to the world at large. Frequent exposés by journalists encourage the belief that only by probing their past can it be discovered who prominent figures really are. Whether it is because Americans have set themselves to find hidden weaknesses in their leaders or because weakness is there to be found, some public figures in the United States have disappointed us in recent decades when hidden details of their characters have come out.

In addition, United States citizens have a poorer treasury of religious and cultural stories to help them grow into better human beings. Children are less able to describe the heroes of religious traditions, past national heroes, or inspiring fictional characters, a sure sign that present-day adults are not passing traditional stories down very well. Parents and community leaders sometimes worry that children are finding role models whose stories they can imitate, but too often these narratives do not promote well-being. The biblical tale of Ruth's fidelity is not as widely known as it once was, but tales of faithlessness are so frequently told in newspapers and on television that infidelity begins to look like acceptable behavior. The Sherlock Holmes or Columbo-like heroes who use their wits to solve problems for others are being jostled aside by protagonists who achieve selfish goals in unpraiseworthy ways. Contemporary stories of heroes and villains who confront difficulties by brute force are the most disturbing, especially when children relive the tales on the playground.

The current deficit in good human mentors and story heroes contrasts with earlier centuries in which the traditional stories of Elijah thrived among many other stories of admirable human beings. By now many of the stories about the prophet that once were widely known have slipped out of view. Like Ruth's biblical tale, many of Elijah's stories described in the previous chapters are not very apt to inspire anyone's imitation since they are no longer commonly known. This book hopes to do something about the disappearance of the Elijah stories from modern lives. It began by retelling stories of the prophet as he appears in Scripture and by retelling his stories as they were changed in later traditions.

Taken up from time to time in this book is the question: How may one allow the past to speak in a serious way to one's own present life? As pieces of the past, traditional narratives come to the present pulling along a great deal in their wake, for they have affected many people before present readers hear them. If the past responses of earlier audiences are rediscovered along with the old Elijan legends themselves, they can enrich the response of present readers to the Israelite prophet.

An unusual retelling of Elijah's oldest story may perhaps encourage present readers to think about him in a new way. Stories told by the Israelites of old and retold by rabbis and preachers; by ordinary Jewish, Christian, and Muslim faithful; and by members of prayer communities may say something particularly challenging or attractive. Readers perhaps will do what so many people have done concerning the prophet and other beloved heroes. Perhaps they will devise tales of them that contain parts of their own life.

This chapter began with the notion that we depend less on imitation than did our elders. Differences in the use of imitation are even greater between present readers and the medieval Carmelite friars whose relation with Elijah is the subject of this chapter. Living in a society that values original achievement so much, it is hard to grasp the extent to which life was carried out by means of imitation in earlier eras. Medieval European society made very heavy use of the act of modeling oneself on others. Younger generations became adept in farming, practicing a trade, and producing all kinds of things by apprenticing themselves to skilled members of an older generation. Formal education required even the youngest students to memorize and then imitate the thought patterns of Scripture, classical poetry, philosophy, and chronicles. Fitting into relationships likewise required imitation. Whether peasant or noble, one learned to engage in conflict, diplomacy, politics, courtship, and childrearing by patterning oneself on the deeds and attitudes of others of one's rank. Public praise and material rewards were bestowed on those who showed themselves to have learned from their models.

Given the capabilities of our technology, it is difficult to imagine that access to models was often greater in the Middle Ages than it is now. Those who could read imitated what they found in the pages of books. The greater part of the population, although illiterate, heard a wealth of tales in storytelling, ballads, popular tunes, public speeches, and sermons in churches and in town squares. Anyone living in a town prosperous enough to support the construction of large buildings could also see episodes of heroic stories carved in stone, painted on walls, or woven in tapestries. Pantheons of religious heroes framed church doors and entryways.

Members of Christian monastic communities lived among an abundance of role models. Heroes and heroines on which nuns and monks sought to pattern their lives were found on walls, in statues, in carvings on pillars, on crucifixes, on painted inlaid ceilings and floors, in carvings on choir stalls, on inscribed or painted mottoes over doors. The stories were recounted in sessions of spiritual direction, read aloud in the refectory and chapel, alluded to in monastic rules, embedded in the monastic names of one's fellow community members, and sewn into the highly symbolic monastic dress that each group wore. Even the poorest monastic foundations, as some early Carmelite houses probably were, were libraries of saints' stories after which life could be patterned.

The reliability of medieval model stories was also much greater than the reliability of model stories today. While current citizens of the United States may worry whether the life story of a respected or prominent figure who might be a candidate for imitation truly is what it seems, the validity of Christian hero stories seems to have been rarely questioned in the Middle Ages, even though disagreement could occur over how Christian stories were to be incorporated into one's life. Medieval trust in the reliability of the stories of Christian heroes did not mean that thirteenth-century men and women were more gullible than people are now. Instead, for earlier Christians, stories such as those that this chapter will tell of the life of Elijah received their persuasive power from being located in a pyramid whose apex was the story of the life of Christ.

Jesus' scriptural and traditional life story lent trustworthiness to all other Christian model stories in several ways. In the past the story of Christ was more influential than now in society as a whole. For one thing, the story of his life, gleaned from Scripture and tradition, was believed to be so true and powerful by medieval European Christians that human history was seen to derive from it. Jesus' incarnation, revelation of the Kingdom of God, passion, and resurrection were the ultimate reference points needed to understand all that happened before and after these events. His life on earth was the center point of time.

For another, many medieval women and men sought to duplicate the story of Jesus' life in their own daily actions. In the twelfth century, young Francis of Assisi left home, plunged into a life of prayer in the wilderness, and emerged to preach conversion of heart, a trajectory that matches the beginning of Jesus' ministry described in the Synoptic Gospels. The thirteenth-century Benedictine anchoress Julian of Norwich asked to suffer as Jesus himself had suffered on the Cross, a grace that she thereafter received. Her own bodily illness prepared her to experience, but also to understand, the interior visions of Jesus' passion, death, and resurrection that came to her as she lay dying. Many ordinary laypeople in the twelfth and thirteenth centuries embraced an apostolic life modeled on the Gospel stories of Jesus.

If Christians took the story of the life of the Savior so seriously as to imitate it, those same individuals were naturally moved by the biographies of saints who acted like Christ as well. Details of the Gospel stories always turn up in saints' lives. To choose an influential text, according to his admiring sixth-century biographer Sulpicius Severus, Martin of Tours performed a large number of miracles obviously like those mentioned in the Gospels: the saintly hermit and bishop converted a thief while he was himself a prisoner about to be executed; restored several people to life, including a young girl; cast out demons and healed a leper. The parallels between his story and the Gospels did much to ensure devotion to the saint.

Medieval stories of the lives of Christian heroes were bits of mirrors that, although small in relation to the person of Christ imaged in them, still could reliably reflect the admirable events, states of mind, and words found in the story of the life of Christ. The ability of stories of Christian heroism to promote Gospel values and behavior protected them against belittlement or disproof since what mattered in the story of the spiritual hero was Christ's story. The life stories of Christian saints sometimes told of human weakness, but their basic intention was to tell a story of human success in imitating Christ. This meant that the narrative, regardless of whose it was, functioned in a powerfully authoritative way.

Their heroes' accomplishments contributed to the reliability of the old model stories. As was said earlier, model stories nowadays—those that are repeated frequently enough to seem possible or normal—sometimes do not describe moral achievements. Tales of generous or courageous individuals are still repeated but so also are stories of scornful tricksters or criminals who burst the bonds of social restraint. In contrast to this mixed bag of present-day tales of achievement, the stories that medieval men and women were encouraged to imitate all describe their heroes succeeding nobly. Medieval model stories never end in human failure, disillusionment, egoistic triumph, or disruption of society. Those human issues did surface in medieval culture—listeners then seem to have appreciated tales of rascals—but these were not narratives that explicitly promoted imitation. Medieval model stories end the way old movies often do, in a celebration of success. Their heroes by the story's end display sacrifice, fidelity, and the ability to restore peace and life to those around them. Regardless of how improbable the medieval epics or the lives of the saints may seem to present-day readers, these narratives encouraged the belief that humans can triumph in their struggles. In stories told of them, medieval saints all overcome personal limitations in response to God. Many were also admired because their stories showed them succeeding in helping other human beings. This was Elijah's case.

Recalling a general culture that strongly encouraged imitation of admirable lives is the place to begin this inquiry into how the prophet Elijah came into the lives of the medieval members of the Order of Blessed Virgin Mary of Mt. Carmel. Already living in a place and time in which many tales of heroes and saints were being told, Carmelites chose to become especially involved with three spiritual heroes. First, as have many other earlier and present-day Christians, medieval hermits of Mt. Carmel sought to imitate the life of Christ.

Scriptural passages describing Jesus' withdrawal into solitary prayer and his relation with his Father appealed to their preference for solitary communion with God, while descriptions of his public ministry inspired their pastoral work. Second, members of the Order imitated the openness to God that the Virgin Mary displays in the Gospels. The Virgin, who soon became the Order's patroness, was a reliable traditional guide concerning purity of heart. As for the Carmelites' third spiritual hero, Elijah, when the belief spread throughout the Order that the old Israelite prophet had established an eremitical community on Mt. Carmel in which their own ancestors participated, medieval members of the Order began to declare that Elijah was their institutional founder as well as their spiritual father.

Chapter 2 of this book began by discussing the phenomenon that Elijah's storytellers, the "peoples" to whom he has been especially meaningful, multiplied over time. Although they shared their stories of the prophet with other groups, each developed legends of him that were particular to each one. Brothers and sisters of the Blessed Virgin of Mt. Carmel are one such Elijan group. Legends that the Order has repeated over the centuries encourage imitation of his zeal, poverty, abandonment to God's will, and purity of heart—all spiritual qualities that Jesus models in the Gospels. Biblical descriptions of Elijah's reliance on God by the brook Carith and of his full-hearted responses to God have profoundly influenced how members of the Order prepare for loving encounter with their Lord. Through the stories they tell of him, Elijah has been an accessible, reliable, and admirable mediator and companion to Carmelites over the centuries.

The First Encounter with Elijah on the Mountain

Carmelites were influenced by the prophet from the beginning of their existence. The Order historically descends from a small group of Latin, possibly Frankish, hermits who, around 1200 C.E., took up occupancy in a group of caves on the western slope of Mt. Carmel, the mountain on which Elijah won back the hearts of the Israelites for Yahweh. The group, numbering a dozen or fifteen, was following the long-standing habit of other Christians who transplanted themselves to places in Palestine associated with outstanding scriptural mentors. In the fifth and sixth centuries, to draw from a host of examples, the Eastern Fathers Euthymius (d. 473) and Sabas (d. 532) founded communities in the Judean wilderness whose members practiced a life inspired by the story of Jesus' withdrawal and struggle with the Tempter in the same site. Others chose to live by the Jordan in imitation of John the Baptist, believed with Elijah to be a founder of Christian monastic life.

The Frankish hermits surely chose Mt. Carmel, a ridge on the coast near Haifa in northern Israel because they believed that Elijah had spent much of his life there. Muslims, Christians, and Jews had long revered Mt. Carmel as the place in which their Scriptures said that the prophet had triumphed over Baal. Local legends collected by medieval travelers added that Elijah had taken up residence on the mountain and had miraculously caused a spring to flow near its base. The locale had a long connection with Khidr, a Muslim figure described in the previous chapter who sometimes was thought to be Elijah. Archaeological excavation has shown that the Cave of Elijah at the base of the promontory, some four kilometers from the hermits' dwellings, had been a worship center for many centuries before the arrival of the ancestors of the Carmelites nearby. Muslim women hoping to have children came to visit Khidr there, but other worshipers had come in other eras as well. Christian pilgrims to the Holy Land had long included the mountain on their itineraries. These details assure us that the Western hermit forebears of the Carmelite Order deliberately chose to live as near as they could to the prophet's legendary home.

In coming to his mountain, they hoped Elijah would help them live profound spiritual lives. We know that the group that came to Mt. Carmel chose to live as solitary contemplatives and penitents, in the same way that medieval Christians generally believed the prophet had lived. The document given to them by the Western patriarch of Jerusalem sometime between 1206 and 1214, which approves and formalizes their manner of life, sketches the outline of a group firmly committed to prayer; solitude; and peaceful, brotherly relations among themselves. It also has been confirmed that when residents of Mt. Carmel were forced to emigrate to Europe in the middle of the thirteenth century, they sought to continue to live as they believed Elijah had and as they themselves had begun: in solitude, in prayer, and in penitence. The earliest European foundations of the brothers of Mt. Carmel were hermitages located some distance from towns.

The group succeeded in transplanting the ideals that they saw expressed in Elijah's eremitical life to Europe, but whether it also cared to transplant local stories of the prophet, some of which descended from Jewish, Islamic, and Christian tales told in chapters 2 and 3 of this book, is less clear. The Carmelite scholar Rudolf Hendriks has noted a surprising silence concerning Elijah in the earliest documents of the Order still in existence. The formula of life, written for the hermits of Mt. Carmel by the patriarch Albert that eventually became the official rule of the Carmelite Order, does not say a word about the prophet, although his mountain is named. Instead, the apostle Paul is presented as a model in the *Rule*, and Carmelites are commanded to live in Christ. Mention of Elijah is also absent from the second earliest document of the Order that we have, the 1271 *Ignea Sagita (Fiery Arrow)*, a call by the Order's prior general Nicholas of France to return to strict eremitical solitude. Important mention of the prophet, however, can be discovered in a few highly influential sentences appearing in the preamble to medieval Carmelite constitutions. The preamble, commonly called the *Rubrica prima,* occupied the opening paragraphs of the eight medieval constitutions whose copies we still have.

Elijah's portrait for the earlier centuries of Christian monasticism needs brief review before an inquiry into his appearance in the preambles is begun. In 1–2 Kings, the prophet zealously challenged his people, massacred competing Baalite prophets, and moved from place to place under the influence of Yahweh. In later Jewish tradition he continued to be a physically mobile figure who traveled between heaven and earth, saving individuals from danger. Beginning around the fourth century, however, early Christian abbots and theologians wrote that Elijah lived as a hermit. These promoters of eremitical life described the prophet moving about in the wilderness but tended to replace his activities on behalf of others with zealous pursuit of his own perfection. Early Christian stories of the prophet were shaped by the beliefs that little real help to others can be given until personal perfection is accomplished and that often the best help one can offer was to become a reliable, attractive model of the spiritual life.

Accordingly, Athanasius, Jerome, Augustine, Cassian, Gregory the Great, and many later Christian writers closer to the medieval lifetime of Carmelites emphasized the prophet's personal life in their stories. Elijah's poverty, suggested in stories of him in the Bible, and his virginity, borrowed from Jewish legend, were declared by the Fathers to be evidence that the prophet had lived a monastic (that is, solitary and dedicated) life. His miraculous rescues of others were replaced with zeal for penitence, prayer, and abstinence. Promoters of saintly Christian life began to mention that Elijah fasted and kept vigils, two other frequent Christian ascetic practices. All this medieval Carmelites and their late twelfth-century hermit forebears on Mt. Carmel would have known and admiringly imitated.

Preambles to medieval Carmelite constitutions draw on these earlier Christian beliefs and stories about Elijah. They also supplement old traditions with new details having to do with Carmelites alone. With only slight variations over the centuries, the *Rubrica prima* instructed medieval friars:

> How to respond to those who inquire from whom and in what way our Order took its origin. Since some of the younger brothers in our Order do not know how to satisfy according to the truth those who inquire from whom and

in what way our Order had its origin, we wish to respond
to them, giving them a written formula for such inquirers.

For we say, bearing witness to the truth, that from the time
of those devout inhabitants of Mount Carmel, the prophets Elijah and Elisha, holy fathers of both the Old Testament and the New have truly loved the solitude of that
same mountain for the sake of contemplation of heavenly
things; that they undoubtedly lived a praiseworthy life
of holy penitence there next to the spring of Elijah;
and that by a holy inheritance this life has been continuously maintained.

In the time of Innocent III, Albert, patriarch of the church
of Jerusalem, gathered their successors into one college,
writing a Rule for them which Pope Honorius, Innocent's
successor, and many of his successors, approving this
Order, have most devoutly confirmed with the testimony
of their bulls.

In this profession we, their followers, serve the Lord in
various parts of the world until the present day. (1281
Constitution; a careful translation by Paul Chandler in
private correspondence. All further citations are taken
from this source.)

This story appeared in the opening paragraphs of constitution after
constitution for hundreds of years. Eventually the Order's name, its
relation to the Blessed Virgin, and its legitimate standing were inserted into the narrative, but the description of the prophet and his
companions on Mt. Carmel remained virtually unchanged. Carmelite
historian Keith Egan comments that monastic constitutions amount
to official interpretations of an order's rule and traditions. Medieval
Carmelites must have understood that the *Rubrica prima* legend expressed realities underlying their *Rule* and daily life.

The story of Elijah and his succession of spiritual companions on
the mountain was very widely known among medieval Carmelites.
Each time a constitution was revised, copies of it were distributed to
all monasteries throughout Europe and put into force immediately,
something that ensured that the *Rubrica prima* was shared, read aloud,

and committed to memory by Carmelites regardless of where they lived. The fact that its language remained much the same for centuries suggested that the Order's eremitical connection with Elijah was unchanging as well. Its repeated appearance must have helped the story become deeply embedded in the Carmelite mentality. Elijah and, it is important to note, the succession of "holy fathers," whom Carmelites also claimed as forebears and who also appear in the *Rubrica prima* tale, were not only reliable and near at hand in the storytelling of each monastery but also perennial and real.

The sentence from the *Rubrica prima*, "from the time of those devout inhabitants of Mount Carmel, the prophets Elijah and Elisha, holy fathers of both the Old Testament and the New have truly loved the solitude of that same mountain for the sake of contemplation of heavenly things," does not suggest anything novel about Elijah himself, as medieval Christians had come to know him from the traditions of the Fathers. Earlier Christian writers had said that the prophet was a devout hermit and had said the same about other Christian spiritual heroes such as John the Baptist and Antony. What made the preamble story a special one were the other occupants of it, its time frame, and the location of its events.

First, by adding themselves to the end of a string of successors in the story—"In this profession we, their followers, serve the Lord in various parts of the world until the present day"—medieval brothers of Mt. Carmel did what others had done when they told stories of the prophet: they wrote themselves into a legend that they saw shaping their life. It is no coincidence that the stories of Elijah carefully preserved in the Talmud by rabbinical sages happen to include rabbis and that stories preserved in oral storytelling by common folk describe the prophet flying to the aid of a poor man or helping a humble husband and wife. Like stories belonging to other groups who cared about their relation with Elijah, the *Rubrica prima* includes in its narrative the very people who have safeguarded and cherished it. Carmelites are thus both participants within the legendary story of the holy life of Elijah and the succession of his disciples on Mt. Carmel, and are as well tellers of it. One result of this is that not only Elijah and Elisha but also previous generations of Carmelites become the earlier-mentioned "bits of mirrors" that reflect Christlike virtue to hearers who want to pursue the spiritual life.

Second, as has been shown in earlier chapters that examined legends belonging to other groups, Carmelites began to say things about Elijah that do not appear in Scripture. Writing their own *haggadot*, Carmelites particularly altered the solitude that Elijah experienced in the 1–2 Kings stories. With the exception of his successor, Elisha, who appeared in the prophet's life in 2 Kings, seemingly near the end of his prophetic career, Elijah had no human companions in his oldest biblical stories. Instead, the vignettes collected in 1–2 Kings stress his independence and solitude. He helped other people but received help only from God. The first chapter of this book advanced the idea that the Tishbite's psychic isolation from other human beings in 1–2 Kings was a story element used to stress the solitary independence of his Creator and Lord. Elijah remained a solitary figure in many legends told worldwide.

The *Rubrica prima* story is, in contrast, a social one. While emphasizing the solitude of its participants, it also suggests ingathering and common life. It says that holy men were drawn to live near Elijah and Elisha, or near their home, out of a common desire for contemplation. They shared Elijah's way of life. The brief story told in the *Rubrica prima* may reflect the daily proximity that the first group of hermits on Mt. Carmel apparently experienced, given the location of their caves. It also allows for the possibility of a more spiritualized sense of community maintained by individuals living in stricter solitude from one another, perhaps as desert fathers such as Antony were said to have lived. They were principally alone but maintained important social contacts that related to their pursuit of the spiritual life:

> For we say, bearing witness to the truth, that from the
> time of those devout inhabitants of Mount Carmel, the

prophets Elijah and Elisha, holy fathers of both the Old
Testament and the New have truly loved the solitude of
that same mountain for the sake of contemplation of heavenly things; that they undoubtedly lived a praiseworthy
life of holy penitence there next to the spring of Elijah;
and that by a holy inheritance this life has been continuously maintained. In the time of Innocent III, Albert, patriarch of the church of Jerusalem, gathered their
successors into one college, writing a Rule for them. (128 ...

Several parts of this passage deserve attention. Where in 1–2 Kings,
Elijah moved the length and breadth of Israel, nearly always alone, in
the Carmelite tale, the mythic founder and spiritual model resided in
a location to which generations of holy men came. The scene of the
Rubrica prima is set at an *axis mundi,* a gathering point. Physically
and socially, Mt. Carmel is like the Ka'bah in Mecca toward which
Muslim pilgrims journey from all over the world or like Mt. Zion
where biblical prophets envision that one day the nations of the world
will gather around God.

Prophets such as Jeremiah or Malachi declared that in the final
days God will purify Mt. Zion and all who are drawn to it. In the
Rubrica prima, what not only attracts individuals to Mt. Carmel but
also sanctifies them is the life of prayer lived on the mountain "from
the time of the prophets Elijah and Elisha." The *Rubrica prima*
certainly praises Elijah's spiritual life on the sacred mount but also
hints that eremitical life creates gatherings of kindred souls. Elijah is
far from spiritually alone in the *Rubrica prima*. The life of prayer,
holiness, the mountain fastness, and the community all converge in
the story.

As has been mentioned, Elijah's stable presence on Mt. Carmel
was unusual. This part of his Carmelite legend coincides with
the tendency in prior spiritual literature to convert the Tishbite from
a zealously active Israelite man of God into a Christian model of
interior sanctification. In contrast with the vigorous mobility that he
displayed in many scriptural and nonscriptural traditions worldwide,

here he is described as not moving at all. He and others who came to live nearby were active in their hearts, performing interior acts of repentance and love. In his legendary stories, Elijah remained at home with Carmelites instead of flying to heaven or suddenly appearing and disappearing as he so often did in the special legends of Muslim and Jewish groups. Throughout the centuries, Carmelites have also remained in their founder's home, for Mt. Carmel remains a very rich mythic ground of the Order's self-understanding even today.

Another unusual feature in the Carmelite story of origins told in the *Rubrica prima* surfaces when its chronology is examined. Time in the preamble story begins in the ancient Israelite lifetime of the prophet, stretches through the Old and New Testament periods, converges with what is now called historical time when the *Rubrica* mentions the small band of hermits on Mt. Carmel, and continues through subsequent Carmelite history to the moment in which the preamble is read. Such a chronology was not all that unusual in medieval writing. Chroniclers frequently began accounts of their own times by retelling scriptural events. Medieval men and women generally believed that their era was part of the patterned flow of events that the Bible describes.

Instead, what is unusual about the chronology is how Carmelite storytellers position their ancestors in it and what is thereby implied concerning the Order's relationship with the prophet. The *Rubrica prima* places Elijah and the latest generations of Carmelites at opposite ends of the time sequence. They arrange earlier Carmelites and the holy fathers whom they saw as their direct forebears along it, like beads strung next to each other in a necklace. Word choice in the original Latin of the *Rubrica prima*—*"In cuius professione nos eorum sequaces usque."* ("In this profession we, their followers, serve the Lord," or more literally, "We are continuously [in an unbroken sequence, one after another] following in their profession")—contributes to the impression that Carmelites came down to the present by means of an unbroken succession.

So many times the unusual features of the foundational legend have to do with its Carmelite participants. In high contrast with what

Carmelites suggested concerning themselves and the prophet, that their forebears were a "string of beads" all following each other in unbroken sequence, most Christians of those earlier centuries believed that Elijah had lived a life wholly in the past, separated from them by gaps in time and space. Similar gaps existed for medieval individuals who expected Elijah to return in the final days, as Malachi prophesied. For most medieval Christians, there were no intermediate beads on the string of time stretching between themselves and the prophet. Access to Elijah could not be tangible since he had prophesied so long ago and had not yet appeared.

Discrepancies between the very unusual features of the Carmelite myths of Elijah and what other Christians tended to believe concerning him require a little more exploring. As has been discussed in some detail in chapter 2, most Christians thought Elijah was a type. He was taken to have been a human being who certainly contributed to the unfolding of sacred history while he lived on earth, but whose mission and way of being was, or would be, more fully accomplished by someone else at a later time. Chapter 2 discussed several ways in which the early Fathers and medieval writers used typology to understand the relation between the Tishbite and John the Baptist, forerunners of the Lord living in different eras.

In the *Rubrica prima* legend, Carmelites filled in the chronological gaps between Elijah's lifetime and their own medieval existence. The story insists on an unbroken, continuous succession of individuals who lived Elijah's way in Elijah's home. Other documents of the Order handle the prophet as a type and model, but in its *Rubrica prima*, the medieval Order had a different intention. The legend said that, due to a successful series of spiritual lives, their Order stretched back to include the prophet. Carmelites thus saw themselves able to touch Elijah's spiritual life by living their own. In time their documents began to assert that the Tishbite was their true historical founder. He provided the means by which their community was established (medieval donors receiving the title of founder provided land, a house, or funds; Elijah provided the mountain) but also introduced to them a way of life, just as Jesus and his imitator Francis of Assisi each founded a new way of life by the example of their own actions. Carmelites greatly expanded upon these beliefs in later writings, as we will see, but the seeds of them are already present in the *Rubrica prima*'s firm insistence that, in times long past, direct forebears had lived with Elijah (or at least near him or near his home and engaged in his way of life), then with each other, and then with their own successors.

Glancing backward to the Church's writings before the *Rubrica prima,* the story of a contemplative community collecting around Elijah on Mt. Carmel surpasses what certain Fathers such as Jerome had said in the fifth century, that Elijah was the first "monk" to "inhabit the desert"; or Sozomene, who said that the prophet and John the Baptist were "leaders of this excellent way of life"; or John Cassian in the *Institutes*, that Elijah and John the Baptist "laid the first foundations of this profession" (see, for example, the citations Hervé of the Incarnation collects in *Élie le prophète*, vol. 1, 194–195). Carmelites said that he inaugurated a group that they claimed still existed, replenished by a succession of spiritual lives. When they said this, they were affirming that they were connected to Elijah not only in memory and in storytelling but also in a perennial communion.

Emanuele Boaga has found a possible prototype for the tradition of Carmelite succession in the writings of the fourth-century Fathers. It is also possible that the Carmelite narrative of Elijah developed some of its unusual features because it was told according to the conventions of foundational stories of Christian religious orders. Biographies of Benedict of Nursia written in the sixth century and Francis of Assisi in the thirteenth similarly explain the genesis of the orders carrying these saints' names as a gathering of devout souls around these holy men. Some monastic founders such as Francis, Benedict, and the eleventh-century Camaldolese founder Romuald were reportedly living as hermits, just as the Carmelite legend says Elijah and Elisha were when their disciples began to gather. It is furthermore true, according to William Pantin, that during the fourteenth century, English Benedictines, at least, were writing treatises that traced the origin of their observance to the Old Testament lives of Samuel, Elijah, Elisha, and the sons of the prophets.

What distinguishes the Carmelite tale of origin from stories told about founders such as Francis or Dominic were that the latter were composed near the lifetime of the founders and drew from what eyewitnesses and companions could say, while Carmelites of course could not do the same for Elijah. Although they insisted that their direct spiritual forebears had shared a life of prayer with the prophet, for many outside the Order, it was just too much to believe that it had been so. Although they sometimes sought to do so, early brothers of Mt. Carmel could not convincingly demonstrate from the Bible or from any authority outside their own writings that any of their number had had direct contact with and personal spiritual guidance from the founder to whom they laid claim.

Nevertheless, the thirteenth- and fourteenth-century European friars stubbornly clung to the very parts of their legend that are most difficult to believe. Carmelite assertions of their lived connection with Elijah expanded rather than withered away as the centuries passed. The sturdy refusal of medieval Carmelites to abandon the parts of the myth that provoked challenges from outsiders because they were so different from other legends of the prophet is noteworthy. Their unhistorical, impossible-to-prove claim of the continuous, unbroken eremitical life on Elijah's mountain must have named something authentic and very real in medieval Carmelite experience, or it would have been abandoned in the centuries in which the Order weathered other profound changes in its identity. It is indeed striking that Carmelites, who had been lovers of contemplation from the start, quickly adopted mendicant activities and even relinquished the highly symbolic habit they had chosen for themselves in the Holy Land, but they could not be pried away from the assertion that their group had existed from the time of the prophet Elijah.

Carmel's declaration that an unceasing succession of forebears shared an Elijan spiritual life down through the ages displays the Order's enduring commitment to an attitude of the heart. The Elijan tale found in the *Rubrica prima* declares optimistically that the prophet, the "holy fathers" who came to live where he was or had been, their successors, and their spiritual descendants truly loved the solitude of that same mountain for the sake of heavenly contemplation regardless of the era. How different was medieval Carmelite faith in the possibility of contemplating heaven while living in a secluded community and how differently their trust in the success of passing that community life down generation after generation are from the hesitancy over models and ruptures in faith in modern American society.

Early Elijan Carmelites

The emigrating hermits apparently brought few written records with them when they left the Holy Land. What they brought were scattered throughout Europe. The *Rule of St. Albert* plus a few references to hermits on Mt. Carmel found in writings outside the Order are the only evidence still in existence of their life on the mountain before their emigration to Europe around 1235. Little direct information remains concerning the Carmelites who lived in the first centuries of the Order.

Thirteenth- and fourteenth-century constitutions offer the best indirect clues to how medieval Carmelites existed, but these should be viewed more as prescriptions than as evidence of what was done in response to their guidelines and obligations. Details of individual lives of course are not found in the constitutions, nor are profiles of particular communities. Most visible are emphases and shifts in the Order as a whole. One can, for example, conclude from constitutional attention to the educational system established to prepare friars to soundly preach Church doctrine; from guidelines in constitutions concerning how Carmelites should perform pastoral work; and from municipal documents that show that houses often requested to build churches, to hear confessions, and to bury the dead that the early Order embraced mendicant service upon their arrival into Europe. The many early Carmelite saints remembered for their preaching also point to early zeal for the mendicant *vita apostolica*.

Similar evidence suggests that during the Order's first European decades, its members sought the geographic and domestic conditions for contemplation originally associated with Elijah by the first group of hermits on Mt. Carmel and commanded of them by their *Rule*. In version after version, constitutions promote solitude and silence within each house. There were surely more early brothers like Blessed Frank of Siena (d. 1291), remembered in the Carmelite calendar for his eremitical perfection. Several of the first priors general of the Order, including Nicholas of France (1266–1271), Raymond of Ile (1294–1297), and possibly Ralph Fryston (1270s), exchanged their administrative duties for eremitical solitude. We can see, in other words, a silhouette of preference for solitary prayer in the constitutions and in a few details we have of individual lives. Elijah's involvement in that preference is visible in the *Rubrica prima* of the constitutions written between 1281 and 1369 and in a handful of apologetic and historical documents.

Elijah's Story Develops

Changes in description of the prophet and his companions in the fourteenth and early fifteenth centuries reveal that the Order gradually deepened its understanding of what it meant to live like Elijah. The *Rubrica prima* eventually began to include a few new story details. Surviving apologetic and historical works written by Carmelites began telling the story of origin in different ways. The first book in a collection of works pertaining to the origin and nature of the Order that began to be disseminated around 1390 repeats some new legendary details of the other works, but far surpasses them in detail concerning Elijah.

Several conditions helped the expansion of the Carmelite legend of origin in the fourteenth and fifteenth centuries. First and most obviously, the Order by then had matured into the organization that would substantially remain. By then, its legitimacy had been repeatedly confirmed by Rome, an internal government had been established, and a system for preparing members of the Order for pastoral service had been placed in operation. The number of foundations throughout Europe had increased, especially in the last part of the thirteenth century. By the end of the fourteenth, Carmelites were known in Europe not only for their evangelical service in areas neighboring their houses but occasionally as advisers to kings or consultants to Rome. The Order had acquired a corporate identity that could be the object of meditation and critique.

The appearance of new features in the legend was probably also aided by the improved education of the men who put the stories on parchment. In contrast with the first Carmelites who, according to the early historian of the Order John Hildesheim, were "simple, unlettered men more accustomed to praying than to writing" (cited in Robinson, 90), those who wrote the versions of the Elijah legend that we are about to examine were trained at Paris and Oxford in Scripture, rhetoric, logic, and theology, all disciplines of immediate use to a writer. The changes in the Carmelite legend of Elijah were surely affected by the fact that fourteenth-century Carmelite writers such as Hildesheim, the scholastic John Baconthorpe, priors general John Grossi and Bernard Oller, and Parisian master John of Cheminot lived in different decades than did the Carmelite leaders who first composed the *Rubrica prima.*

Baconthorpe and Cheminot were born in the last part of the thirteenth century; Hildesheim, either then or in the beginning of the fourteenth; Grossi and Oller, sometime during the first half of the fourteenth. They could not have had personal memories of life on Mt. Carmel and had not been members of the Order during its difficult transition during the midthirteenth century from hermit life in

Palestine to an eremitical and mendicant life in Europe. As a result, their view of their Order must have differed from that of Nicholas of France, believed to have been a member of the original Mt. Carmel community. As one of the first priors general, Nicholas penned an urgent call in 1271 to his brethren to abandon apostolic work and to turn back to the "primitive spirit" of the Order, "in shame from their erring paths to the right way," which for Nicholas could be one and only one thing, solitary prayer in deserted places (Nicholas of France, prologue). Grossi, Cheminot, Baconthorpe, Hildesheim, and Oller never described the Order in such a univocal way. In their experience, two calls, not one, had always been in place. It is quite possible—even probable—that these later authors chose to become Carmelites, instead of Dominican preachers or enclosed Carthusians, because they were attracted to the Order's simultaneous pursuit of contemplation and apostolic service. When they wrote about Elijah and his successors, many of these leaders of the Order did what would have scandalized Nicholas of France. They retold Carmel's Elijan legend in ways that promoted both solitary prayer and evangelical service.

Boaga, following Carlo Cicconetti and Elias Friedman, observes that the *Rubrica prima* falls into three parts, each with its own agents. Elijah and Elisha first appear, followed by the holy fathers of both testaments, and finally their successors who include medieval Carmelites. Boaga notes that in the thirteenth century, the "Elijan *haggadah*," or amplification of each of the three parts, expands "in a continuous crescendo" (cited in Chandler, *A Journey with Elijah*, 97). Closer examination shows that Carmelites were particularly interested in expanding the story of Elijah and themselves by adding a later time period to it (much as the second chapter of this book showed Malachi adding a new segment to Elijah's life). In Carmelite histories and apologies for the Order, the scene, actor, and actions of the prophet and his Mt. Carmel companions appear very much as they are found in the *Rubrica prima*. Cheminot, for example, declares in a work composed around 1337, "It is known that Elijah and Elisha lived above all in the holy place, Mt. Carmel, and their successors and also the holy Fathers of both the Mosaic and New law also served God there with devotion" (Cheminot, *Speculum*, ch. 2, cited in Hendriks, *Élie le prophète*, vol. 2, 50–51). As Cheminot begins to tell his legend, Elijah remained an example of the spiritual perfection possible to attain in seclusion from the clanging secular world, and the sequence of the *Rubrica prima* is followed. The few new details added to what Boaga identifies as the Elijan part of the *Rubrica prima* are usually emphases on what it already says.

The real changes to the story occur in a period embracing the lifetime of Christ. Documents begin to say that Elijah's successors left their Mt. Carmel home to go to Jerusalem. Reasons given for the move vary. Some writers say that the hermits wanted to establish contact with Mary. Sometimes Jesus or the Gospel being preached by the apostles attracted the group to the capital. Whatever the version, the expanded first-century part of the legend says that the Mt. Carmel hermits were converted to Christianity and devoted themselves to preaching throughout the region.

About this time, the *Rubrica prima* also begins to include a few references to Christ's lifetime. Earlier versions had said of Elijah's companions, "In the time of Innocent III, Albert, patriarch of the church of Jerusalem, gathered their successors into one college, writing a Rule for them...." The 1324 and 1327 versions of the *Rubrica prima* modify the sentence to say, "After the incarnation of Christ, their successors built a church in that place in honor of the Blessed Virgin Mary, and took their title from her and for that reason have since, by apostolic privilege, been called Brothers of Blessed Mary of Mt. Carmel" (for the 1327 version, see Hendriks, *Élie le prophète*, vol. 2, 58). Later versions of the *Rubrica prima* retain the references to the incarnation, the Virgin, and the first-century Carmelite forebears' devotion to her.

The new legendary details in the *Rubrica prima* do not completely match other documentary tellings of the legend. Cheminot, for example, did not mention the church built for Mary after the incarnation, saying instead that Elijah's followers

persevered in holy penitence from the times of the holy
prophets Elijah and Elisha under Ahab's reign, which preceded the Incarnation of Our Lord Jesus Christ by nine
hundred thirty three years. Then darkness fled and light
came to the world, the promise of God the Father which
they had heard preached by the mouth of prophets. They
believed that God had sent his Son, born of woman, and
they received witness of the truth through the preaching
of Blessed John the Baptist and then Christ. And devoutly
confessing the universal faith they were baptized in
Christ. Then, persevering in the doctrine of the Apostles,
with the favor of all the people, they became faithful messengers of the evangelical truth, and authorized defenders
of the holy Christian faith. (Cheminot in Hendriks, *Élie le
prophète*, vol. 2, 50–51)

In spite of obvious differences between this story and that told in the
Rubrica prima, Cheminot most likely did not invent the unusual first-
century features. A variant of the story exists in an earlier document,
the *Universis Christifidelibus* (*Let All Christians*). Cheminot's work
is entitled, *Mirror of the Brothers of the Order of Blessed Mary of Mt.
Carmel*. He must have at least partly repeated what other Carmelites
thought at the time, or he couldn't promote the story as a reflection (a
"mirror") of Carmelite life.

The present-day reader of these stories of origin is likely to have
quite a few sticking points concerning the authenticity of the events
told in the legends. Legendary passages such as the one just cited will
obviously fail to meet the demands of those who need ordinary historical proofs before they believe a story to be true. Sometimes, indeed, the content of the legends told by Cheminot, his peers, and the
Rubrica prima has been dismissed as false history. There has been
some twentieth-century embarrassment over the fact that in the seventeenth, eighteenth, and even nineteenth centuries, Carmelites in both
branches officially defended the stories as literally true. While one
should not think legends historically accurate, it may be trusted that
the stories told by Cheminot and the *Rubrica prima* do have an important connection to the medieval Order. Although they are not fact,

legends are serious business, since groups devise and maintain them. We will return in a moment to Cheminot's story. Now perhaps it is sufficient to make the point that in some way, each story of Elijah and his Carmelite descendants reflects something about the collective thinking of the medieval order.

In considering how these very old documents may have meaningfulness to present-day readers, it is useful to note the wide variety in the fourteenth-century versions of the Carmelite legend of origin, once the myth of the Mt. Carmel genesis of the Order in Elijah's lifetime is retold. Some later fourteenth- and early fifteenth-century documents copy from earlier ones in the group, but no telling of the story of origins goes in quite the same direction once the nucleus of the *Rubrica prima* account is retold. Cheminot rather heavily emphasized first-century preaching as an important activity of the early Carmelites. He was joined in this by colleagues such as Grossi and Hildesheim. However, not even this feature of the fourteenth-century additions is universal.

A passage from *In Praise of Carmelites,* attributed to the Carmelite "Doctor Resolutus" John Baconthorpe, expands its version of the legend of origin differently:

> The brothers of Carmel chose the title of the Blessed Mary and resided religiously, carrying out contemplative life on Carmel in imitation of Elijah, because the Master [Peter Comestor] says in his *Histories* I.III that Samuel was the first to constitute a community of religious called a school of prophets whose office it was to contemplate God. In time the sons of the prophets became attached to the contemplative Elisha as 4 Kings 2 [i.e., 2 Kings 2] says. And Carmelites took it to heart to continue this contemplation which the community and the sons of the prophets had begun on this same Mt. Carmel. (Hendriks, *Élie le prophète*, vol. 2, 46)

This brief story of Carmelite origins makes no mention of Jesus, the apostles, the legendary first-century decision of the hermit forebears to leave Mt. Carmel or, for that matter, the cohabitation with Elijah insisted on by the *Rubrica prima.* Most striking is the omission of any reference to continuous succession. Specific time references are absent, allowing much of the passage to be applied to any era the reader chooses. Contemplation is shown to be the activity that allowed the Order to continue over time. The *Mirror of the Institution of the Order Established for the Veneration of Blessed Mary* and the *Compendium of History and Laws*, which are definitely Baconthorpe's works, also view prayer as the central activity of the Order.

One thing that all the storytellers are sure to do, whichever way they tell the story of the Order's beginning, is to say that contemplation continued in the Order as the centuries wound along. Even the legends that emphasized the hermits' journey from their mountain to Jerusalem shows that the Carmelite ancestors continued to be men of contemplative prayer. In Cheminot's story, the hermits became peripatetic evangelists, but eventually settled down together in monastic quiet under the guidance of Albert's *Rule.* In a defense of the Order written in 1370, Hildesheim cited the comment of Joseph of Antioch that the hermits were "devoured by zeal and committed to contemplation. Following in the footsteps of Elijah and descending Mt. Carmel, [they] disseminated the faith of Christ with great constancy throughout Galilee, Samaria and Palestine" (Hildesheim, *Dialogus*, cited in Hendriks, *Élie le prophète*, vol. 2, 61). Bernard Oller's *Informatio,* written around the time of Hildesheim's document, duplicates Hildesheim's language to say that the group continued its contemplative life while involved in proclaiming the "faith of Christ with great constancy throughout Galilee, Samaria and Palestine" (Oller, *Informatio*, cited in Hendriks, op. cit., 65).

As the examples given here have perhaps shown, the fourteenth-century additions almost all emphasize legendary events in the first century. This suggests that, like other groups in the Church at the time, the Order as a whole was pondering its relation to events recounted in the Gospels and the Book of Acts. Cheminot's telling of the New Testament events of the legend shows this. He uses the preaching of the newly converted successors as a linchpin connecting the story of life shared with Elijah on Mt. Carmel—by then well accepted in the Order—to the first-century story line of Acts in the New Testament.

This is an important feat. It splices a story that Carmelites developed among themselves into the powerfully authoritative story of sacred history found in the Bible. If fourteenth-century Carmelites possessed a story of origin that began in Elijah's lifetime and merged with Christian history near, or in, the first-century lifetime of Christ, they could believe that their Order was indeed most holy and ancient. Legends of origin like Cheminot's told them that not only had their observance begun under the tutelage of Elijah, a supurb model of Christian spiritual life, but that it had become what it was in the Middle Ages—a Christian Order committed to prayer and service—through the effect of lived contact with the originators of Christianity itself: Christ, Mary, John the Baptist, and the apostles. By inserting material found in the New Testament—the references to the incarnation and the preaching of John the Baptist, Christ, and the Apostles—into the Carmelite legend, Cheminot asks his readers to believe that forebears in the Order had been actual participants in the beginning of the Church.

The Parisian master's mingling of Scripture, Carmelite myth, and details from Carmelite history is a meditation on changes that his Order experienced over the previous century. It also argues that Carmelites had a more ancient and admirable origin than that of all other Christian observances, including the hoary Benedictines and the still more ancient eremitical and cenobitic communities of fourth-century Syria and Egypt. Cheminot tells a story "mirroring" his contemporary Carmelite brethren (reflecting their own lives but also providing them a model to imitate) in which the legendary Mt. Carmel hermits fulfilled their baptism not by returning to their beloved mountain but by joining the apostles in preaching the faith of Christ. Obviously he and others in the Order at the time believed that their identity as Carmelites and Christians involved both solitary prayer and apostolic service.

Several more points may be made about the new features of the legend surfacing in the fourteenth and fifteenth centuries. One important result of expanding the details of the legend in the period between Elijah's lifetime and the present era is that the legend acquires a very important second beginning. In the expanded legends, Carmelite spiritual life is inaugurated on Mt. Carmel during the lifetime of the Order's founder. Its membership in the Christian Church, expressed in its baptism and apostolate, is inaugurated in the new first-century time period of the legend. Extraordinary spiritual figures assist each moment of birth. Legends relate that the original Carmelite ancestors began their spiritual lives under the influence of Elijah and Elisha. In the new phase of Carmelite legend that begins to appear in the fourteenth- and fifteenth-century documents (including the *Rubrica prima*), Christ, Mary, John the Baptist, or Christ's followers influenced the hermits as they made their passage into the community of Christian faith.

Second, the Order's distinctive pursuit of contemplation and ministerial service surfaces in its legends in the early fourteenth century and thereafter remains a part of them. Over the centuries, Carmelites have at times wrestled with tensions that have arisen from simultaneous pursuit of the two calls. Although the documents discussed here describe legendary hermits living out the double call in different ways, it is perhaps most noteworthy that none resolve its possible tensions by rolling back the clock to the first days of Mt. Carmel solitude, when by all counts there was one aspiration, not two. Legends found in medieval Carmelite documents instead describe a group that retained its initial response to God's first call to it and added new ways when God called it in new ways.

Finally, it should be noted that in the documents examined thus far, the protoCarmelite followers were the ones who changed. Fourteenth-century legends begin to say that Elijah's followers came down from their mountain in willing response to the call of Christian ministry but never show their spiritual model Elijah leaving his soli-tude. Despite what one would expect, given his powerful public ac-tions in 1–2 Kings, the prophet never moved from his place of prayer in the brief stories told by Grossi and his peers. In written versions of the legend examined thus far, Elijah continued to behave like an ideal Christian hermit such as Antony. His spiritual descendants left their mountain to find and follow Christ, but Elijah remained on his moun-tain, a consistent, reliable, and indeed, immutable example of zeal in solitude and contemplation for the Order.

The Institution of the First Monks

There seems to be only one exception to this among the legends told in Carmelite documents surviving to the present day, but it is a very important one for the Order. *The Institution of the First Monks,* which was circulated in the Order beginning in 1390, is the first of a collection of works entitled *The Ten Books about the Institution and Notable Deeds of the Carmelite Religious* that was edited and per-haps partially written by the provincial of Catalonia Felip Ribot some time around 1370. Its impact on the Order in the centuries that fol-lowed has not yet been fully determined, but reiterated appeal to it by many shapers of the Order including John Soreth, Jerónimo Gracián, Michael of St. Augustine, and Titus Brandsma indicate that it has been a seminal document whose influence has been especially felt in moments in which the Order has sought renewal.

The legend of the Order recounted in the *Institution* far exceeds other surviving medieval ones in length and spiritual depth. Elijah's interior life is developed and the impact of his spirituality on other souls is explored. Elisée de la Nativité remarked that until the *Institu-tion* appeared, medieval Carmelites could only study the "actions and gestures of his religious life in the books of Kings, collecting refer-ences [to the prophet] that were certainly suggestive but were equally brief" (Elisée de la Nativité in *Élie le prophète*, vol. 2, 85). The prophet certainly pursues the eremitical life ascribed to him in earlier Carmelite documents, but for most of the story told about him in the *Institution*, he is engaged in a remarkably active life. He is a spiritual but also a practical founder. *The Institution of the First Monks* makes the large claim that first the Carmelite Order and eventually all of Christian monastic life sprang from the prophet's zealous interior response to the call of God.

Many questions remain unanswered concerning the authorship of the *Ten Books*. If one took literally what the documents in the collection say about their authors, one would believe that John 44, bishop of Jerusalem from 387 to 417, wrote *The Institution of the First Monks;* that a thirteenth-century Carmelite prior general Cyril wrote the second text, a letter explaining certain details of the *Institution* and sketching the Order's history until the beginning of the thirteenth century when the band of hermits received their formula of life from Albert of Jerusalem; that theologian and/prior general Sibert de Beka wrote a commentary on the changes sustained in the *Rule of St. Albert* in 1247; that the Mt. Carmel hermit William of Sanvico contributed the fourth document; and that Ribot edited the papal bulls and privileges rounding out the collection. There are several obstacles, however, to taking all this at face value: Cyril exists only in legend, John 44 could not have been the Carmelite that the *Institution* indicates that he is, and it is not clear how much of the collection is owed to Ribot's hand.

The *Institution* is an allusive, multileveled work that quickly dispels any prejudice that the older a writing is, the more unsophisticated it must be. For one thing, it possesses a series of narrative frames that nest inside each other. At least two of the narrative levels differ from each other in style and vocabulary, suggesting that what we now can read may be a composite text. Other fourteenth-century Carmelite writers such as Cheminot display a thorough knowledge of Scripture and authoritative sources and often weave them deftly into their story of origins. They are not a match, however, for the author or authors of the *Institution*. Whether its complex levels of narration, rhetoric, and knowledge of spiritual tradition are the result of one writer or of some other effort, the *Institution* is an important contribution to Western spiritual thought whose words are composed very capably.

The "outer" narrative frame provides the situation for the whole of the *Institution*. It is a conversation, apparently already underway in the opening paragraph of the work, between a speaker and Caprasius, who seems to be a young Carmelite asking the same questions the *Rubrica prima* declares that it will answer for new recruits: how and from whom did the Order come forth? In a 1995 article on the *Institution*, Joseph Baudry observes that the dialogic format of the *Institution* may have reminded its early readers of the apothegms of the fathers of the desert or the tendency of earlier monastic rules to be cast as a dialogue in which a master answers questions put by novices. Any medieval Carmelite readers making such literary connections surely felt that they were reading a most ancient rule for their Order.

Caprasius is named but does not speak throughout the *Institution;* he and the reader of the *Institution* listen to the speeches of the other interlocutor together. A few more passages in the *Institution* suggest that Caprasius continues to ask questions. From his interlocutor's replies we know that the friar knows some of the medieval objections to the Order's claims to an ancient origin. Caprasius wants to know why "monks" in Elijah's lifetime should be called Carmelites and how ancient Israelites and their Jewish successors could belong to the same group as the Christian hermits who occupied the mountain later. The text of the *Institution*, however, only records the voice of the one who answers him.

Who might this speaker be in the outer frame of the *Institution*? The initial paragraphs of the work suggest that the speaker is able and inclined to describe the "holy deeds and glorious virtues" of Elijah and his successors according to the way "our predecessors before us understood these things and taught them to us in the Old Law and the New" (1:1; all citations of the *Institution* are drawn from Chandler, *The Book of the First Monks: A Workbook*). He is apparently well

versed in monastic life and in the Order's legendary history. A difference in generation, in status, or in eremitical experience is suggested
in the speaker's stance in relation to Caprasius. The speaker's full
identity seems to emerge in the last sentences of book 1: "Thus ends
the institution, that is the manner of coming to prophetic perfection
and the goal of the monastic eremitical life, which God gave to the
prophet Elijah to observe, and which has been commented on and
expounded by John 44, bishop of Jerusalem, from the sayings of both
the Old Law and the New" (1:8).

The speaker and, it is implied, the writer of the *Institution,* who
talks with Caprasius concerning Elijah's legendary life, is more
than an ordinary Carmelite elder eager to teach a fellow community
member about the Order's way of perfection. The sentences appearing at the end of book 1 declare what Carmelites came to believe, that
the *Institution* was the work of a bishop living in the Holy Land
during the formative centuries of the Church. The speaker's authority
for medieval Carmelite readers was derived from a legend persisting
among Carmelites that John 44 had been an early prior in their Order.
Any friar believing this accepted that the author of the *Institution*
satisfied the criterion invoked in its first paragraph (and long invoked
by spiritual writers worldwide) that "an understanding of this way
of life consists in experience alone, and this understanding cannot
be given fully in a teaching of words except by an experienced person" (1:1).

If Carmelites could believe that the speaker was John 44—and
indications are that they did believe this for a long time—then they
could believe that they were reading a copy of an ancient document
whose author lived during the era of the fathers of monasticism Antony
the Hermit, Pachomius, John Cassian, Gregory the Great, and Jerome.
Manuscripts of *The Institution of the First Monks* must have felt holy
to the friars who held them in their hands. For a medieval reader, the
authorial voice of the frame narrative spoke from an era of first and
purest things. In various ways the *Institution* claims to be the history

of the origin of the Carmelite Order and, as its title indicates, the history of the institution, or beginning, of Christian monasticism. Possession of the *Institution* must have given brothers and sisters of Carmel great pride and security but also humility, for it told them that their actions should reflect the pristine origins of their way of life.

Imitation of Christ

Something even more powerful and authoritative happens on another narrative level of the *Institution*. The conversation between Caprasius and John 44, which continues throughout the work, can be thought of as a first level of narration because it has the elements of a story: characters, a narrator, a situation (intimate conversation), and the implied plot of the spiritual life that the two men pursue. The content of what John 44 tells Caprasius is a considerably fuller second story, to which this discussion will soon turn. While Caprasius listens, John 44 relates events in the life story of Elijah the hermit, who founded monastic life and the Carmelite Order.

However, in a long passage filling most of book 1, the *Institution* dips down to a third story level. John 44 does more than tell a long story about Elijah and the Order. Within that story is another story told at a deeper level. It is from this deeper level that the *Institution*'s most powerful teaching authority derives, and it is there, at the level of the third story, that its most important messages are delivered. On the deepest level, the speaking voice of John 44 sometimes merges with, and most often is entirely replaced by, the voice of God. Rudolf Hendriks remarks that the explanation of what the monk must perform step by step come from the Divine Being who speaks "one moment *ex persona Dei* and the next *ex persona Christi*" (Hendriks, "Elias in the Carmelite Tradition," 99). On this level the identity of the person addressed shifts as well. Here, as in the long conversation running on the first level, Caprasius is indistinguishable from the reader of the *Institution*: they receive what is said at the same time. On the third level, these two listeners merge with Elijah, in a wonderful turn, as he is called to imitate the deepest story, the life of Christ.

The three levels need to be shown from details in the text. After opening on the first level ("With good reason, beloved Caprasius, you inquire about the beginning of the Order...." 1:1), the *Institution* quickly moves to the second level, the story beginning in Elijah's lifetime ("Know this, therefore, and give heed: From the beginning of the reign of Ahab, king of Israel, until the coming of Christ in the flesh, there passed about nine hundred and forty years.... During his time and in his kingdom there was a great prophet of the tribe of Aaron named Elijah, born in the city of Tishbe." 1:1). A few paragraphs later, at the end of the second chapter of its first book, the *Institution* prepares its audience for the powerful shift of narrative and voice about to take place:

> And so by what he proposed to the holy prophet Elijah in all the above words, *God earnestly wished to urge him the first and principal leader of monks, and also to urge us his imitators,* to be "perfect as our heavenly father is perfect" (Matt. 5:43), "having above all things charity, which is the bond of perfection" (Col. 3:14). In order to attain the gifts of his perfection and the promised vision of glory, then, let us try to understand clearly, attentively and in order, and to fulfill in deeds, the form of life for achieving this given by God to blessed Elijah in the above words. *For when he speaks to Elijah the Lord also says to every hermit monk, in the Old Law and the New,* "Depart from here, namely from the perishable and transitory things of earth" (my emphases). (1:2)

Those to whom God speaks on the third level must include the *Institution*'s readers. Elijah's life story, occupying most of the rest of the *Institution*, will be told in the third person and narrated in the past tense, allowing its audience to feel that it is distanced from what happened in earlier eras of the Order. The third story level uses, in contrast, the "I" and "you" of conversation (as does the first level). This move brings readers, whoever they may be, into the story. After signaling the reader that the Lord not only spoke to Elijah but speaks to "us," book 1 continues:

> Therefore, my son, if you wish to be perfect and to arrive at the goal of the eremitical monastic life and to drink of the torrent there, "Depart from here," namely from the perishable things of the world, relinquishing in spirit and in fact for my sake all earthly possessions and powers, because this is an easier and safer way of tending towards prophetic perfection and finally of coming to the kingdom of heaven. (1:3)

While this passage may, on a glance, seem to be more conversation between John 44 and Caprasius, the demand to give up all "for my sake" identifies the speech as belonging to Jesus, who in the Gospels tells his disciples, "If any man would come after me, let him deny himself and take up his cross and follow me. For whoever would save his life will lose it, and whoever loses his life for my sake will find it" (Matt. 16:24–25).

Christian life has always involved imitation of Christ, at the very least as an ideal. The apostle Paul's letters reminded first-century Christian groups throughout the Mediterranean how closely tied they should understand their own sufferings and humility to be to the voluntary acts of God and Christ who Paul taught brought about the world's salvation. Fourth- and fifth-century Syrian and Egyptian Christians who withdrew to the desert as hermits recast the early Church's understanding of how to imitate Christ's suffering. Their offerings of body and soul in imitation of Christ were not the acts of public martyrdom so often praised by the Church until then but solitary gifts to God informed by a never-ending interior pursuit of spiritual purity. For the early Christian hermits, progress in detachment from the impediments of possessions, ordinary human relationship, and even ordinary needs, coupled with progress in acceptance of God's initiative in their life, constituted imitation of Christ.

Medieval European Christians, including the laity and originally lay organizations such as the Franciscans or Carmelites, retained the early Fathers' emphasis on interior transformation in imitation of Christ. To this they often added literal imitation of Christ's material poverty and missionary tours to preach conversion of heart. Through the story that it tells of Elijah, *The Institution of the First Monks* explores what it means, or could mean, to be a follower of Christ as a member of a religious order. Not only the oldest motifs of Christian imitation, such as the willingness to suffer as Christ had suffered, but also medieval emphases on Jesus' material poverty and preaching are at the center of the document. Its greatest attention is to the imitation of Christ's love, which encompasses the other themes.

In a moment we will examine passages in which the voice of God more obviously utters the call to imitate Christ. First, we need to address the question: how may such shifts in voice and narrative level have affected the medieval Carmelites who encountered the book? This topic deserves more thorough discussion than will be given it here, but several things can be said. First, monastic culture has been, and definitely was in the Middle Ages, a culture in which the speaking voice was highly valued. Carmelite historian Redemptus Maria Valabek has shown from several medieval sources (including later passages of *The Institution of the First Monks* that describe Elijah's legendary hermit followers engaged in singing the liturgy) that the medieval Order believed that speech had important functions in the interior life.

Some of the best evidence for this is found in the Carmelite *Rule* whose text received its final form in the first half of the thirteenth century. First, it required medieval Carmelites to read and hear the scriptural word of God in the most sacred areas of their daily living space. The "law of the Lord" was the Carmelite's daily companion in the cell (1247, ch. 7). Brothers and, in time, sisters were instructed to "eat whatever may have been given to you in a common refectory, listening in common to some reading from Sacred Scripture" (ch. 4). Whether in their cells, as it seems had been the practice on Mt. Carmel, or gathered in the oratory, as became the habit in medieval European houses, Carmelites were instructed to "say" the Psalms (in the 1207 *Rule*; in the 1247 *Rule*, "say the canonical hours") or "say the *Our Father*" daily (ch. 8). Mass was to be heard daily in the oratory (ch. 10). The meditated, heard, and recited word of God was to be wholly taken into their lives. It was to lodge in medieval Carmelites' hearts, to be on their lips, and to inform their actions: "May you possess the sword of the spirit, which is God's word, abundantly in your mouth and in your hearts. Just so, whatever you do, let it be done in the Lord's word" (ch. 14).

The document that governed medieval Carmelite daily life addresses other features of utterance as well. It explains the spiritual benefits to be gained in the long night silence it required. Throughout the daytime hours, it calls Carmelites to "studiously cultivate silence, in which lies the fostering of righteousness" (ch. 16). Needless to say, the daily experiences of physical silence and restrained speech tends to heighten the effect of the scriptural word when it is chanted with other members of the community in the oratory or read, silently or aloud, in the cell. The voice of Christ could furthermore break into medieval Carmelites' attentive silence when their prior or prioress spoke to them. The *Rule* commands, "Reverence your Prior humbly, thinking of Christ rather than of the one he has set up as your head, and he has said to the leaders of the Church: Who hears you, hears me" (ch. 18). In sum, their *Rule* shows us that medieval Carmelites were indeed sensitized to the voice of God. They knew that they could hear it speak in the written word and in words uttered by those around them.

God's voice predominates in the long third-level discussion of the implications for spiritual life of the command given to Elijah, "Depart from here and turn eastward, and hide yourself by the brook Cherith, that is east of the Jordan. You shall drink from the brook, and I have commanded the ravens to feed you there" (1 Kings 17:2–4). At key moments, the voice, sometimes seeming to belong to the Father and often to the Son, shifts from an explanation of the spiritual life to a compellingly personal address. These personal moments—in which God seems simultaneously to be speaking to Elijah, to "every hermit monk," and to "you"—are the ocean floor, the deepest level of *The Institution of the First Monks*. What is said at these moments invests everything else in the document with meaning. Here there is no confusing the speaker with a fourth-century bishop or Carmelite elder. The calls are too absolute, and the final offer of a gift is too great for any human to make them. For a Christian, only God could say such things.

Each of the urgent speeches of the divine voice completes the discussion that precedes it, naming a final act in a phase of spiritual perfection. The speeches call the listener to a sequence of peak events in the interior life that, if they are accomplished, conform to the spiritual life of Christ reflected in the Gospels. In chapter 4, after explaining why desire for possessions and certain kinds of relations obstructs the spiritual life, Christ urges his listeners to renounce not only the objects of desire but also self-will:

> Indeed, I am the Lord and master of the prophets and "I came down from heaven not to do my own will but the will of him who sent me," the Father (John 6:38), "becoming obedient to him unto death, even to the death of the cross" (Phil. 2:8). …If you wish, therefore, to come after me "towards the East," that is, against the original cupidity of your flesh, consider how you must carry the cross…just so must you be crucified and deny yourself, so that you do not turn your will to what pleases you and at the moment delights you, but instead apply your whole will to that to which my will has bound you. In this way "you may live in the rest of your time in the flesh not by human desires but by the will of God" (1 Pet. 4:2). (1:4)

If they wish to arrive at the goal of prophetic, eremitical life, Christ urges hearers to be spiritually crucified as he was, fastened to the will of the Father.

In chapter 6 of the first book, the divine voice, perhaps belonging to Christ, perhaps to his Father, urges hearer/readers to accomplish the next great step of spiritual perfection. They are to love God with their whole being:

> If you love anything more than you love me, you do not yet love me with your whole heart, and you are not in Carith, that is in charity, and therefore you are not worthy to see me. ...If however, you offer me your heart with such love and commit yourself to me with so much affection that whatever I discountenance and forbid to you, however difficult it may be to avoid it, yet for love of me you completely avoid and hate; and whatever I wish and command, however difficult it may be to do it, you nevertheless observe and do for love of me, then you begin to love me "with your whole heart and whole soul and whole mind." (1:6)

This, too, heavily echoes the Gospels. In John 14, on the occasion of the Last Supper, Jesus declares to his disciples: "He who has my commandments and keeps them, he it is who loves me; and he who loves me will be loved by my Father, and I will love him and manifest myself to him" (14:21). What Jesus says next in the Gospel describes the very interior acts that *The Institution of the First Monks* calls its readers to perform: "I do as the Father has commanded me, so that the world may know that I love the Father" (14:31).

Paul Chandler observes concerning the whole of Ribot's remarkable document, "For the *Institution* everything in religious life, all its structures and energies, are directed to this end: total transformation in divine love" (Chandler, *The Book of the First Monks*, 8). This and other passages in which the divine voice speaks make Chandler's point very powerfully. Echoes of the voice of God in the Hebrew Scriptures and the voice of Christ in the Gospels resound in the call to love recorded in chapter 6 of book 1. Psychically standing with Caprasius and Elijah, the reader "hears" once again the *Shema* of Deuteronomy 6:4–5 ("Hear, O Israel: Yahweh our God is one...and you shall love Yahweh your God with all your heart, and with all your soul, and with all your might") and the double commandment of love found the Gospels (Matt. 22:34–40, Mark 12:28–31, Luke 10:25–28).

Medieval Carmelites also surely heard the insistence on the double commandment in their own familiar *Rule*: "Put on the breastplate of justice so that you may love the Lord your God with your whole heart and your whole soul and your whole strength, and your neighbors as yourselves" (ch. 14).

Each time that it shifts to direct address, the divine voice urges readers first to abandon themselves to Christlike obedience and then to Christlike love. Late in book 1, it explains what may happen if one does these things. Relinquishing all personal desire and delivering oneself into the love of God, one may be united briefly with God in love:

> Whatever I command or advise you in my law—whether to flee unclean thoughts and the passions of the flesh and the world so that you may keep your heart from them; or to serve your neighbor and avoid offending him so that you may preserve a good conscience toward him without reproach, or to render the service of my worship so that you might serve me with a faith that is not feigned but sincere—all these things I urge on you to this end, that from your "pure heart and good conscience and sincere faith" there may freely rise a love which is so fervent and powerful and yet so peaceful and complete in binding your heart to me, without any resistance at all, that your heart feels nothing whatsoever in it contrary to my love or hindering it, but rests absolutely at peace in my love. ...When...you arrive at this...in this perfect union of yourself with me I shall give you and your companions to drink from that torrent of which the prophet says to me: "You shall give them to drink of the torrent of your pleasure" (Ps. 35:9). (1:7)

Obedience and love are commanded once more. The extraordinarily attractive speech describes an unimpeded flow of the spiritual life in which self-abandonment unfolds into the powerful, peaceful love in which union occurs. Prior steps of perfection have freed and purified the soul for the flowing experience that the voice describes.

The passage is laden with implications for Christian imitation of Christ, and Carmelite imitation of Christ in particular. It teaches that preparation for loving union with God needs eremitical seclusion but also can occur outside of strict solitude, in acts of service to fellow human beings and in the "service of worship," liturgical prayer, which, Valabek observes, other Carmelites such as John Soreth (following Bernard of Clairvaux) believed was an occasion for contact with God. It also speaks to the heart. The voice on the third level is too power-fully authoritative, personally compelling and clear in its communi-cations to miss the fact that its messages are meant to have priority over all others in the document.

Imitation of Elijah

Details in *The Institution of the First Monks* suggest that the long passage in which the divine voice speaks may have been written by one author, while another person may have been responsible for story levels one and two. The divine voice speaks only on the third story level, never on the first and second. The passage in which the Father and the Son speak does not mention the Carmelite Order or, as Chan-dler has noted, the mountain that is so central to the group's sense of identity. Baudry observes that the divine voice always addresses hermits in general, not any specific group. (Level two speaks of both the Order and Mt. Carmel. Level one mentions the Order but not the mountain.) On the third level, Elijah is called to live as a Christian hermit. He is not the busily active monastic founder that he becomes on level two. What most suggests that the long third-level passage originally existed on its own, then was embedded in what is now the whole document of *The Institution of the First Monks*, is the fact that the third-level passage has no need of the other two to make its points. It is cogent when read on its own (a fact that members of the Order have corroborated in the last century by repeatedly extract-ing book 1 and the first part of book 2 for publication. The passage in book 1 which the divine voice speaks points forward to later phases of its own discussion and recalls its earlier remarks but does not refer to levels one and two that extend throughout books 1–7.

Although nothing in the level-three passage suggests that it was composed with the Carmelite Order in mind, whoever wrote the rest of *The Institution of the First Monks*—levels one and two—certainly believed that the content of level three mattered to the Order. The Elijan legend told on level two repeats the teachings of level three at several points. While the author of level three gives no sign of being a member of the Order, the devisor of the long legend on level two must have been a fourteenth-century Carmelite (such as Felip Ribot). The devisor knew the content of the *Rubrica prima* and probably had read some of the Carmelite documents described earlier in this chapter, since some of their details are repeated on level two. The mendicant service that Carmelites undertook in the thirteenth century is mentioned in the legend. Whoever wrote the long Carmelite saga repeated the great themes of the third-level passage. Someone—most likely the writer of the second level of narration—set the saga and the third-level passage in the frame of a dialogue between John 44 and Caprasius. As a result, the speeches of the divine voice are the core of a multilayered exploration of how the imitation of Christ has inspired the Carmelite Order from its beginning.

According to the second-tier story, the Order sprang from a spiritual response to God's initiative:

> Once he had heard from God the above law for arriving at prophetic perfection and the goal of the monastic eremitical life and persevering in it, Elijah reflected that it is "not the hearers of the law who are just before God, but the doers of the law who will be justified" (Rom. 2:13). Therefore he strove with all his heart to reach this prophetic perfection and goal of the monastic eremitical life, and to live out in practice the law he had heard from God for attaining it. (2:1)

Elijah wholeheartedly accomplished everything his Lord commanded. He obeyed Christ's call to deny his own will. He chose solitude, silence, and chastity. He loved God. Finally "earning the right to stand before the majesty of God," he was given the gift of union "as he tasted frequently the inexpressible glory of God and dwelt (that is rested) in the torrent of divine pleasure" (2:1). He continued to seek perfection, nourished by the example of holy men described in Scripture. "In this way Elijah observed the prophetic monastic life in the desert" (2:1). Where the Bible makes no comment on his life before his prophetic career, in the Carmelite document, God first calls Elijah to perfect his own soul before sending him to reclaim the hearts of the northern Israelites.

The *Institution* promotes imitation of models whose exemplar is Christ himself. Elijah and the prophetic hermits who succeeded in imitating the patterns of his spiritual life are mirrors of Christ's life. In book 1, the divine voice calls hearers to achieve Christlike self-offering and love. After Elijah molded his life according to the steps of perfection given in his call, disciples patterned their lives on his. At the end of book 2, the point is made that the Carmelite Order and all other observances owe their existence to Elijah's example: "Because God decreed that the perfection of the prophetic institute consists in imitating Elijah, Elijah gave to the members of the Order the great models of prophetic discipline and monastic life; namely, his actions and good works. ...Thus, those leaders of the monks were, one might say, by their sound teachings on the monastic life individual streams flowing from Elijah as from the first and universal source of all streams" (2:8, Werling numbering).

It may be recalled that learning by imitation happened very often in the Middle Ages and that medieval religious life constantly reminded its adherents of the deeds of many figures. Carmelites who read the *Institution* must have concluded that they needed to accomplish all of the steps of purification commanded by the divine voice. Elijah had mastered them, and so, according to the legend, had very many of their spiritual forebears. Encouraging models abounded. Early readers most likely saw that Christ's life underlay the story of the Order's origins, given that the second-level story so clearly demonstrates that Elijah succeeded in imitating Jesus' greatest spiritual achievements.

The Carmelite founder is also held up as a model of organizational leadership, which is quite an unusual role for him in the whole body of legends told about him worldwide. Given historical pressures on the Order, contemporary readers most likely noticed this feature of the document as well. Friars who lived during the decades that ended the fourteenth and began the fifteenth century (that is, in the very decades in which Carmelites such as Cheminot, Baconthorpe, and Ribot were circulating new versions of the Order's legend of origin) had seen the damage done to their observance by the Hundred Years War (1337–1453), which kept England and France in turmoil for so long, and by the Western Schism (1378–1417), which split the Order and the Church. Fourteenth-century privileges and exemptions bestowed by Rome on friars involved in academic and political pursuits weakened the corporate life of the Order.

Medieval Carmelites reading the *Institution* were also well aware that their Order had lost a great deal to the Black Plague that had swept through densely populated areas throughout Europe in the middle of the fourteenth century. The disease heavily damaged religious orders in Europe as whole communities were wiped out overnight and leadership positions were suddenly vacant. Houses in all the orders often took in members they would have found unacceptable in other times. In his study of these difficult years, Carmelite historian Benedict Zimmerman comments that in the immediate wake of the Plague, it was nearly impossible to achieve full observance of the *Rule*.

The contrast between the picture painted in the *Institution* of capable leaders who, following Elijah's example, oversaw the peaceful, constant expansion of a new religious order and the recent decades of struggle to keep the Carmelite Order from foundering due to low membership, absenteeism, and weak or inexperienced leadership must have been obvious. A letter written by English provincial Thomas Netter to his prior general John Grossi suggests that a strong leadership class had yet to be reestablished even by 1425. His complaint,

"Reverend Father, it is a very remarkable thing that in many countries where the Order has been introduced only recently, it is entrusted to some raw recruit and inexperienced guardian" (Letter 27 in Fitzgerald-Lombard, 359), was part of an attempt to persuade the aging Grossi to remain at the helm of Carmel, but it also named a situation within the Order. Netter's "inexperienced guardians" were quite different from Elijah and the leaders he appointed in the *Institution,* who attended to their own spiritual maturation before attempting to guide others.

Netter's letters to Grossi yield more information about the *Institution*. It appears from additional comments that the English leader makes in his correspondence with Grossi that *The Institution of the First Monks* had impressed many in the Order within a few decades after Ribot began to circulate it in 1390. Netter served as provincial between 1414 and 1430. He wrote to Grossi to request a copy of the *Institution* on two occasions. In what seems to have been his first petition he mentions the *Institution*, the first work in the collection of the *Ten Books:*

> May you also deign to let me have through [the definitor William Thorpe, sent by the English province to a general chapter in 1425] the work of John 44 addressed to the monk Caprasius or another of the requested books if you have any, at my expense. (Letter 27, op. cit., 360)

Grossi seems not to have responded. Netter wrote again. His second letter stresses his desire to obtain the *Institution* and explains that others in England are also eager to see it:

> Finally, I ask you, and many other people with me, to have the book of John 44 to the monk Caprasius copied at our expense, a book which would be of great value and honor to us if it could be purchased for us in ancient script. (Letter 28, op. cit., 362)

Regardless of why Grossi kept it and how Netter knew that he could request a copy of it, it is clear from the correspondence that the fame of the *Institution* and respect for its contents had spread by around 1425. Dissemination of it continued. Joachim Smet, author of a five-volume history of the Order, notes that Thomas Scrope made an English translation of the work at the end of the fifteenth century and that Teresa of Avila consulted a Spanish translation of it in the sixteenth century. Otger Steggink and Kilian Healy find traces of it in later works, Healy, for example, detecting evidence of its influence in the *Directory* of the Touraine Reform. Additional details concerning its influence will be presented in the next chapter.

Netter surely found the text useful to communities in his province because of what it taught about the spiritual life. It may also be imagined that he found its serenely positive model of leadership personally inspiring in an age of the Church now remembered for its laxity and loss of fervor. In it, Elijah displays wisdom, decisiveness, foresight, and an ability to foster leaders under him. Everything to which he puts his hand flourishes. As a result of his efforts, many communities are founded, all seemingly at peace within themselves. The prophet's leadership in the *Institution* generally resembles positive accounts of the foundational activities of Benedict of Nursia or Francis of Assisi. It also resembles the leadership of Jesus, who, the Gospels say, similarly taught an inner circle of followers the spiritual principles of the way of life he promoted and challenged them to conform their lives to his. In the *Institution*, Elijah's extraordinary success as a leader was a result of his full-hearted response to the call of God to become like Christ.

In the *Institution*, the prophet begins his promotion of prophetic eremitical life by choosing an inner circle of disciples from those attracted to him for his sanctity. He shepherds his special group of companions through the biblical period of Ahab and Jezebel's vengeance, eventually establishing them on Mt. Carmel, a place that the *Institution* says he chooses because it is especially appropriate for eremitical life. Elijah's selection of Mt. Carmel as a place to establish a community is unparalleled in his traditions worldwide. Although the prophet's settlement of his group on the mountain accounts for the Order's historical beginning, what the *Institution* says happened reconfigures the true order of events, in which, instead of being led by their founder to the mountain in the ninth century before the common era, a small band of Western hermits two millennia later chose to dwell where they believed Elijah had once lived. In the legend, Elijah teaches the new residents "to observe the monastic life according to the form given him by God" and to sing psalms to God, in which they "devoutly opened the interior of their minds to the Lord, so that he frequently sent the spirit of prophecy into their hearts" (2:11).

The story expands geographically, involving the lives of more and more people. As adherents to his way of life begin to multiply, some taking up residence elsewhere in Israel, Elijah selects "hermit-prophets" to help him oversee all the groups:

> From this time, under the guidance of divine Wisdom, those monks established by Elijah increased in number, and he chose from them certain foremost ones who prophesied the future to accompany him and succeed him in this office: to carefully teach those monks the monastic life given to Elijah by God, to organize them in the prophetic school and in singing psalms with the psaltery, and to take care of them as diligently as if they were their own sons. Moreover, these monks, who were at first called prophets (as we have said), were afterwards called sons of the prophets because they were the disciples of the foremost prophets of the Order: they lived in the prophetic and monastic discipline under the guidance of those prophets who were like their fathers, and were true imitators of the holy lives and virtues of these prophets. (2:11)

Elijah's actions duplicate the governance structure of the medieval orders. When disciples first gather around him, he acts like a novice master or prior directly involved in the welfare of his companions. His support of them is both material and spiritual, as can be seen when he teaches them to sing liturgies that open their hearts to the presence of God. When the number of his followers increase, he begins to act like a provincial or prior general, preparing leaders to teach and organize communities. He eventually visits all the foundations throughout the region. This continues to the end of his life on earth: "Before Elijah was taken from this world to the paradise of delight, he took care, right before his translation, to visit each of his monastic disciples, the sons of the prophets, and to provide a father for them to rule and govern them all in his place" (4:3). He even performs a task somewhat similar to the bestowal of a formula for life by Patriarch Albert of Jerusalem on the historical hermits of Mt. Carmel. He carefully transmits the spirit and practices of eremitical life to those who will succeed him. The story often stops to note that he teaches his way of life to his successors.

Stories told in the *Rubrica prima* and in documents predating the *Institution* mentioned earlier in this discussion give the impression that the Order endured because a constantly replenished group of hermits prayed continually. They tell stories in which the desire for prayer attracted the first inhabitants of the mountain and attracted a succession of followers. In *The Institution of the First Monks,* continuity in Carmelite life is achieved as much through effective leadership as through the continuous prayer of individuals. The emphasis on leadership and on the success of leaders in instituting practices of community life, including the spiritual training of new members, distinguishes the *Institution* from other Carmelite accounts of origin. Legends found in documents by Ribot's contemporaries such as Cheminot, Grossi, or Oller do not comment on Elijah's leadership.

The story of Elijah on the second level of the *Institution* has quite a lot to show about the issue. It promotes the view, which perhaps existed in the Order but is not expressed in the *Rubrica prima* or other documents, that God was the true founder of Carmel and continued to be its leader. It claims that the Order arose because the Holy Spirit called Elijah to pursue eremitical perfection by the Wadi Cherith. God and his Son called Elijah to live as a hermit. The God-given ability to see into the future and to access God through mystical experience helped the leaders and ordinary members of the group. The *Institution* promotes the belief that God instituted the Carmelite Order and all monastic observance.

Descriptions of divine aid extended to Elijah and his legendary followers sometimes resemble similar moments in the New Testament Book of Acts which so affected Christian thinking during the Middle Ages. In Acts, the two great early leaders of the Church, Peter and Paul, receive constant supernatural support. Many similar instances of heavenly guidance occur in the *Institution*. For example, in contrast with the story told of him in 2 Kings in which Elijah is taken to heaven without knowing whether God will choose to transfer his prophetic call to Elisha, in the *Institution* Elijah deliberately waits to transfer leadership of the new order to Elisha until he observes that God has confirmed his disciple. Elisha's peers bow before him just as the sons of the prophets bow before him in 2 Kings:

> By this act they showed a method to their descendants that when their chief father was taken from them, they should humbly receive in his place as their father, him who, like Elisha, will be sent to them by God through signs and prodigies. If the signs do not appear, they should try with all diligence as of one mind, to put over themselves as their father, one of their number who should then precede the others who received him as their father. (4:3)

The *Institution* adds that thereafter the group regularly sought divine confirmation when it needed to name a new leader.

Leaders who use God-given knowledge or capabilities to pilot the expanding Order along its trajectory are constantly before the reader's eyes. Elijah, Elisha, and other legendary leaders rely on the gift of knowing the future. When John the Baptist becomes the leader of a group of Elijan hermits living by the Jordan River, he uses the spiritual gift to prepare his flock to understand the miracle of tongues in the upcoming Pentecost after Jesus' resurrection and to prepare them to accept the second baptism that will usher them into the Church. The *Institution* places so many critical decisions and actions in the hands of the leaders that it is easy to gather the impression from it that the Order's historical leaders, guided by God, ensured its survival. The many prescient, effective decisions of Elijah, Elisha, and John the Baptist demonstrate that the actions of priors and provincials are critically important, especially at junctures in which the Order needs to change its response to the times. Flesh-and-blood Carmelite leaders familiar with the *Institution* may well have mulled over these details. The call of Jesus Christ to follow his spiritual way of life is the strongest challenge of the *Institution*, but the document presents other challenges to its readers as well.

Followers of the Founder

Carmelite legends always say interesting things about Elijah's successors. As has been mentioned, the legend declares that Elijah first chose a group of disciples to receive his teaching and then, when the number of his followers was very large, chose a group to lead separate communities. The second-level story also claims that the biblical figures Jonah, Elisha, Michaiah (a prophet mentioned in 2 Kings), and Obadiah (a conflation of Ahab's majordomo with the prophet who lends his name to the Book of Obadiah) were "called to monastic life by Elijah" (2:12). The four are members of Elijah's original group of disciples. The prophet recruits Elisha in 1 Kings, but no other disciples appear in his story there. Christian legend sometimes identifies the widow's son whom Elijah returned to life as the prophet Jonah. However, the induction of the biblical prophets Michaiah and Obadiah into eremitical life seems to be a novelty. (In his earlier *Speculum*, John of Cheminot says that Elijah founded a community whose members include Elisha, Jonah, and Abiah.)

What matters most to the work's great themes is not that the *Institution*'s story so freely absorbs the lives of figures unrelated to each other in Scripture, but that Michaiah, Obadiah, Jonah, and Elisha are shown to have carbon-copy spiritual lives matching Elijah's.

Identical phrases in four short chapters affirm that each figure was "introduced into the prophetic discipline of monastic life by Elijah" before beginning his prophetic activity mentioned in Scripture. The Tishbite and four disciples were selected and were taught the way of eremitical life. They succeed in it and performed the prophetic service of God in the larger world for which the Bible remembers them.

The close similarity between substories in the *Institution* accomplishes several more ends. Cheminot's legend that was described earlier in this chapter weaves the history of the Order into the events recorded in the Book of Acts. The *Institution*'s writer interlaces his tale of Carmelite beginnings with sacred history as well. The connection of the Carmelite legend to recognizable parts of Scripture—here, to the lives of several prophets mentioned in the Hebrew Bible, and in other passages, to the Book of Acts—asked medieval readers to believe that some ancestors of the Order had actually lived in this earlier age. In an era in which mendicant orders often quarreled over the legitimacy of each other's origins, the *Institution* was saying (as Cheminot, Hildesheim, and others also suggest in their legends) that the Carmelite Order began in biblical times, long before other Christian monastic groups appeared.

A reader able to believe that Jonah, Elisha, Obadiah, and Michaiah were protoCarmelites was invited to wonder whether other vestiges of Carmelite history might be found in the Bible. If details of the history of the Order could be detected in Elijah's resuscitation of the widow's son in 1 Kings or in the book of Jonah, where else on the sacred page might evidence of it be found?

The exact repetitions of the accomplishments of Elijah and his prophet-disciples also stress the idea, of special importance to Carmelite formation during the difficult fifteenth century, that growth in an orderly life of solitary prayer must precede involvement in leadership and public service. Most important, the redundancy of lives in the legend stresses the core teachings of chapter 1. The reader cannot miss the point, made in identical language in each of the chapters dedicated to Jonah, Elisha, Obadiah, and Michaiah, and in earlier descriptions of Elijah's own prayer life, that growth in the spiritual life must follow a progression of obedient detachment from all save God, followed by wholehearted love. Other unnamed "hermit-prophets" whom Elijah chooses to lead the developing Order follow the same trajectory, as does the whole body of disciples. Members of the group imitate Christ by imitating Elijah.

When the whole group's actions are being described, the passages often seem to comment on events in the early European history of the Order. One passage critiques the Order's double call to solitary prayer and apostolic service. In the legend, Elijah and his followers "stayed mostly in the deserts at God's command" but sometimes went into the neighboring towns "for the sake of the people" to preach, prophesy, perform miracles and attract new recruits to the "prophetic Order" (2:22). Although set in the prophet's ancient lifetime, the passage lists what Carmelites were in fact doing among the laity in the thirteenth and fourteenth centuries. Saints from these centuries are still remembered for their prophecy, miracles, and preaching. Nonhagiographic documents account for Carmelites' pastoral work in areas surrounding their houses during the period.

The legendary portrait of the Order diverges from medieval Carmelite life in one important feature. Although it continued to establish hermitages, the historical Order chose to place most of its new communities near towns and cities. It did this so that friars could serve the laity without the need to venture long distances from their houses. Urban areas also provided material support for the mendicants. In the *Institution* legend, however, monasteries established in towns were not the permanent dwelling places that they were in real life in the Middle Ages:

> In the surrounding districts of certain towns and villages
> of the Promised Land, especially in Galgala, Bethel, Jeri-
> cho, and Samaria, they established schools for religious
> men, sons of the prophets (as is read in the Book of
> Kings), where the monks lodged when they came to the

> towns and villages. Those of the people whom they were
> able to enroll in the prophetic institute, they first instructed
> in these monasteries concerning the prophetic discipline
> and the rudiments of the monastic religious life in order
> that they might wean them from the life of the city and
> then afterwards send them into the deserts. (3:7)

Even the house that the legendary hermits established in Jerusalem
was a temporary dwelling, used when brethren gathered in the Holy
City for the annual feasts and as a place to prepare recruits for desert
life. "These, after the religious instructed them in the rudiments of the
discipline of the prophetic, monastic and eremitical life, were then
transferred to the solitudes" (5:4).

Carmelite constitutions of the day trace a life for new members
that does not match the one described in the *Institution*. In real life,
medieval recruits often underwent a course of study that prepared
them to be good priests. Those with the aptitude were sent to priories
in cities or towns, where, instead of studying to prepare themselves
for desert retreat, they were prepared in philosophy and other disciplines. A small group of the most promising students moved on to
"general schools" (*studia generalia*) located in cities housing major
universities for final training as theologians and teachers. These few
highly educated Carmelites—whose maturation in religious life included experience of several monastic communities, contact with secular life, and contact with members of other observances—returned to
leadership or teaching positions in the Order, not to solitary life in the
desert. The medieval Order was committed to this educational itiner-
ary. Its first general school was established in Paris in the late thirteenth century. Between roughly 1320 and the date the *Institution*
was written, general schools were established in cities along the Mediterranean coastline and in the university towns of Oxford, London,
Cambridge, Cologne, and Bologna. Judging from his handling of
Scripture and rhetoric, the person who composed the second-level
legend had benefited from studying in the system.

In other words, the highly educated, fourteenth-century author of
the second-level saga of Carmelite origins chose to promote to his

readers a physical seclusion that was no longer possible for the Order as a whole to achieve and a formation that varied from what the constitutions prescribed. This was not wishful thinking but a deliberate promotion of the medieval Order's spiritual ideals. The Order has always attracted those who are especially moved by the original story of a small group of hermits who loved contemplation. That many of these also have felt a call to preaching, teaching, or missionary work does not erase an appreciation of the asceticism and contemplation invested in the hermit ideal.

According to monastic historian C. H. Lawrence, many groups turned to idealized primitive models during the long intellectual revival that began in the eleventh century. Monastic reformers especially recalled the "eremitical life of the desert fathers, an obvious model for individuals who had read the early classics of monastic literature" (Lawrence, 126). The author of the second-level story in the *Institution* followed the trend. Like the desert fathers (and in accord with the call to solitude uttered by the divine voice in book 1), the Carmelite saga indicates that the mountains or desert is the best place for the spiritual life. Fourteenth-century Carmelite readers, remembering their historical beginnings on Mt. Carmel, surely would have agreed. The problem they needed to solve was where to find the best equivalents of the wilderness and the hermit's spiritual formation in their urban life. The answer often had to be found in their inner life.

Lawrence reports that writers adapted ancient prototypes. The author of the *Institution* revised the ideals that he borrowed. Incidents of combat with the devil or harrowing personal struggle that are so essential to fourth- and fifth-century stories of perfection are absent from the late fourteenth-century document, as are tales of extraordinary fasts or other challenges to the body. Instead, the legendary hermits of the *Institution* enjoy remarkable peace and quiet away from the secular world. In the document, Mt. Carmel was "indeed suitable for the hermit: it offered silence and quiet because of its solitude;

shelter in its caves; peace in its woodlands; healthful air from its elevation; abundant food from its herbs and fruits; and delicious water from its springs" (3:3). Medieval European readers could imagine that their Order's sacred mountain truly possessed all these charms. They would have known that they were being told a story about ideals, not historical fact, once they read the *Institution*'s description of community life: each hermit on Mt. Carmel lived in "a little dwelling or cave or grotto or cell near the spring of Elijah" in unblemished communion with his companions. "Ceasing from all quarrels and discussions through the practice of silence and harmony and unity of spirit, they came together at stated hours to their assembly place to praise the Creator in peace" (3:5).

Although it certainly calls readers to aspire to what it describes, *The Institution of the First Monks* is not a call to return to earlier times nor is it naive. It is a complex commentary on the way the Order saw itself in the late Middle Ages. Memories, facts of daily life, myths, and ideals are all included in the second-level story of the *Institution*. One strand of the story does follow the lead of European monastic reformers in harking back to eremitical heroes of the dawning centuries of the Church (somewhat idealized by their own promoters), but the author of the second-level legend is engaged in promoting later ideals as well.

Apostles of the Lord

The story also places a second ancient prototype before its readers. "Another antique model that provided inspiration for many new kinds of monasticism," remarks Lawrence, "was what men called 'the apostolic life'" (Lawrence, 126). That phrase meant more than one thing in the Middle Ages, but regardless of its application, the "apostolic life" always took its inspiration from New Testament descriptions of the actions of Jesus and his followers. Older monastic orders such as the Benedictines found features of their cenobitic way

of life in the apostles' peaceful community life described in the opening chapters of Acts. Mendicant groups such as the Carmelites and
Franciscans were especially influenced by descriptions in the Gospels and Acts of the apostles' preaching tours, poverty, and fraternal
care of the poor and humble.

The Institution of the First Monks promotes apostolic life in all
these senses. In it, personal perfection, communal relations, and evangelical service all have a New Testament stamp. Its description of the
hermits' involvement in the first Pentecost after Jesus' ascension to
heaven supplements the report of this event in Acts with nonscriptural
details having to do with their Carmelite ancestors. Acts 2:42 and
2:46 are quoted to describe relations among the newly converted hermits. The hermits in the *Institution* eventually begin to preach, an
element of the *vita apostolica* to which the Order historically committed itself in the middle of the thirteenth century.

Speeches of the divine voice in book 1 explain the spiritual motive for the preaching in which the legendary hermits later engage. In
book 1, Christ and his Father declare that seclusion, service of one's
neighbor, and "the service of my worship" (1:7) all train hermits for
mystical union. The speaker reminds readers of the paradox amply
explored in the Bible that loving God, the ultimate activity for which
human beings were created, is insufficient if that love is given only to
God. In book 1 the divine voice requires the hermit to pursue solitude, silence, and celibacy—all states that free the individual from
ordinary human attachments. This is the "third step of perfection,"
according to the *Institution*. The fourth step requires action on behalf
of others:

> [Love of God] cannot be observed without love of neigh-
> bor.... If you understand this clearly, you must love
> God because of himself, and yourself not because of
> yourself but because of God. And, since you must
> love your neighbor as yourself, you must love him also
> not because of himself, nor because of yourself, but be-
> cause of God. What else is this but to love God in your

> neighbor? …Behold, I have shown you the fourth step
> by which you can attain the goal of prophetic perfection
> which you desire. (1:6)

In other words, imitation of Christ is impossible if one does not love those whom he loved.

In its foundational teachings in book 1, the *Institution* resolves the tension between withdrawal from the world and care for it that has always existed in Christian monastic life. Pope Gregory's twelfth-century reforms, which sent monks back to their cloisters, aimed to resolve the tension by increasing seclusion. In the thirteenth century some groups were resolving it by shifting the balance toward apostolic service. Carmelites appear to have decided that while their personal salvation continued to require solitude, it would not be complete without apostolic service in society at large. A sign of this Carmelite attitude can be found in the third step of perfection described in the *Institution,* which, if it was taken, oriented the hermit's desire toward God; the fourth led the hermit to love others in an unselfish, integrated way.

Louis Dupré observes that the lives of the Christian saints throughout the centuries amply demonstrate that contemplation and active service are not superimposed on each other. Instead, in these outstanding lives, the unitive love of God and care of other human beings "intimately collaborate and reinforce each other. …Having come to participate in God's life, the contemplative also comes to share God's life-giving love. Mystical marriage invariably leads to spiritual parenthood" (Dupré, 8). The *Institution* and passages in earlier Carmelite works that say that the mythic ancestors were both contemplatives and preachers suggest that the Order was inclined to balance the monastic tension by the collaboration that Dupré describes.

This balance is promoted in the second-level story of the *Institution.* After striving "with all his heart to reach…prophetic perfection" (2:1), Elijah does two things of his own will: he decides to leave his solitude to teach others the way of perfection that God has conveyed

to him (2:2), and he undertakes the prophetic service of God that the
Old Testament records (3:1). Some of Elijah's vigorous activity as a
classic Old Testament messenger of God, long shorn from him in
Christian and Carmelite storytelling, is finally returned to him in *The
Institution of the First Monks*. As might be expected, Elijah's service
to others as a Christian monastic founder is given much more space in
the story than his service as an Israelite prophet, but it is significant
that his contact with the larger secular world is in the Christian legend
at all. In the *Institution*, he challenges Ahab and Jezebel and wins
back the hearts of his listeners on Mt. Carmel, just as 1 Kings records.
More important, the prophet teaches his followers the Christlike way
of life that God revealed to him and prepares others to carry on the
tradition of it.

Once his own period of spiritual maturation is complete, the legend ceases to describe Elijah acting like an idealized hermit. While
his legendary followers frequently are described at prayer, living in
the isolation of Mt. Carmel, preparing to go to the desert or, in their
Jerusalem phase, living in the seclusion of their own house, Elijah is
constantly on the move, organizing the Order, teaching its members,
or prophesying to society at large. He more resembles the excellent
fifteenth-century prior general John Soreth whom he antedates (and
perhaps the apostle Paul, a model in Albert's *Rule* and a major figure
in the Book of Acts) than he does Nicholas of France and other thirteenth-century priors general who returned to seclusion, sometimes,
as in Nicholas's case, relinquishing administrative charges in order to
do it. As Soreth would do in real life later, in the *Institution*, Elijah
constantly occupies himself in teaching, visiting, founding communities, and generally worrying about the well-being of his many spiritual descendants. He resembles a busy Carmelite leader—John of the
Cross and Teresa of Avila also come to mind—instead of the rigorously solitary hermit whom the desert fathers idealized. While in
the *Rubrica prima* and other contemporary Carmelite legends Elijah
remains in seclusion on Mt. Carmel, in the *Institution* the Carmelite
founder labors in the vineyard of the Lord. Elijah's life, the best

example of imitation of Christ in the *Institution,* demonstrates that love of God must overflow into active love of other human beings.

This explains why the figure, who had been a solitary hermit in early legends of the Order, contacting only those who came to him on Mt. Carmel, left his solitude by the Wadi Cherith in *The Institution of the First Monks* to become an extraordinarily active founder. It also may be a clue as to why the medieval Order never seems to have tried, corporately at least, to become more like the secluded Camaldolese or Carthusians, returning to its old physical habits of life on Mt. Carmel. Different events and conditions affect the way a particular group's identity unfolds over time, of course, but it does seem that during an era in which many in the Church were meditating on the significance of Christ, Carmelites as a group concluded that they could best imitate their Savior in ways that reinforced both contemplative solitude and active service.

Cicconetti provides an interesting sidelight on the question of the relation of solitude and ministerial service in the medieval Order. He concluded from his studies of the *Rule of St. Albert* that there was more opportunity for particular medieval communities to opt for eremitical or mendicant emphases in their identity than might be thought. "Existing side by side, then, both styles of life were foreseen and equally prized" although "naturally the cradle of the order, the hermitage on Mt. Carmel, with its prestige and glamour, was especially cherished" (Cicconetti, *The Rule of Carmel,* 292–293). Cicconetti expressly rejects the thought that the thirteenth-century *Rule,* the formative document of the Order, reflects any conflict between eremitical and mendicant life. It is possible that the variations in the ways that early Carmelite legends promoted solitude and apostolic service point to latitude that allowed medieval communities or another to choose certain emphases in the two calls.

The author of the outer narrative on the first level of the *Institution* reversed the "solitude-service" paradigm from what it is in the *Rubrica prima* and other contemporary documents of the Order. Where in these latter Elijah remains in solitary prayer on Mt. Carmel and his

descendants become preachers, in the *Institution,* the ordinary followers seem to spend more time in solitude than does their founder.
Nevertheless, even they leave it at times to serve those outside their
ranks. Others follow where Elijah leads. According to the *Institution,*
his followers spend many generations at home on Mt. Carmel, to which
the ordinary faithful sometimes come just as laypeople have always
done in real life if a monastery or hermitage was nearby: "Devout
persons were accustomed to visit Elisha and the other monks of Mt.
Carmel on feast days to obtain a blessing on their food, but especially,
out of devotion to hear the Word of God from Elisha and the other
prophets" (4:4). The detail validates similar actions of the historical
friars. A second, equally brief comment reports that descendants of
the legendary hermits began preaching tours after they were converted
to Christianity: "Finally, many of them, pouring out to others the doc-
trines they had drawn from the apostles, preached the faith of Christ
in Phoenicia and Palestine, explaining the dogmas of faith and, by the
practices of monastic life, demonstrating the marvelous way of life
taught by the Church of Christ" (5:8).

Given the many details from the Book of Acts that appear in the
Carmelite work, one might expect the saga to end here. In Acts, the
sequel to the Gospel of Luke, the apostles, patterning themselves on
their Master, venture out to more and more remote communities,
preaching, baptizing, and founding churches. The ending of the Luke-
Acts story is left open. Paul and his companions are last described
preaching in Rome.

The hermits under Elijah's care continue the teachings the prophet
gave them after he is taken to heaven, just as Jesus' followers carry on
his work after his ascension. In Acts, Christ's followers obviously
respond to the commandment of their risen Savior to proclaim the
Gospel to all the nations. Here the story lines of Acts and the *Institution* converge, for the latter document's protagonists are said to join
other followers of Jesus on preaching tours. The Carmelite hermits
not only preach the good news of Christ but also demonstrate the

good news of their eremitical and prophetic calling. The crowds of Phoenicia and Palestine hear the "dogmas of faith" and see the hermits modeling "by the practices of monastic life" the "marvelous way of life taught by the Church of Christ" (5:8).

Mary's Brothers

The story nevertheless ends more intimately. Elijah's spiritual descendants are last seen in community, at rest between preaching tours of the region. After they were baptized into the Church, the group had begun studying Scripture with new eyes (fulfilling the instruction of chapter 7 of the *Rule* that their descendants would be given to meditate "day and night on the law of the Lord"). Using allegorical techniques taught them by Christ's apostles, the Carmelite hermits uncover the "hidden soul" of the "spiritual and invisible meaning of…profound and divine mystery" under the letter of the Bible (5:7). This prepares them to preach the Gospel of Christ, but they are also finally able to understand the enigmatic report of Elijah's sighting of a little cloud from the top of Mt. Carmel recorded in 1 Kings 18:42–44 that had left them puzzled for a long time.

The allegory unfolded from this biblical event introduces the Order's second patron into the final episode of the legend. Examined piece by piece for its hidden meaning, the scene of the cloud appearing on the horizon, which in 1 Kings brought much needed rain to northern Israel, reveals to the hermits that the Virgin had accomplished the steps of the spiritual life urged by the divine voice in Elijah's call. Chaste from birth, Mary "resolved to vow virginity to God, after the example of Elijah" (6:3), a detail of her inner life that the New Testament of course does not mention. By saying that the Carmelite patroness deliberately chose to remain a virgin, in imitation of Elijah's chastity and solitude, the *Institution* is able to find in her life the sequence of self-emptying and divine filling that were first promoted by the divine voice and subsequently promoted in the second-level story of the success of Elijah and his disciples in patterning themselves on Christ.

The Gospels say that Jesus bowed to the will of the Father, loved the Father above all else, and eventually reunited with him. The *Institution* says that Elijah and his followers followed the same pattern, achieving detachment from self, love of God, and divine union through the practices of the eremitical life. The allegorical meditation on Elijah's vision of the cloud inserted at the end of the story conveys that Mary lived the life to which Christ called Elijah, too. She removed herself from "all the pleasures of the flesh" out of love for God. This admirably accomplished the "first goal of eremitic life," to "offer to God a heart that is holy and pure from all actual stain of sin" (1:2). The two great steps of Christlike obedience and love are needed to attain the first goal. The second goal of eremitical life that book 1 proposed is the gift of divine union. According to legend, Elijah and his hermits at times experienced this gift from God in their heart and mind. Mary achieved this goal as well, for her whole being received the gift of union from whose perfection the Savior was born. All this the first-century hermits came to understand from the enigma of the little cloud that Elijah saw from the top of Mt. Carmel in 1 Kings 18.

Mention of Mary in the story is sudden and late. The present-day reader may well find the shift of attention to her awkward. Nevertheless, by positioning the allegory of Mary's life at the end of his story, the Carmelite writer turns his readers' attention from what for many pages has been principally a tale of spiritually motivated exterior actions toward the interior life. The late appearance of Mary brings the legend into a certain balance. Placed at opposite ends of the second-level saga—Elijah's at its beginning and Mary's at its end—the stories of the personal lives of the Order's two patrons fulfill John 44's intention to recount to Caprasius the "dignity of its authors and founders" and to provide the "original sure models of the monastic life" (1:1). The beneficial effects on the Order of Elijah's purity of heart and love of God are described throughout the long second-level saga. The beneficial effects of Mary's spiritual life are left for readers to meditate, but they are well known by Christians.

Medieval readers would have been hard put to reject the spiritual models that *The Institution of the First Monks* promotes. If it were not enough that the Father, the Son, and the Holy Spirit call Elijah to Christian eremitical life in a way that draws the reader in, or enough that the story told in the last six books shows that the prophet was able to help others because he responded to the call, or even enough that Elijah's spiritual disciples in their turn learned to love the Lord with all their might and so receive the blessing of his intimate presence, the persuasion of the last story of the book must have been irresistible in an age when Mary was widely loved. If the Virgin, the patroness of the Order, chose purity and openness to God as had her spiritual peer Elijah long before, and if so much good had come of her choices, what medieval Carmelite could not seek to do the same?

An Examination of Medieval Models

Medieval Carmelite legends of Elijah have some common themes. One is the patron's accessibility. If they believed what their legends said, which is that Elijah had begun the extended spiritual community of which they were living members, Carmelites must have had the sense that by living their traditional lives, they were putting themselves in contact with Elijah and his ways. They were his brothers, separated by time, but united by their shared life. The emphasis on continuous succession encouraged this attitude.

Elijah is also accessible as a personal model in these legends, as he often is in the legends of him preserved in prayer communities. Although impressive in his love of God and zeal for perfection and astonishing in his success, the prophet is not, in these stories, a hero so perfect that modeling one's life on him is impossible. In the *Rubrica prima* and in other tellings of Carmelite origins, Elijah's mythic followers are always shown achieving their model's challengingly high level of religious life. They, like he, repent, purify their soul, love God, and know God's presence. Whether they thought of themselves as living in the Order that Elijah founded or whether they thought of themselves as living among descendants of those who gained the spiritual riches of their founder's life, medieval Carmelite friars must have deduced from their legends that Elijah's spiritual life was possible for them.

    Variety is also an important theme in the legends. The story of Elijah's hermit life on Mt. Carmel is very consistently retold everywhere except in *The Institution of the First Monks*. However, once Carmelite writers turn to the founder's followers, they seem quite willing to vary from each other in what they say. The many differences in the pictures painted of legendary protoCarmelites suggest that perhaps the friars of the first centuries believed it was possible to view themselves in a variety of ways. Elijah, expressing their spiritual ideals, had a stable identity in the tales. His mythic followers, who demonstrated the learning and applying of those ideals, varied. Who Elijah's descendants were in these legends changed and developed over time.

    Third, these stories are very concerned with Christ. Thirteenth- and fourteenth-century Carmelite stories of Elijah involve Christ so much that it is not too far-fetched to think that by means of their storytelling, early Carmelites engaged in a meditation on the place of the Son in their way of life. Carmelite legends of origin say that it was Christ, or knowledge of his advent, that drew protoCarmelites out of their seclusion on Mt. Carmel. The stories say that it was Christ who drew the legendary Carmelite ancestors into baptism, participation in the larger community of followers of Christ, and the more active life of evangelical service that echoes the Order's historical embrace of apostolic mendicancy. In *The Institution of the First Monks*, the Holy Spirit, the Father, and especially Christ call Elijah—and through Elijah, others—to a life of self-abandonment and love.

    Chapter 2 in this book shows that Christian tradition transferred Elijah's biblical powers and messianic role to God's Son and had much less to say about the prophet than Jewish tradition did. In the Order and certainly in *The Institution of the First Monks,* Elijah is not replaced by Christ. Instead, he is a mediating human being called by God to show others how to be Christlike. In the *Institution* and in the Order, Elijah has been a reliable, accessible mirror of Christ. The patron's similarity to the Savior heartened medieval Carmelites to think that they also could imitate their Lord.

The first chapter of this book noted challenges that the ancient stories of Elijah in 1–2 Kings pose to present-day Western readers. This discussion will end with a few more thoughts on challenging differences, in this case, between the content of medieval Carmelite legends and life today. Some present-day readers may notice the unvaryingly positive pictures that these legends paint. Success abounds. The life that Elijah and his companions pursue is shown to be deeply effective. People in these stories enjoy contact with God and succeed in benefiting others. The confident successes of the prophet and his followers may provoke thought.

These legends may also be provocative because they tend to show that good things are accomplished by swimming against the tide of the past or against the current state of things. Food for thought may be found in the fact that these are stories of individuals who depart from their earlier ways. Elijah turned from his earlier habits when Christ called him. His followers left their solitary life on Mt. Carmel to join the Church (although they found ways to continue in contemplation). While the stories promote certain elements of Carmelite life as perennial, including a love of God and a desire for solitude, the tales also describe substantial changes in the ways of doing things, even radical departures from the norms. Additional features of the legends provoke response, as well. It deserves attention that during the historical period in which the Carmelite Order was zealously expanding its evangelical calling, it was keeping alive its legends that told attractive stories of secluded life. The very least that we can see from this is that medieval Carmelites tolerated and even maintained mechanisms by which they could question their own ways.

These old stories may also provoke present-day readers to think about God in certain ways. The God implied in these early legends does not overlap with all the views of God in all medieval Christian texts. On the whole, these are not stories of God above and separate from human beings. Even in the *Rubrica prima,* which does not mention divinity directly, spiritual men are attracted to a mountain on which God had once made his nature especially visible. The beliefs that God desires contact with humans and that humans may have intimate contact with God are visible in the medieval Carmelite stories. The experience of God's presence by large numbers of Elijah's legendary followers also suggests that such experiences are not restricted to the perfect. The legends indicate that many of Elijah's followers, not just an inner core of the especially advanced, knew God by experience. This is noteworthy, for the stories were produced in an era of the Church in which clerical authority and mediation were consciously being elevated. In medieval Carmelite legends, God does not reserve himself an elite.

Finally, these are stories of God's fullness. In the view of these legends, especially in the view of *The Institution of the First Monks,* the increasingly inclusive love of God is the alpha and the omega, the cause, goal, and means of Carmelite life. In the *Institution,* it is grammatically impossible to separate statements about the love of human beings for God from those that describe the love of God for human beings (1:7). The *Rubrica prima*'s insistence that an unending succession of human beings had been drawn by love into solitude for contemplation suggests an expansion of divine love across time. Stories that describe the legendary followers' movement out of solitude into the fellowship of the Christian Church suggest the expanding fullness in God in another way. Full and increasing love is expressed in the comment of the *Institution* that humans "have above all things charity, which is the bond of perfection" (Col. 3:14, cited in 1:2) and in its story of Elijah's generous response to his call. The prophet zealously pursued personal perfection, but that was not enough: his love poured out in beneficial influence on more and more people. Even the sudden moment at the end of the *Institution*, in which the legendary followers of Elijah discover the depths of Mary's spiritual life by studying Scripture, opens up vistas.

It will matter to many present-day readers that *The Institution of the First Monks,* which does not mention women except to recommend avoidance of marriage and sexual contact, ends by telling the story of Mary. At the last moment, briefly but clearly, it shows that Christ's generous life of love is attainable by women. The last story shows that both spiritual father and mother of the Carmelites imitated Christ. So also did Mary's female companions, for "love of chastity was afterwards inaugurated among women by the Mother of God" (6:5). This is one more instance, an important one for the present day, of the many ways that Carmelite legends suggest that the love of God always inclines to inclusion.

Examples of divine fullness and flourishing in the legends constitute a broad challenge to the present-day reader, whether the person is monastic or not. Descriptions of the positive, serene, and expanding effect of God's love and of the attainment of spiritual love by ever-increasing numbers of Elijah's eremitical descendents were kept alive during what clearly were not the best of times. These stories ask readers living inside and outside monastic walls the following: What reliable sense can be made of the dissonance between the undeniable difficulties of real life and the confident witness of these legends to an inclusion and to a plenary love that are in their essence divine? One way or another, a reader's core beliefs are likely touched by the legendary testimony to the possibility of loving contact with God and Christlike love of other human beings.

For Further Reading

Cicconetti, Carlo, O. Carm. *The Rule of Carmel: An Abridgment.* Translated by G. Paulsback. Edited by P. Hoban. Darien, Ill.: Carmelite Spiritual Center, 1984.

Dupré, Louis. "The Christian Experience of Mystical Union," *Journal of Religion* 69 (1989): 1:1–13.

Egan, Keith. "Carmelite Spirituality" in *The New Dictionary of Catholic Spirituality.* Edited by Michael Downey. Collegeville, Minn.: The Liturgical Press, 1993.

Friedman, Elias, OCD. *The Latin Hermits of Mount Carmel: A Study in Carmelite Origins.* Rome: Teresianum, 1979.

Hendriks, Rudolf, O. Carm. "Elias in the Carmelite Tradition," *Carmel in the World* 4 (1964): 1:87–100.

Lawrence, C. H. *Medieval Monasticism: Forms of Religious Life in Western Europe in the Middle Ages.* London: Longman, 1984.

Le Goff, Jacques, ed. *Medieval Callings.* Translated by L. G. Cochrane. Chicago: University of Chicago Press, 1990.

Mulhall, Michael, O. Carm., ed. *Albert's Way: The First North American Congress on the Carmelite Rule.* Barrington, Ill.: Province of the Most Pure Heart of Mary, 1989.

Smet, Joachim, O. Carm. *The Carmelites: A History of the Brothers of Our Lady of Mount Carmel*. 5 vols. Darien, Ill: Carmelite Spiritual Center, 1976–1985; vol. 1 revised 1988.

Valabek, Redemptus Maria, O. Carm. "Prayer Among Carmelites of the Ancient Observance," *Carmelus* 28 (1981): 1:68–143.

Chapter 5
Elijah and Carmelite Renewal

Pope Innocent IV's changes in the Carmelite *Rule* in 1247 affected the identity of the Order. Carlo Cicconetti observes that the inserted sentence, "If the Prior and brothers see fit, you may also have foundations in solitary places, or where you are given a site that is suitable and convenient for the observance of your Order" (*The Rule of St. Albert*, ch. 2), allowed new houses options. The choice of a more secluded location suited an eremitical emphasis in community life. Placing a foundation near a town or city facilitated preaching and hearing confessions. Innocent's added permissions to Carmelites to use animals and to eat meat when they traveled also aided pastoral work. Decisions regarding the use of these options were left to the judgment of the interpreters of the *Rule*.

Other modifications in 1247 were not subject to choice. The formula of life written in 1207 by the Patriarch of Jerusalem Albert Avogadro required the hermits of Mt. Carmel to remain in the solitude of their caves: "Let each one remain in his cell, or near it, meditating day and night on the law of the Lord and keeping vigil in prayer unless occupied with other lawful duties" (ch. 7). It obliged contact only in the daily Eucharist and in weekly sessions of spiritual guidance. For six days of the week, the hermits of Mt. Carmel could minimize communication with each other despite the proximity of their dwellings. Pope Innocent altered this when he required shared meals and recitation of the Divine Office in the oratory. He also shortened the silence stretching from the last Office of the evening into the following morning by about three hours. Anastasio Ballestrero notes that daily assembly in the oratory and the refectory produced an alternation between solitude and communal life throughout the day. Regular movement between these two poles has distinguished the Carmelite way from others, in Ballestrero's estimation.

The additions of 1247 contributed to the flexibility and stability of Carmelite identity. Emphases on variation and constancy are visible in other early Carmelite works as well. As was shown in the last chapter, the claim promoted in the *Rubrica prima* that Elijah and Elisha pursued a life of solitude on Mt. Carmel, and eventually attracted Carmelite ancestors to the site, remained very much the same from document to document, but descriptions of first-century events relating to the Order varied. Carmelites handled their expressions of relationship to Mary flexibly as well. Alternative versions of legends continued to develop. By the end of the fourteenth century, it was possible to emphasize a motif in a well-known cluster, or perhaps counterpoise one tradition with another. Ballestrero observes that the obligatory modifications of 1247 in the *Rule* produced a carefully balanced day. Thoughtful balances began to appear elsewhere. Mary and Elijah were described in a complementary pair. Praise of solitary contemplation could immediately be followed by exhortation to apostolic service. Nevertheless, deep, unvarying concerns always underlay newly cast legends or new combinations of motifs. However flexible they were, early Carmelite descriptions of the Order promoted desire for contemplative intimacy with God, reverence for the Virgin, appreciation of Elijah's solitude, and zealous imitation of Christ.

The ways that later Carmelites have responded to Mary, Elijah, and Christ demonstrate the freedom with which members of the Order have handled their traditions and their desire to express enduring values. Carmelites have always chosen to open themselves to a special relationship with one or perhaps two of the three. True to their religious names, for example, Teresa of Jesus and John of the Cross especially dwell on Christ—Teresa explicitly, in written prayers, accounts of visions and spiritual guidance of her sisters, and John more implicitly in his doctrine of interior transformation. They allude to their two patrons Mary and Elijah less often, although the two Spanish leaders unquestionably held all three models of Carmelite life in high regard. Many Carmelite women and some men have adopted Mary's name or perhaps the name of an event in her life as their own, and many in the Order especially revere her. Carmelite men have often taken Elijah as their namesake and hero. Monasteries and provinces signal special relationship by including the name of Mary, Christ, or Elijah in their own name.

Early Carmelites developed a variety of descriptions of how they related the three figures to the Order and to each other. In the fourteenth century, John Baconthorpe claimed that Elijah, the founder of the Order, revered Mary before she was born. Arnold Bostius wrote in the following century that the Virgin protected the prophet from Ahab and Jezebel. Writing around 1600, the Discalced Carmelite Jerónimo Gracián explained how Elijah related to Christ:

> The first Rule, the most perfect of all belonging to any order, is the life and image of Jesus Christ, who by his example and word taught perfection, poverty, chastity, obedience and love of God and of one's neighbor. All Rules belonging to all religious orders come from this. The apostles put this Rule into practice. The Carmelite Rule was also practiced by St. Elijah and given to his disciples in his words and actions. It was written down by John, Patriarch of Jerusalem in the book of the *Institution of the First Monks*. (*On the Discipline of the Rule*, 1:4, cited in Elisée de la Nativité, *Élie le prophète*, vol. 2, 100)

Baconthorpe thought forward in history, from Elijah to Mary. Bostius thought backward, from the Virgin to the prophet. Gracián sees in Christ's life a radiating power that encourages holy people to imitate him whenever they have lived in history. His appreciation of Christ's timeless power moved him to say that his Savior's life was the pattern on which the Carmelite *Rule* was modeled, which is true, and that

Elijah not only followed the *Rule* in the ninth century B.C.E., but passed it down to his disciples orally, which is historically impossible. What mattered to Gracián above all else was Carmelite imitation of Christ. Varying explanations of how Elijah, Mary, and Christ related to each other and to the Order continued to appear. In 1766, for example, Manuel García Calahorra declared in his *Brief Compendium of the Origin and Antiquity of the Holy Carmelite Order* that Elijah, Father and Patriarch, merited the title of founder as the efficient cause of the Order, since he actually founded it, while Mary, Most Holy Virgin, Mother of God and Lady, merited being called foundress because she was its final, exemplary, and meritorious cause, since she inspired it—another statement that contains both anachronisms and spiritual truths.

It may be worthwhile to note here that from the Middle Ages through the nineteenth century, Carmelites tended to write about their Order in a transhistorical mode. A mythical, timeless self-view is not as univocal as a modern historical one. Their patrons Elijah and Mary not only were, but also could be, many things to Carmelites. History, in the present-day sense of being a stable, reliable story founded on data, did not matter to earlier writers as much as did their expression of the higher life. Their perennial truths could be expressed in a variety of stories. With their attention on spiritual verities, early writers sometimes freely remodeled traditions that expressed the core Carmelite motifs.

Recombination and flexibility were made possible by juxtaposing Elijah with other figures. Allusions surrounding him, if traced far enough along their evocative lines, often end up moving out of "Elijan" mythic territory and into other zones of Carmelite identity. A hermit in his legends, Elijah is by no means an independent mythic figure in the Order. When they write about him, Carmelites always relate the prophet to something or perhaps someone else in the Order that matters to them. Memory of him may lead to thoughts about Mt. Carmel or to Christ or to the *Rule* or to Mary. How he is connected to these other radiating centers of identity varies from legend to legend. Nevertheless, Elijah has a stable set of associations that we can call his own. This chapter will trace how the Order has spoken of these associations in recent centuries.

First, members of the Order have had much to say about the prophet's solitude. Affected by the traditions passed down to them by the desert fathers and certainly by the *Rubrica prima*'s influence on their constitutions, Carmelites have thought of their patron as a hermit living in the wilderness. Motivated by changing circumstances in their lives, Carmelite writers sometimes take up a new feature of Elijah's isolation that matters to them or shift emphasis on an old one.

Second, writers in the Order insisted for centuries that Elijah founded their continuously existing way of religious life. Treatment of this claim as historical fact waned in the first decades of the twentieth century. Present-day Carmelite writers seem to have little use for the legend of continuous succession, but while it flourished, it helped the Order preserve itself.

Third, as are Mary and Jesus Christ, Elijah is habitually remembered for his purity of heart. From the earliest centuries, Christian holy men and women have sought to acquire such purity. After *The Institution of the First Monks* explicitly associated him with the desired state, Carmelites regularly praised it in his legendary profile among them.

Fourth, late medieval and early modern writers bequeathed an appreciation for their patron's zeal to later generations. The prophet's extroverted vigor has always appealed to people. Legends worldwide relate his daring, spectacular miracles. Among Carmelites, Elijah's zeal was inward. Beginning in the fifteenth century, they began associating it with full-hearted love of Christ. Thereafter, zealous love of Christ became an identifying feature of the Carmelite way.

The Order seems to have pondered Elijah's solitude, purity, zeal, and his continuous succession during its moments of change. Writers producing works during reform movements often appealed to the

mythic founder. Substantial additions to his legends most often appeared in moments of change (although not every renewal movement
produced new stories). As is generally known, the first great shift in
Carmelite identity occurred in the midthirteenth century, when Rome
approved the request of the Mt. Carmel hermits to become a mendicant order and when Innocent modified their rule to accommodate
their change in life. The *Rubrica prima* and a handful of other works
produced around the time dwell on the prophet's withdrawn life of
repentance and prayer on Mt. Carmel. Expansion of detail in apologies and historical works suggests that the Order may have been thinking about its identity in the last decades of the fourteenth century and
the first years of the fifteenth. In that period, between 1370 and 1415,
Carmelites writers began attaching a first-century segment to their
legend of origin that had many variations.

The fifteenth century, not a happy one in the Church, saw several
reform attempts in the Order. In midcentury, prior general John Soreth
returned as many Carmelite men as he could to a more traditionally
monastic, liturgically centered life. His establishment of the Second
Order implanted his reform in new communities for women. Consistent with his desire to return Carmelite life to the cloister, Soreth particularly comments on Elijah's inner orientation to God. The great
prior general's remarks revealing his understanding that Elijan zeal
amounts to love, inflamed by the Holy Spirit, are one of the earliest
signs available to the present day of a new emphasis in traditions
surrounding the patron. Comments by reforming generals Nicholas
Audet and John Baptist Rossi suggest that the belief that Elijah was a
great lover of Christ continued to unfold after Soreth's day. Thought
about zealous love, if not always of Elijah as a lover of Christ, appears in works produced by Teresa of Jesus and John of the Cross, as
they promoted the Discalced return to "primitive" observance of the
Rule in sixteenth-century Spain. Teresa also added a new understanding of poverty to the cluster of values surrounding the mythic founder.

Carmelites continued to turn to Elijah for inspiration in times of
renewal. Touraine reformers of the Ancient Observance invoked his

inner solitude in the seventeenth century. As also will be discussed later, present-day Carmelites are emphasizing a feature of Elijah's biblical profile that did not occupy the attention of their forebears in any previous era. What they are saying about the prophet's double spirit certainly suggests that they have heard the call of *Perfectae Caritatis* to renew themselves by returning "to the sources of the whole of Christian life and to the primitive inspiration of the institutes" of their traditional way of life and by adapting "to the changed conditions of the time" in a way that deepens their identity, instead of diluting it (*Perfectae Caritatis* in *Vatican Council II*, vol. 1, 612). The new Carmelite tradition of Elijah's double spirit seems especially suited to these goals.

The Founder's Wildernesses

The life that old documents say the prophet led on Mt. Carmel dovetails with some of what is known about the group of men that were located near the Spring of Elijah in 1195 or 1197. "Wanting to embrace a more elevated and perfect life," Bernard Oller wrote in 1370, Elijah "began eremitical and solitary life on Mt. Carmel, a place that greatly lent itself to contemplation" (cited in Hendriks, *Élie le prophète*, vol. 2, 63). This, of course, describes why the historical group made its long journey from Europe to Mt. Carmel. While legends native to the Holy Land placed the prophet's residence in a grotto at the foot of the promontory, medieval Carmelites tended to place their hero at the site of the historical settlement, the anonymous author of *In Praise of Carmelites* saying that Carmelites "inhabited the location where these prophets had lived, long before [the Order's] confirmation and in an era more ancient than that in which other orders arose" (cited in op. cit., 47). Surely the first hermits understood that they were pursuing a spiritual life like the one Elijah had led in the place in which he lived. It mattered to emigrated Carmelites that they continue to believe this.

In his legends Elijah lived in stricter solitude than what the first hermits enjoyed. The spring near which the historical hermits resided was in a withdrawn but not entirely secluded location. Pilgrims mentioning that they had visited the monastery needed only to make a long climb up from the trade route that skirted the shoreline below. Acre was a few kilometers away. A monastery inhabited by Greek and Syrian monks lay nearby, as did a church for pilgrims staffed by Cluniac monks. The Carmelites lived with the same degree of remoteness that Peter Brown reports was frequent for Christian holy men and women of the fourth or fifth century—far enough away from population centers for psychic seclusion, but close enough for support if an emergency arose, or to acquire goods from time to time. In contrast, the *Rubrica prima* and works from the first European century and a half do not mention the mythic founder having any contact with pilgrims or the local faithful and do not mention him leaving his retreat on Mt. Carmel. Elijah's isolation from those who were not hermits has been a staple in Carmelite storytelling.

Stress on Elijah's physical seclusion continues the traditions of the Fathers and is consistent with the comment of Hebrews 11:37–38 that biblical prophets lived in desert places, but it contrasts with most Jewish and Muslim legends in which he is vigorously active. In the Bible, Elijah's periods of withdrawal alternate with prophetic activity. Carmelites have preferred to think of him as living a stable life secluded from society at large. Their appreciation for the Elijan traditions of the Church Fathers may be sufficient to explain their preference, but one wonders as well if the circumstances of early Carmelite lives had something to do with the insistence on seeing their patron in one or another wilderness setting—on Mt. Carmel most of all, but also at Cherith as will be seen and on Mt. Horeb as well. Is it possible that they insisted on thinking of their founder in a more secluded wilderness than they could hope for themselves out of a desire to name what they had cherished in times when they needed to remember it? Living near the walls of towns, in farmhouses, and in buildings within towns and cities, and moving back and forth between eremitical life and mendicant service, they read in the *Rubrica prima* of their constitutions that their founder "truly loved the solitude" of Mt. Carmel "for the sake of holy contemplation."

The persona of Elijah developed among Carmelites as time passed. So also did the "persona" of the first wilderness in which he was thought to have lived. Mt. Carmel became a powerful symbolic aid to the interior life. When early Carmelites comment on the prophet, they rarely speak of his psychic detachment separately from the seclusion that Mt. Carmel was thought to have offered. As Kilian Healy remarks, mountain and spiritual father have been inseparable in the mind of the Order. Descriptions of Mt. Carmel multiplied. The Sicilian Nicolas Calciuri (d. 1466), a member of the Mantuan reform, composed a description of the spiritual life on the mountain for tertiaries in Florence. Calciuri's modern editor, Graziano di Santa Teresa, notes that other verbal portraits of the lovely isolation of Mt. Carmel may be found in Phillip of the Holy Trinity's *Carmelite Theology* (1665), his *Oriental Journeys* (1667), Leander of St. Cecilia's *Palestine* (1753), John Baptist of St. Alessio's *Historical Compendium of the Ancient and Modern State of Carmel* (1780), and Mary-Joseph of the Sacred Heart's *Sacred Topography of Mount Carmel in Palestine* (1911). A splendid evocation of the mountain, complete with photographs, meditations, legends, and historical fact, appears in *Carmel in the Holy Land: From Its Beginning to the Present Day* (1995).

Carmelites such as the tertiaries, who had little hope of visiting Mt. Carmel themselves, were also aided in imagining Mt. Carmel by occasional news of others' contact with the mountain. Pilgrimages to Mt. Carmel resumed in the fourteenth century. In the seventeenth century, the tenacious Discalced Carmelite Prosper of the Holy Spirit set up camp in the ruins of the thirteenth-century monastery, clinging to life there until he was able to purchase part of the mountain from a local Muslim ruler. When the monastery Stella Maris was built on the promontory of Mt. Carmel in the early nineteenth century, Carmelites in both observances could feel that the Order had returned home, at least in some ways.

However, for most Carmelites over the centuries, visits to the site of Elijah's legendary spiritual life had to be imagined. Written descriptions of Mt. Carmel helped them to go to Mt. Carmel in the mind's eye, entering its seclusion for the sake of holy contemplation and renewal. Travelers' reports occasionally relayed eyewitness details about the mountain, but most early descriptions of it were created from more than fact. Graziano di Santa Teresa observes that Calciuri compiled his description of Mt. Carmel from the *Life of the Brothers of Holy Mt. Carmel*, from John Grossi's *Viridarium* written in the previous century, from reports of fifteenth-century Carmelite pilgrims (studied in a 1931 article by Benedict Zimmerman), and from the "fruit of his fantasy" since "in that century nothing remained of the ancient construction except scattered ruins" (Calciuri, 286), the monastery on Mt. Carmel having been destroyed in 1291. Calciuri connects Elijah with solitude and with the mountain in much the same way that other Carmelite writers do. Repeating earlier traditions of the Order, he says that the prophet was one of many hermits who lived on Mt. Carmel. According to Graziano, he handily draws the claims of the *Rubrica prima* concerning the prophet and those contained in Ribot's *Ten Books* into one story line, saying that later inhabitants lived on the mountain "in imitation of Elijah and his disciples" until the time that Basil of Caesarea wrote a rule for them that was "modeled on their Elijan customs" and that John 44 eventually extended the rule to govern all Christian hermits (op. cit., 287). Calciuri presents myth, fact, and fancy as if they were equally descriptive.

The Sicilian Carmelite's representational methods were not unusual for his time. Contemporary reports of faraway lands tended to mix factual detail with myth and fiction. Cosmologies of the time included maps reflecting explorers' information, line drawings of exotic animals about which the author had only heard (which resulted in elephants looking like big dogs with noses like tree trunks), and the "fruit of fantasy." Inhabitants of the equator, some authors speculated, had feet pointing one way and their heads the other. Despite his sometimes imaginative speculations about how Mt. Carmel looked, Calciuri provided the tertiaries and anyone else unable to visit the site a mental picture of its physical features. Misperceptions about the history of occupancy of the mountain became embedded in the Order when fantasy was juxtaposed with fact; nevertheless, aided by such descriptions, Carmelites could more vividly claim the site as part of their own lives.

Those telling the story of life on the mountain continued to mix historical detail with tradition well into the first decades of the twentieth century. A 1927 introduction to an American Discalced Carmelite history of the Order blends fact and legend to say that the grotto of the prophet "served the Saint as an asylum and oratory," and "had attached to it a Chapel, regarded as the most ancient ever erected in honor of Our Lady of Mt. Carmel; it dates back to the year of Our Lord, 83" (*Carmel: Its History, Spirit, and Saints*, 4–5). Admittedly full of historical inaccuracies, the description seeks to promote an ethos of secluded devotional life. Other early twentieth-century writers explain the connections among Elijah, solitude, the mountain, and the Order with more care. Titus Brandsma's widely read discussion of Carmelite spirituality, first presented as a lecture in the 1930s, evokes the attractive spiritual seclusion of the mountain while avoiding contested beliefs about it.

Studies using modern methods of research have replaced the imaginative, partly mythic portraits of the secluded mountain in the second half of the twentieth century. Florence of the Child Jesus, Clemens Kopp, Elias Friedman, and others began to help Carmelite readers to distinguish myth about the solitude of Elijah on Mt. Carmel from corroborated facts. Archaeological excavations and intensive study of the *Rule of St. Albert* have also helped Carmelites envision the life the first hermits led near the Spring of Elijah. The prophet's seclusion on Mt. Carmel now is accepted in the Order as a legend expressing important values, not as history in any modern sense. As such, it continues to help Carmelite members of both observances connect the ideal of contemplative solitude to their own existence.

The solitude of Mt. Carmel claimed more and more power over the Carmelite imagination. The symbol of Elijah's worldly detachment and encounter with God has been equated with the cells in which the friars and nuns have lived, with whole communities (called Carmels) and with "hermitages," a term members of the Order have used to designate places of special seclusion within a community compound. John Soreth's fifteenth-century biographer and companion Gauthier of New Land records that the general chose a site for a house near Puy because it recalled Mt. Carmel and the spiritual life Elijah led on it:

> Having examined at leisure…the plan of the monastery
> that could be built in that place, which would be the hope
> of the nascent reform movement, he saw the image of the
> ancient desert and, deeply moved, beheld a little mountain
> that resembled the great Mt. Carmel, and grottos reminis-
> cent of the grottos so important to the piety of our Fathers
> and so famous because of the residence in them of Elijah
> and his disciples. At the thought of this celestial way of
> life which our ancestors experienced so devoutly long
> ago, far from the contact with men in the caves of Carmel,
> tears sprang to his eyes and he deplored the barbarousness
> of the Saracens. He suggested that the mountainous loca-
> tion be called "Carmel." (cited in Elisée de la Nativité,
> *Élie le prophète*, vol. 2, 92–93)

The equation in the general's mind was clear: as Elijah pursued solitary prayer on the mountain of God in the Holy Land, so a community of Carmelites could also hope to attain his quality of life in grottos in a remote location in France.

The first Discalced desert was also carefully situated in a place that would naturally recall Mt. Carmel. The Spanish prior Gregory of Nazianzus, assigned to evaluate Bolarque, Spain in 1592, enthusiastically reported that "the location was situated on the slope of a mountain that descended sharply into the valley carved out by the flow of water; it was surrounded by higher summits on both sides of the River Tajo. The site was covered with abundant vegetation, trees, bushes, plants of all kinds and flowers of many colors" (Baudry, "Thomas de Jesús," 41). When Carmelites entered one of these physical locations in their daily lives, they could know that they were entering the fastness of Mt. Carmel. Nuns or friars who retired to a secluded monastery (such as those founded near Bolarque and Puy), to a hermitage, or to their cell went to Elijah's mountain abode, and as they did, they entered more deeply into his life. All these elements added to the ethos of Elijah and Mt. Carmel.

The Bible says that God sent Elijah to the Wadi Cherith (east of the Jordan) during a drought. The prophet called his people back to God on Mt. Carmel. After he fled to the desert south of Beersheba, God compelled the prophet to journey farther into it to Mt. Horeb. Carmelites at first wrote about Elijah only on Mt. Carmel, but in time they thought about him in his other two wilderness locations as well. Each of the three wilderness sites came to symbolize a particular kind of encounter with God for Carmelites. As the solitary sites associated with him multiplied, Elijah became a more and more allusive emblem of secluded spiritual life.

The 1370 *Institution of the First Monks* is the earliest surviving work that comments on the spiritual significance of Elijah's period of withdrawal by the Wadi Cherith. First Kings says that God told Elijah to cross the Jordan, going east until he found the Wadi—"You shall drink from the brook, and I have commanded the ravens to feed you there" (17:3–4). The first book of the *Institution* amplifies the scene: it is in Cherith, the place of his spiritual detachment, that Elijah learns the "prophetic eremitic" love to which Christ, the Father, and the Holy Spirit call him. Later Carmelite works that mention his stay at Cherith usually repeat the claim of the *Institution* that Elijah chose or began a spiritual way of life during his stay in that wilderness. In 1956, Paul-Marie of the Cross remarks concerning the lack of shelter in the site:

"The prophet didn't need a cave to escape from the pursuits of men and to be lost in God. It was enough for him...to plunge into the depths" (*Élie le prophète*, vol. 1, 14). Cherith became an emblem for the patron's willing response to God's call to interior life.

John of the Cross may have originated the Carmelite habit of meditating on Elijah's experiences in the wilderness of Horeb. There is certainly biblical justification for associating the prophet with the place and with mystical experience. First Kings says that God revealed himself to Elijah on the sacred mountain. Given the power and mystery of the biblical episode, it is surprising that Carmelites scarcely mention Elijah at Horeb before John of the Cross comments on the scene. The *Institution*'s reference to Horeb is a brief, rather wooden, and undeveloped allegorization of what the Bible says happened there. The Spanish mystic departs from the trend in his Order. In five of his six allusions to Elijah, he places the prophet at Horeb. Despite the symbolic importance of Mt. Carmel in his writing, John does not connect Elijah by name with the promontory near Haifa.

The Spanish saint is ambivalent about Mt. Horeb or, for that matter, any other location for the spiritual life. His poem "The Spiritual Canticle," which he composed while imprisoned in a small cell, suggests that wilderness locations aid the spiritual life. The soul in his poem expects to find the one she loves beyond the ordinary boundaries of social life. She says that she sought her Beloved "up through the sheepfolds to the hill" (stanza 2). She is eager to go even farther into the wilderness to find him: "I will head for the mountains and for watersides,.../ I will go beyond strong men and frontiers" (stanza 3). When her Bridegroom suddenly addresses her, showing her that he is, after all, right next to her, the only words the enamored soul can find to describe him are descriptions of remote nature: "My Beloved, the mountains, / and lonely wooded valleys, / strange islands, / and resounding rivers, / the whistling of love-stirred breezes, // the tranquil night / at the time of the rising dawn" (stanza 14). The literal level of "The Spiritual Canticle" encourages readers to think that the wilderness is a place where God may be encountered. John of the Cross is known to have appreciated the fields and mountain fastnesses.

However, in book 3, chapter 42 of *The Ascent*, John of the Cross says that physical seclusion such as Elijah knew on Mt. Carmel, at Cherith, or on Horeb matters only if God gives it meaning. "There are three different kinds of places...by which God usually moves the will," John says. Of pleasant natural locations that "provide solitary quietude" (3:42:1), he says:

> It is advantageous to use these places if one immediately directs the will to God in forgetfulness of the place itself, since one should not be detained by the means and motive more than necessary to attain the end.... The anchorites and other holy hermits, while in the loveliest and vastest wildernesses, chose for themselves as small an area as possible, built narrow cells and caves, and enclosed themselves within.... For those saints clearly understood that without extinguishing their appetite and covetousness for spiritual gratification and delight they would never become truly spiritual. (3:42:1)

No matter what narrow cells and caves in whatever wilderness John had in mind as he wrote this passage—one wonders if he thought of the laurae of Mt. Carmel—his point surely is that whatever attractive remoteness it possessed did not matter in the final analysis.

A second kind of devotional place, he says, is one in which God has particularly affected the person in prayer. But he counsels the seeker not to see such a place any differently from any other: "on returning, that person discovers that the place is not what it was before because these favors do not lie within one's own power. God bestows these graces when and how and where he wills without being bound to place or time or to the free will of the recipient" (3:42:2).

John counts Horeb a third kind of devotional place, "in which God chooses to be invoked and worshipped" (3:42:5). The second kind of site is one in which a favor is received. The third is a place of response to God. For the Spanish saint, places of this third kind include Mt. Sinai; "Mount Horeb, to which he sent our Father Elijah that he might appear to him there" (3:42:5); Mount Garganus in Italy, the site of a vision of St. Michael; and a location in Rome in which a miracle attributed to the Virgin occurred. Carmel, the sacred mountain of John's religious order, does not appear in his list, despite the testimony of the Bible that the assembled northern Israelite nation worshiped God there and despite the insistence of his Order that his ancestors duplicated Elijah's secluded life of prayer there. "God alone knows why he chooses one place in which to receive praise more than another" (3:42:6), says John.

However, in his other references to it (displaying, perhaps, the Order's characteristic flexibility in speaking of the spiritual dimensions of its identity), John of the Cross treats Horeb as the second kind of wilderness, in which God gives a particular gift. When the Spanish saint writes of Elijah at Horeb, he focuses on the event, not the place, of the epiphany. It is the audition of the small sound by which God reveals himself at Horeb that matters, the "whistling of the love-stirred breeze" that the soul equates with her Beloved in *The Spiritual Canticle*. He cares only to write about the impact of the sound on the prophet's soul. In his hands, Mt. Horeb is related not to detachment (the usual state associated with Mt. Carmel) or to response to a call (associated with Cherith) but to a very advanced mystical experience. He explains that the sound occurred in "a high state and union of love...called spiritual betrothal with the Word, the Son of God. ...Since this whistling refers to the substantial knowledge mentioned, some theologians think our Father Elijah saw God in this whistling of the gentle breeze heard on the mount at the mouth of his cave. Scripture calls it 'the whistling of the gentle breeze' because knowledge was begotten in his intellect from the delicate communication" (for the quotation and his full exposition, see *The Spiritual Canticle*, 14:12–21).

Similarly, in book 2, chapter 24 of *The Ascent of Mount Carmel*, he says that in the whistling of the gentle breeze at Horeb, Elijah experienced a substantial, spiritual vision such as "occur rarely or hardly ever, and to only a few" (2:24:3). "For God imparts this kind of vision only to those who are very strong in the spirit of the Church and God's law, as were these three" whom John earlier identifies as "St. Paul, Moses and our Father Elijah" (2:24:3). Elsewhere in the *Ascent* (book 2, chapter 8) he says Elijah's experience is a moment of unknowing. In *The Living Flame of Love* he explains that the whistling breeze is the

> delicate touch, the Word, the Son of God…after overthrowing the mountains and smashing the rocks to pieces on Mount Horeb with the shadow of might and power that went before you, you gave the prophet the sweetest and strongest experience of yourself in the gentle breeze! O gentle breeze, since you are a delicate and mild breeze, tell us: How do you, the Word, the Son of God, touch mildly and gently, since you are so awesome and mighty? (2:17)

Present-day Carmelite writers who place Elijah at Horeb often bring up the conditions of isolation, thirst, lack of food, or lack of shelter that make the figure's encounter with God in the location more extreme. The attention of John of the Cross is entirely on the contact point between God and Elijah in the soft sound.

For a long time, writers in the Order claimed that Elijah underwent a period of wilderness preparation before he began his prophetic mission. Expressions of this belief, which would qualify as the kind of "haggadic amplification" that Boaga often detected in Carmelite legends of the prophet, can be found in *The Institution of the First Monks* and in an eighteenth-century history by Manuel García Calahorra, the latter author saying:

> Although the year of [Elijah's] birth and his mother are unknown, it is known that, like Christ and the Baptist, he retired to the desert, or solitary places, of Gilead, where his bed was the hard ground, his clothing poor skins, his tears his bread and fasting his refreshment. With these disciplines the Divine Majesty prepared him for the office destined by his wise providence. When he had grown up,

> God told him through an Angel to appear before Ahab and
> prophesy against his evilness and blind idolatry. He hum-
> bly obeyed. Given the keys to heaven he went to Samaria
> and appearing before King Ahab, said "he Lord God of
> Israel lives before whom I stand. There shall be neither
> dew nor rain from heaven on your fields unless it is when
> and how I choose." (García Calahorra, 2)

García Calahorra adapts the biblical story to fit the eremitical and apostolic charisms of the Order. His remarks on the prophet's training in the wilderness of Gilead are meant to remind the reader of Hebrews 11:37–38, which says that biblical prophets wore garments of skins, slept on the hard ground, and wandered in solitary places. He also makes connections between the 1–2 Kings story and the New Testament. Adding a preparatory episode in solitary places to the story of Elijah's life makes it parallel that of Jesus', who also prepared in the wilderness before beginning his mission. It also makes Elijah resemble John the Baptist, who "grew and became strong in spirit...in the wilderness till the day of his manifestation to Israel" (Luke 1:80).

Members of the Order have meditated on two kinds of wilderness seclusion. When they think about communion with God, they often say that it occurs in a beautiful, flower-laden place of pleasure. The best biblical models for the nuptial wilderness are the enclosed gardens and flourishing meadows of the Song of Songs and certain lovely visions of a restored, fertile world found in the books of the prophets. Prior general Nicholas of France, thought to have been an early inhabitant of Mt. Carmel, meant to lure what he saw were wayward Carmelites back into this kind of wilderness. He contrasted the dangers of urban life, which he clothed in images from the Apocalypse, with the spiritual solace of the desert:

> In the desert all the elements conspire to favor us. The
> heavens, resplendent with the stars and planets in their
> amazing order, bear witness by their beauties to mysteries
> higher still.... When we sing the praises of our Creator,
> the mountains about us, our brother conventuals, resound
> with corresponding hymns of praise to the Lord. (Nicho-
> las of France, ch. 11)

Carmelites will remember other lovely depictions of solitude. Images of a pleasure-bower fill "The Spiritual Canticle." In 1697, the Discalced Carmelite friar Blas of St. Joseph published *Paradise in the Desert in the Sweet Company of Jesus*. Photography in the recently issued *Carmel in the Holy Land* emphasizes the green, blooming season on Mt. Carmel.

When they write about the experience of God's absence, or perhaps about the transformative shattering of their own expectations of God, Carmelites often describe seclusion as a barren, waterless wasteland. They frequently place Elijah in such a desert. This kind of wilderness perhaps suits the prophet's audacious style, but it is also the kind of place in which absolute questions must be addressed. Lacking vegetation, water, or animal life, the desert, as Scripture describes it, is a place of supernatural agency. As Alexander Vella has remarked, it is an appropriate abode for Yahweh, who is free, powerful, and unknowable. The early Fathers agreed with the Bible that such a place can also be an arena for temptation. Carmelites have thought of Elijah's physical solitude most often, as a place of hunger and challenge, not a place of edenic plenitude, although life can issue even from rocky soil. The final document of the general chapter of Carmelites of the Ancient Observance held in Rome in 1995 says, for example, that "instead of bringing on his death, the desert [at Horeb] turns out to be the place of new encounter with the Word of God" ("Final Document," 240).

Flourishing meadows and rocky, Elijan desert places have been more than mental landscapes, although it has been said that Carmelite life has a high quotient of yearning for such unbounded locations. Given their early history and their insistence on their spiritual model's solitude, it is no surprise at all that the friars of Mt. Carmel have always sought physical seclusion. Keith Egan remarks that the first Carmelite houses in England at Hulne, Aylesford, Losenham, and Bradmer (founded between 1242 and 1247) were in isolated locations "very much in keeping with the eremitic character of the order"

(Egan, "An Essay," 90). After the Order took up mendicant service, constitutions continued to safeguard silence, cloister, and poverty, the physical conditions internal to each house that supported psychic seclusion. Zimmerman's study of the Italian community of Monte Oliveto founded in 1516 indicates that its location some distance from the nearest village promoted its eremitical life according to the primitive (1247) *Rule*. In the seventeenth century, Thomas de Jesus helped found Discalced deserts in "vast and beautiful sites that would elevate the soul" (Baudry, "Thomas de Jesús," 41), some, as noted above, deliberately recalling Elijah's mountain. Deserts were constructed so that cells surrounded the oratory, perhaps imitating what was then known of the life of the thirteenth-century hermits who had lived on Mt. Carmel. Baudry concludes that the leader of the Teresian reform did not intend the deserts to replace urban Discalced houses. Instead, Thomas saw them as a counterbalance that would ensure the eremitical life that the *Rule* encouraged. Urban Discalced houses, which were more numerous, already facilitated the apostolate. The number of deserts rose to thirty-two before the religious suppressions of the eighteenth century. Several are still in existence.

Individuals have also sought the stricter seclusion that stories of Elijah on Mt. Carmel, at the Brook Cherith, and at Mt. Horeb evoke. Several early priors general relinquished administrative work to become recluses. The names of solitaries such as Blessed Frank of Siena (d. 1291) and Henry Hane (d. 1299) or Thomas Scrope of Bradley, a fifteenth-century preacher who retired to a hermitage, continue to surface in documents from time to time. Pablo Maria Garrido reports that in 1563, the Portuguese Carmelite John of Piety was allowed to establish a hermitage in Castille and live in it in perpetuity. The Aragonese friar Albert of St. Augustine was granted a similar permission in 1568. Teresa's descriptions of secluded foundations, whether Discalced or not, indicate her great appreciation for them. John of the Cross expressed relief when he was assigned to the hermitage at El Calvario near the end of his life.

Absence of physical access to natural wilderness is perhaps one reason why Carmelite women mention Elijah rarely in their works available outside their communities. In the Middle Ages, women ordinarily lived in more confinement than did men. As did their sisters in other forms of vowed life, Carmelite women entered strict enclosure when they entered the Order. Their houses needed to be placed in urban areas, since their gender and their vow of enclosure precluded travel, preaching, and soliciting alms. Commitment to enclosure, which exceeds the ordinary cloistering of monastic life, is still valued in women's communities. Since the inception of the Second Order, Carmelite women most often have found the best physical equivalent of Elijah's wilderness in the interior spaces of buildings or in the interior of their monastic compounds. Cloister (for men as well as for women) produces some of the social isolations of wilderness life but cannot, of course, entirely match Elijah's legendary existence in a cave near the summit of Mt. Carmel, his sojourn during a drought near the Wadi Cherith, his long journey alone through the desert to Mt. Horeb, or his experience of the crashing rocks that preceded the eerie sound that showed him God. Until recently, wilderness for Carmelite women has been spiritual and symbolic and less frequently has involved the desert in a literal, physical way. Perhaps this is one reason why they write of Elijah infrequently.

Spiritual Solitude and Its Transmission

This, however, is not a fully satisfactory conjecture, because interior life has always mattered to Carmelite women and men more than any physical condition for it. The wilderness, the cell, the hermitage, and the geography of Mt. Carmel are precious but not the heart of the matter. Albert of Avogadro called the thirteenth-century hermits and their descendants not to physical isolation but to "allegiance," a "pure heart and a good conscience," obedience, meditation, and the "armor of God" (*Rule*, ch. 1). The essential space of Carmelite life is the space of the mind and the heart, and Carmelite nuns as well as friars have had access to this domain. On the long view, Elijah has been more a sign of spiritual solitude than he has been of physical location. Two better conjectures about why Carmelite women mention the prophet so infrequently when they write are that in Mary they have a radiantly appealing feminine model of spiritual life available to them, along with Christ, and that Elijah's prophetic activity is more easily identified with the public preaching reserved to men than it is with the kinds of service usually available to religious women.

Secluded locations have been seen as auxiliaries to spiritual life, not assurance for it. Few writers in the Order have agreed with Nicholas of France that true Carmelite life can only be lived in the desert. Evocation of physical seclusion in order to say that inner life matters more became commonplace. Michael of Bologna's fourteenth-century remarks are typical:

> Love of eternal realities expels love of temporal things....
> In this way such a man retreats from evil not physically
> but interiorly.... By taking flight he retreats, because by
> leaving behind an accumulation of earthly desires, he is
> raised to a sublime contemplation of God. "I would make
> a new home in the desert," that is, in the mind, where there
> is no one with him but God. That man reaches tranquil[ity]
> in solitude, who in contemplating God remains in the re-
> mote reaches of his mind. (Cited by Valabek, 91–92)

Valuing interior above physical solitude was more than a capitulation to urban life. The *Directory of Novices* produced by the seventeenth-century Touraine Reform of the Ancient Observance explains that inner seclusion is where one meets God:

> The first and principal obligation of our Institute is to at-
> tend and stand with God in solitude, silence and continual
> prayer, following the wish of our first father and founder
> St. Elias, the prophet. For this reason our dwelling has
> been placed in the desert, where the express command of
> our Rule orders us to remain continually withdrawn in our
> cells, meditating day and night on the law of God. And

although after many centuries we have been transported
from the deserts of Palestine to the cities and populated
towns of Europe, nevertheless, this obligation of continually being attentive to God in prayer has always remained
the same. Our Rule on this point has never been changed.
Hence, the principal work of the Order is prayer, solitude
and silence, all other work should be considered acces-
sory, and should never destroy or be prejudicial in any
manner to the principal work. (Cited in Healy, *Methods of
Prayer*, 18)

First in order of value is the Carmelite's silent communion with God
in the solitude of the cell; second, the memory that the mythic founder
wished later Carmelites to achieve this communion; and third, the
desert, which was greatly desired, but the *Directory* makes clear, not
absolutely necessary to Carmelite spiritual life.

Robert Stefanotti comments that the Touraine reformers "sought a
synthesis of the traditional and original. The task, as they saw it, was
to bring the strict observance of the *Rule*, the early constitutions and
the living models of Elijah and Mary (the two primary symbols of the
Order) into dialogue with lived faith, the contemporary reality of personal and communal religious life" (Stefanotti, 12). In addition to the
works Stefanotti mentions, the group seems to have been particularly
interested in the commentary on the *Rule* that the prior general John
Soreth had composed during a reform of the Order two centuries earlier. Soreth had praised life in remote locations: "Our vocation is to
leave the cities and their crowds and to search for solitude. The place
makes no difference, provided you follow Christ into the country or
look for him in the desert or pray with him alone on the mountain"
(Barry, 102). However, Soreth turns to the commonplace: it is quality
of life spent in such locations that makes them places of solitude.
This is true even of the cell, the most available "wilderness" Carmelites
have: "The cell is a holy land where you meet God. But it is in the
inner cell of a pure heart that you really meet him" (Barry, 102).

Touraine reformer Michael of Saint Augustine (1621–1684)
drew on Soreth, *The Institution of the First Monks*, and other early

apologetic works to compose his lengthy discussion of how Elijah's life exemplified the *Rule. The Introduction to the Interior Life and Fruitful Practice of the Mystical Life* comments on the patron's abstinence, fasting, mortification, zeal, and care for others:

> [Albert's *Rule*] is a vivid expression of the prophetic life, the limpid mirror in which we may contemplate the principal virtues of our holy Fathers Elijah and Elisha so that we may learn to practice them. In effect, does it not call us in its first chapter to angelic chastity, to voluntary poverty (virtues which they were the first to teach their disciple by means of their example) and to the religious obedience that the sons of the Prophets rendered them as the first Priors ever to exist in our Order? (Michael of St. Augustine, 261)

Where the *Institution* remarked, "For all these reasons Elijah chose not only to live on that mountain but also to build there a house consecrated to prayer, called the *semnion*…" (bk. 3, ch. 17 in Werling's notation). Michael of Saint Augustine explains that the chapel which the *Rule* ordered the first hermits to construct is "the first oratory, called a *semnio*, which our holy Father Elijah built on the slope of Mt. Carmel in honor of the Mother of God, whom he foresaw in the spirit, and which was reconstructed by the holy Prophet Agabus in the time of the Apostles" (Michael of St. Augustine, 262).

Wanting to impress the necessity of retirement and contemplation on his readers, Touraine spiritual director John of St. Samson recalls the scene of Elijah living on Mt. Carmel that appeared in the *Rubrica prima* and other early works:

> Before the mystery of the Incarnation God chose certain great servants…to live in certain places which they sanctified by their virtuous, heroic life. Our Father St. Elijah was such a one, chosen at a particular time in sacred history to live a retired and solitary life on Mt. Carmel. There he had disciples as time passed, and together they lived a holy life spent in authentic retirement and advanced contemplation of divine things. (John of St.

Samson, *Observations Concerning the Carmelite Rule*, 848, cited in Elisée de la Nativité, *Élie le prophète*, vol. 2, 111)

He then conventionally asserts the primacy of interior over exterior spiritual life: "It will do us no good at all to be the legitimate offspring of these holy Patriarchs if we are not animated by their spirit.... We would be like a body without a soul" (John of St. Samson, op. cit., 111).

Whenever the Order underwent periodic self-examination and renewal, its writers retold earlier traditions of Elijah. Returning to trustworthy works in the Order and adding their own expressions of tradition, they forged a chain of transmission concerning the founder that mythically anchored the Order more and more firmly. Transmissional lines, of course, were also being forged for Mary's traditions and for those of Jesus Christ. From time to time, new links—that is, new emphases or details in the foundational stories—were added to the lengthening Elijan cable. These were accepted by later generations because they expressed the inner life of the Order in some way.

The *Rule*, the Bible, the *Rubrica prima* and contemporary documents telling the story of the founder on Mt. Carmel, *The Institution of the First Monks*, and Soreth's commentary were principal sources of authority and inspiration on which Touraine writers drew to argue for their reform. In time Carmelites (in both branches, but especially in the Ancient Observance) drew on works produced by Touraine for help in naming what it meant to belong to their Order. John Brenninger's 1940 *Carmelite Directory of the Spiritual Life* for Carmelites of the Ancient Observance cites beliefs concerning Elijah at Cherith found in the *Institution* (which Brenninger believed was written by John 44 in the fifth century).

> Rightly is our holy Father Elias said to have laid the foundation of the monastic life.... He was concealed for a long time in the solitude of the torrent Carith..., lived in

Breninger

poverty and in perfect perpetual chastity and consecrated himself entirely to God, having no other desire than to walk in the sight of God...and to fight for his honor. With zeal he was zealous for the Lord God of hosts.... All those who were afterwards received on Mount Carmel strove to imitate his example. (*Carmelite Directory*, sec. 194, "Devotion to our Holy Father Elias")

Brenninger's work explicitly claims influence by the *Directory of Novices*, the works of Michael of Saint Augustine and John of St. Samson. Formed by the *Carmelite Directory*, many Carmelites of the Ancient Observance today think of Elijah as did Soreth, the writer of the medieval *Rubrica prima* and the writer of the two-goal passage of the *Institution of the First Monks*. Because later writers explaining the charism of the Order have habitually repeated key phrases, traditions, and teachings of earlier documents, it has been possible for Carmelites to learn traditions of the Order without having studied the older works directly.

Discalced Carmelite descriptions of Elijah's inner life have hardly differed from those of their confreres in the Ancient Observance. In a passage from his 1953 *Carmelite Spirituality in the Teresian Tradition*, Paul-Marie of the Cross comments on the relation of physical and spiritual solitudes:

The exercise of prayer at Carmel is accompanied by a minimum of material conditions. Prayer involves no rigorously prescribed methods. For its development it requires the liberty and fidelity of a soul constantly visited and vivified by the spirit. The rule faithfully preserves this conception of life with God. The central obligation there laid down is "to meditate day and night on the Law of the Lord." But the example of Elijah, as well as an inner demand, urges the hermits to realize, both within and outside themselves, a spirit of silence and solitude eminently favorable to prayer, of which the desert is the most perfect expression. The desert calls out to the spirit and the spirit calls out to the desert. Between the spirit of Carmel and the desert there is a living relation. Carmel's prayer is the desert in which the spirit dwells.... This search for God in

> silence and solitude, this absence of imposed forms of
> prayer, a conversation that is free and truly heart-to-heart
> in "the place of the espousals"—this is what the desert
> means, this is what has characterized Carmel from the
> beginning. Life of God and desert: these timeless realities
> are never separated in the Old Testament or in the New.
> The desert of the soul is the very place of God's commu-
> nication. (Paul-Marie of the Cross, 19–20)

As do so many other Carmelite writers, Paul-Marie of the Cross values the physical desert, but once again he cites the "spirit of silence
and solitude" in the "desert of the soul" as the true arena of spiritual
life. He elsewhere cites the two-goals passage of the *Institution of the
First Monks* as an excellent expression of the Carmelite way of life.
The influences of the *Rule*, the Bible, and John of the Cross's doctrine of freedom are evident in his work.

Each century seems to find its own note in the melody of Elijah's
legendary spiritual life. Whether it is because society at large, at least
in the West, has lost its center, or for some other reason, present-day
Carmelites (or at least, a sizable number of their writers) portray the
mythic founder's spiritual life as a *via negativa*. His inner solitude is
most often characterized by silence, darkness, and radical need. The
writer of the "Final Document" of the 1995 General Chapter of the
Ancient Observance characterizes Elijah on his way to Mt. Horeb as
a "broken man" heading for the desert, "a place where there is no life,
a symbol of nothingness. He feels empty and without hope" ("Final
Document," 240). Thinking of Elijah relating to God in an empty
solitude is a recent emphasis on the prophet's interior life, not a perennial one.

More than their sisters and brothers of earlier centuries, twentieth-
century Carmelites tended to retrieve from Elijah's legends of solitude his human experiences of thirst, loss of a sense of self, and lack
of protection in moments of encounter with God. In a 1977 article,
the Discalced Carmelite Joseph Baudry comments, "To live in the
desert is to experience thirst, hunger, fasting, radical stripping. It is to

learn to detach oneself from everything that is not essential...the one who accepts such a stripping will find growing in himself a thirst that only God can slake" (Baudry, "Élie et le Carmel," 166–167).

Many have meditated on how the patron's experiences, especially at Horeb, may teach them about the absolute concerns of the spiritual life. In a 1985 article, Discalced friar John Abiven remarks that members of both observances share a "certain way of envisioning religious life" expressed in the ideals of "continual prayer" and "the test of the desert" (Abiven, 163). The trial, which Abiven sees as characteristically Carmelite, happens in the heart:

> But it is pertinent to note that [it] is a spiritual experience. The desert can be entirely interior, and the "long journey" can occur in a dechristianized ambience; in the boredoms of the apostolate; in the personal tests of aging, illness, aridity in prayer, difficult conditions of existence or relationship, etc. ...Carmel, given its eremitical origins, has the charism and the mission to highlight this traditional treasure. A religious institute committed to an apostolate and claiming Mt. Carmel for itself cannot ignore the need to be an effective, visible witness to the riches of its experience in this domain, and make them available to the Church. (Abiven, 163)

Chapters 1 and 2 of the 1995 *Constitutions of the Ancient Observance* portray Elijah's desert as a dark, boundary-shattering experience from which a gift comes: "From Elijah," solitary, contemplative and prophet, "Carmelites learn to be people of the desert, with heart undivided standing before God and entirely dedicated to his service" (pt. 1, ch. 2, sec. 26, p. 19). The experience of the desert is an apophatic zeroing out, until all that is left is faith, hope, and love:

> Down the ages the Carmelites have emphasized the dynamic of the desert experience as a crucial factor in unifying these values. The desert experience is a Carmelite commitment to make the crucified Christ—stripped and emptied—the very foundation of their lives; to channel their energies entirely toward him in faith, tearing down

> any obstacles which may stand in the way of perfect de-
> pendence on him or impede perfect charity towards God
> and towards others. (Pt. 1, ch. 2, sec. 15, p. 13)

Carmelites now more often use Elijah's psychic experiences in the desert to help them imagine Christ's absolute destitution on the cross and to encourage themselves to follow in that service of their Lord.

Formative Carmelite works of earlier centuries stand behind such recent expressions of the identity of the Order. The emphasis on the stripping and emptying that occurs in Elijan solitude echoes with John of the Cross's teaching on radical emptying of the soul, with the *Institution*'s insistence that Elijah must be nailed to the cross of God's will, with the prophet's dependence on his Lord for sustenance at Cherith and in the southern desert, and, of course, with resonances of individual Carmelite lives. Other masterpieces of the Christian apophatic tradition also contribute to the present tendency to think of Elijah as a man undergoing loss before gain.

Elijah's Purity of Heart

Carmelites have always sought purity of heart. Their *Rule* opens by requiring them to "live a life of allegiance to Jesus Christ and serve him faithfully with a pure heart and a good conscience" (Intro-duction). Michael Hayek suggests that the belief that Elijah had achieved purity of heart came into the Christian tradition from the Syriac Fathers. It is found among the early Latin Fathers as well, John Cassian commenting, for example: "Certain ones directed all their effort to the seclusion of the desert and purifying their heart. Such, in past days, were Elijah and Elisha, and in our own the blessed An-thony and others who pursue the same ideals" (Conference 14:4). Works by Gregory of Nyssa, Chrysostom, and Cassian appear on book lists from early Carmelite houses. It can be expected that from the beginning, members of the Order thought about purity of heart as did the Fathers, who were their models in many things.

The Institution of the First Monks appears to have cemented the connection between the prophet and interior purification for the Order. The instructions it says that the Father, Son, and Holy Spirit gave Elijah on how to live as a prophet-hermit contain passages that are strongly reminiscent of Cassian's teaching on the matter. Cassian addresses the topic in the first of his twenty-four conferences containing the lessons he absorbed from Egyptian masters of desert life. In his view, the desert monk constantly pursues two goals. The immediate aim of monastic life is purity of heart. The monk finally hopes to enter the Kingdom of God, that is, to come into God's presence in "simple and unified contemplation," and to live "solely on the beauty of God." The famous two-goals passages of the *Institution* deliberately echoes Cassian:

> The goal of this life is twofold. One part we acquire by our own effort and the exercise of the virtues, with the help of divine grace. This is to offer God a heart that is holy and pure from all actual stain of sin.... The other goal of this life is granted to us as the free gift of God: namely, not only after death but even in this mortal life to taste somewhat in the heart and to experience in the mind the power of the divine presence and the sweetness of heavenly glory. (1:2)

Cassian explains that purity of heart is not perfection itself. Neither is it fulfillment. It is not a state. It is, instead, the "right path" to the ultimate goal of the presence of God, a "marked road," "standard" or "reference-point" helping the monk move toward the ultimate destination (Conference 1:4):

> Perfection, then, is clearly not achieved simply by being naked, by the lack of wealth or by the rejection of honors, unless there is also that love whose ingredients the apostle described and which is to be found solely in purity of heart. Not to be jealous, not to be puffed up, not to act heedlessly, not to seek what does not belong to one, not to rejoice over some injustice, not to plan evil—what is this and its like if not the continuous offering to God of a heart

that is perfect and truly pure, a heart kept free from all
disturbance? (1:5)

In the *Institution* Christ similarly tells Elijah that exterior ascetic acts
are not the point of the life he is about to undertake. What matters in
all cases is interior detachment, which replaces "clinging to the things
one enjoys," "care" and "greed" (1:3) with "obedience to God's will"
(1:4). Purity of heart is for Cassian a "path" or "marked road" (1:4).
The *Institution* insists that Elijah must humbly persevere, since purification of the heart in this life never ends.

The story told in the remaining books of the *Institution* ensures
that readers will remember Elijah as an example of purity of heart:

> Therefore Elijah, in order to live perfectly in the spirit,
> "crucified his flesh with its vices and passionate desires"
> (Gal. 5:24). ...This he did in a more eminent way than
> anyone before him, for he was the first man to freely dedi-
> cate himself to perpetual virginity for God's sake: thus he
> sought to imitate the life of the angels and to become like
> them in the purity of chastity and the incorruption of the
> flesh. (*Institution* 2:1)

Books 2–6 of the work portray not only the founder but also his disciples achieving the final goal of monastic life to experience the power
of divine presence. Like no other Carmelite work before it that we
may now examine, Ribot's saga associates the classic conditions for
purity of heart, including detachment, chastity, and perpetual effort,
with the mythic founder of the Order. "What is proper to the teaching
of the *Institution*," says Kilian Healy, "is that it proposes purity of
heart not only as preparation for entering the kingdom of heaven but
as the proximate preparation for the reception of the gift of contemplation in this world" (Healy, *Prophet of Fire*, 51).

Teresa, Elijah, and Poverty

Whether or not Teresa of Jesus knew the content of the *Institution*,
as some have thought, she was undeniably committed to the spiritual

states that it associates with Elijah. She especially prized detachment from self and love of Christ that the work said the prophet was called to seek. Her reform was modeled, first and foremost, on Christ's life and, second, on what she knew of the lives of the "holy fathers" of the Order, chief of whom, of course, was Elijah. In *The Interior Castle* (1577), Teresa reminds her sisters of the spiritual life that legend said their ancestors had achieved on Mt. Carmel:

> So I say now that all of us who wear this holy habit of Carmel are called to prayer and contemplation. This call explains our origin; we are the descendants of men who felt this call, of those holy fathers on Mount Carmel who in such great solitude and contempt for the world sought this treasure, this precious pearl of contemplation that we are speaking about. (*Interior Castle* 5:1:2)

In *The Book of Her Foundations*, she relates what she saw in 1580 as she approached Our Lady of Succor, a hermitage for Discalced men:

> This house stood in a delightfully isolated and solitary spot. And as we approached, the friars came out in a procession to meet their prior. Since they were discalced and wore their poor, coarse woolen mantles, they inspired us all with devotion and moved me to tender feelings since it seemed to me that I was present in the flourishing time of our holy Fathers of old. In that field, they appeared to be like white fragrant flowers, and indeed I believe that before God they are, for in my opinion He is authentically served there. They entered the church singing the Te Deum with voices very restrained. The entrance to it is underground, as though through a cave, which represented that of our Father Elijah. (28:20)

In the following chapter, she comments again on the holy prophets: "For the love of our Lord I beg you to remember how soon everything comes to an end, and to remember the favor our Lord has granted us in bringing us to this order and the great punishment that will befall anyone who might introduce some mitigation." For the foundress, unmitigated Carmelite life achieved great solitude and the precious pearl of contemplation: "...fix your eyes always on the ancestry from which we come, those holy prophets. How many saints we have in heaven who have worn this habit! Let us adopt the holy presumption that with the Lord's help we will be like them. The battle will be brief, my Sisters, and the end is eternal" (29:33).

Father Elijah, the holy prophets, and the holy fathers were stamped on her mind. She may have seen Elijah's coat of skins in the coarse woolen mantles of those who approached her in 1580. The cordial, reverent hermits coming to greet their prior, embodied the fraternal relations, solitude, contempt for the world, and contemplation on Mt. Carmel. In Teresa's mind, her whole Order, her sisters, and she were spiritual descendants of those holy prophets.

Phillip of the Trinity has remarked that Teresa's great contribution to earlier Carmelite tradition consisted in grafting an apostolic desire to save souls onto the eremitical, contemplative spirit of the Order. This overlooks centuries of sincere Carmelite labor in mendicant service that coincided with an equally sincere orientation to contemplation before Teresa's lifetime. Adding desire to win souls for Christ to an inclination to solitude did not begin with the great foundress. Instead, her innovative contribution to the traditions of Elijan spiritual life that by her day included solitude, silence, repentance, humility, chastity, purity of heart, and zealous love was a fuller understanding of the poverty that she believed Elijah and the holy fathers experienced on Mt. Carmel.

Remembering the comment in 2 Kings 1:8 regarding the prophet's haircloth garment and his dependence on God in 1 Kings, as well as the reference to the destitution of the prophets in Hebrews, Christians often portrayed Elijah without possessions, clothed "in skins of sheep and goats, destitute," living in "deserts and mountains, and in dens and caves of the earth" (Heb. 11:37–38). The association of Elijah with poverty existed in the Order from its beginning. The first Western residents of Mt. Carmel pursued a modest lifestyle in imitation of him. When they emigrated to Europe, the group appealed to Rome to become mendicant—that is, a "begging" order—during a period when the Church was divided over whether or not Christ had been materially poor. Carmelites chose institutional poverty for themselves. In the fifteenth century, Soreth dedicated a large portion of his commentary on the *Rule* to encouraging a return to evangelical standards of poverty, although his modern commentator Gabriel Barry notes that this "apparently did not penetrate too deeply in the Order" (Barry, 104), and an early foundress Frances of Amboise insisted on a very restricted material life in the convents she established. Although it lapsed from its ideal at times, the Order related poverty to its spiritual concerns and to its origin.

Teresa's innovation, then, was not to introduce stricter collective and individual poverty into her reformed houses—others had sought that reform before her and the ideal had always resided in the Order—but to deepen a spirituality of this long-standing element of Carmelite life and to link it explicitly to the "holy fathers" whose excellent existence on Mt. Carmel inspired her. Many things may have caused her to impress on her sisters how necessary poverty was to contemplation. She must have been affected by the writings of Frances of Amboise, with which she was acquainted, and may have been influenced by translations of the French Carmelite women's constitutions, which, according to Vital Wilderink, were models for Spanish ones in the sixteenth century. These especially stress the destitution of Christ's passion. Teresa's thoughts on the place of poverty in Carmelite life were probably affected by Franciscans Clare of Assisi and Francisco de Osuna, whose works she knew, and certainly were affected by her Franciscan confessor Pedro de Alcántara, who insisted to her that material poverty was necessary to spiritual life.

Christ's spiritual suffering and humble service of his Father were the greatest influence on Teresa's thoughts on the matter. She constantly wrote to her sisters about his willing self-impoverishment. Given the magnitude of his self-offering, Carmelites could not attain the poverty he experienced, she taught. By calling them to their way of life, Christ made Teresa and her sisters poor. This, she said, was a gift that they should accept as a particular favor (*Meditations on the Song of Songs* 2). It was God's will that they be poor (*Life* 35, 36). Carmelites needed to learn to trust that God indeed would provide for their material needs (*Way of Perfection* 2, *Foundations* 18, *Spiritual Testimonies* 2). Spiritual poverty, which was fostered by material poverty, yielded happiness (*Foundations* 15), freedom from care (*Life* 35), and equality in relations with members of a community. It was accomplished through trust in God accompanied by continual efforts at detachment. Spiritual poverty even included refusing to cling to the fruits of prayer. Advancement in loving union with Christ could not be possessed or retained; to attempt to do so violated its nature. Spiritual marriage was not a personal gift to the soul who received it; it was the essence of spiritual poverty, since it was participation in Christ's self-emptying love for others (*Interior Castle* 7:4).

Teresa emblematizes her beliefs on poverty in her brief descriptions of the ideal life spent on Mt. Carmel by Elijah and his followers. While Carmelites in earlier centuries occasionally say that inhabitants of the mountain were poor, the remark is made in passing. Elijah's seclusion, his contemplation, or his foundation of continuous succession instead draw attention. Teresa treats poverty as a cornerstone of Elijan life. In chapter 14 of her *Foundations*, she exclaims concerning the poor state of the farmhouse at Duruelo that briefly housed the first male Discalced Carmelite community:

> Oh, God help me! What little these buildings and exterior comforts do interiorly. Out of love for Him, I ask you my Sisters and Fathers, that you never fail to be very moderate in this matter of large and magnificent houses. Let us keep before us our true founders, those holy fathers from whom we descend, for we know that by means of that path of poverty and humility they now enjoy God.

Three chapters later she speaks of the residents of El Tardón, a hermitage near Seville: "Each one lived apart in a cell. They did not recite the divine office together but did gather in an oratory for Mass. They had no fixed income; neither did they want to receive alms, nor did they. But they supported themselves by the work of their hands, and each one ate alone and very poorly. When I heard about this it seemed to me to be a living picture of the life of our own holy fathers." In chapter 2 of the *Way of Perfection*, entitled "Treats of how one should not worry about bodily needs and of the blessing there is in poverty," she exclaims:

> Holy poverty is our insignia and a virtue which at the beginning, when our order was founded, was so esteemed and well kept by our holy fathers. For I have been told, by someone who knows, that they did not keep anything for the next day. If exteriorly we do not carry out this practice so perfectly, let us strive to do so interiorly. Life lasts but a couple of hours; exceedingly great will be the reward. If we should do nothing else but what the Lord counseled us to do, the pay of just being able in some way to imitate Him would be great. (2:8)

Teresa persuasively brackets the life of the sisters to whom she writes between two excellent models of the poverty they should seek: the holy fathers whose spiritual lives inaugurated the Order and Christ whose poverty made the Order possible.

The great Spanish reformer comments on the material conditions of poverty that pertained to cloistered life. Not at all surprising for her times and gender, she almost always preoccupies herself with advancing spiritual life within community walls. Like Frances of Amboise in the preceding century, Teresa saw that rank, especially rank based on possessions, disturbed sisterly relations within her groups of nuns. At times she sought novices for new houses who had few resources, commenting that these, being freer of family attachments and social obligations, were better prepared for the material poverty and humility of Carmelite life. Focusing her attention on the poverty of the religious life of women in a mendicant order (who, due to their vow of cloister and their gender, were constrained from begging and, at least at first, sought to maintain communities without endowments), she has little to say about what Carmelites should do about the destitute outside the walls of their houses.

Recent publications suggest that the Discalced Carmelites and the Carmelites of the Ancient Observance may be shifting their views on the kinds of poverty that should affect their spiritual life. Long-standing attitudes and practices concerning material life continue. Possessions are held in common. Communities deliberately maintain a modestly supplied life. The view promoted by Teresa that poverty is an intramural spiritual affair is still influential. In a 1990 article, Healy promotes a traditional understanding of spiritual life whose poverty is hidden from the world: "But does this hidden life [dedicated solely to prayer] far from the anxieties and sufferings of the people demand courage? Is it not rather a cowardly withdrawal from the lives of the poor and oppressed? On the contrary, one who commits himself or herself to the contemplative life with sincerity chooses not only to be poor and chaste, but for the love of God and others chooses to put to death all that is selfish. The contemplative leaves the world for the good of the world" (Healy, *Prophet of Fire*, 38).

There are Carmelite voices saying other things about the issue as well. Affected by the call of Vatican II to religious orders to be a sign in the world of God's grace, Carmelites also participate deliberately in the lives of the suffering and destitute outside the doors of their houses. Whether nourished by Teresa's meditation on the Christlike features of the poverty she believed the holy fathers on Mt. Carmel possessed or drawing from other resources, Carmelites of both observances now often ask how they as vowed religious relate to the poor of the world. Terence Cyr, O. Carm., reported in the Discalced *Carmelite Digest* in 1992:

> Recent Carmelite provincial and general chapters have issued challenges to individual Carmelites and local communities to re-examine the vow of poverty in such a way that Carmelites adopt a lifestyle that demonstrates a

"preferential option for the poor." Carmelites hope to give witness by their corporate and individual lifestyle to the fact that the political and social structures of our modern world need to be purified and impregnated with authentic Gospel values. (Cyr, 34)

This Cyr finds entirely consistent with the mendicant identity of the Order. He lists ways this new attitude toward poverty is being carried out in practice. Corporate financial decisions are made in ways intended to ease the ills of society at large. Individual Carmelites "consider themselves with the poor"—a mendicant view inherited from the Middle Ages (Cyr, 36). Members of the Order act to welcome the poor of the larger society (in his brief article, Cyr did not mention what these ways are). John Abiven, OCD, also alludes to the chosen proximity of Carmelite communities to the most destitute, and the 1995 constitution of the Ancient Observance, citing a document from the 1980 General Congregation, affirms the "choice to share in the lives of the 'little ones' (*minores*) of history, so that we may speak a word of hope and salvation from the midst—more by our life than by our words" (pt. 1, ch. 2, sec. 24, p. 18).

When Elijah is evoked in current discussions of poverty in Carmelite life, he tends to appear in his old biblical role of an Israelite prophet, whose words and actions demonstrate the nature of God, and in his experiences of powerlessness before God in which Carmelites have found signs of mystical encounter. It appears from their writing, then, that a significant number of Carmelites have shifted their understanding of poverty. It continues to include eremitical asceticisms summed up in the first goal of *The Institution of the First Monks*, and it continues to accept Teresa's teaching that Carmelites need to welcome spiritual poverty and chosen lack as avenues to participation in Christ's love for others, Healy's emphases in his 1990 article. Additionally, Carmelites now encourage themselves to participate in the life of the poor in society at large.

To do the latter places pressure on earlier monastic understandings of poverty. The deliberate physical impoverishments of the fourth- and fifth-century desert fathers, who claimed Elijah along with Antony and John the Baptist as models, were often reported to be extreme, but they were carried out in a carefully balanced lifestyle. Ancient holy women and men supported themselves with sedentary labor such as gardening or other tasks that could be pursued while fasting or while engaging in vigils. Their ascetic practices—their voluntary practices of bodily impoverishment, one might say—were validated by an understanding of the relation of body to spirit that is not as widely accepted now as it was in their day. Minimal food and water or the deliberate relinquishment of sensual pleasure helped ancient ascetics maintain what they saw was a state of physical and spiritual incorruption that for them was a true (that is, direct, not symbolic) foretaste of heaven. In other words, as a fourth-century hermit, with God's grace one made oneself otherworldly through chosen physical restrictions that encouraged inner detachment.

The amount of detailed attention Teresa of Jesus pays in her writing to establishing, and then improving, balances in communities that elected to survive on meager resources shows that she agreed with the desert fathers that religious poverty needed to be constructed with care. Her worries about how her sisters tolerated crowding and lack of food show that the foundress knew that there was a line near which she wished her communities to live, but below which material poverty would be too crushing. Teresa knew that material poverty needed to be carefully balanced and tended if it was to support spiritual life. It needed to be regular and disciplined.

The destitute to whom Carmelites increasingly have turned rarely have the opportunity to hope for such a balanced situation. Most of the world's hungry have not chosen their state. Lacking resources, they are subject to many disturbances. The poor of the world rarely report that their dark nights are brought on by God in prayer. In a word, the poverty they know is not monastic poverty, no matter how their conditions affect their spirit. Carmelites who now live among the poor, not as visitors who can return to a more comfortable home when they choose, but as companions, have removed themselves from the well-thought-out isolations and careful balances of fourth-century desert life and medieval monastic life. They have moved into something more like the psychic space that Elijah occupies in his biblical stories.

In 1–2 Kings, Elijah also cannot construct his poverty or bring it to an end. When God tells him to go to the desert and wait to be fed, Elijah must go and wait. When the prophet wants to die, he is required to eat and continue his journey. When he enters a cave, he is required to come out. When he says he has given up prophecy, he is sent to prophesy. He cannot claim or pattern his own life. He is destitute, dependent on what God does or does not do to him. The shift in Carmelite commitments to poverty will almost surely change how it defines the solitude that surrounds contemplation in the Order. Those whose own lives are disrupted by the disruptions of the poor around them may ponder where they can find the best equivalent of the life of peace on Mt. Carmel that the Carmelite tradition has so often said that Elijah enjoyed with other contemplatives. Elijah of the harsh desert may help in thinking about this.

Elijan Succession, a Faded Tradition

One of the most vigorous traditions of the Order claimed that Carmelites were part of an unbroken succession of spiritual lives tracing back to Elijah and Elisha. Although there were always those in the Order who handled the claim critically, many writers repeated the legend as if it were a historical truth. Documents were destroyed in the religious suppressions of the eighteenth and nineteenth centuries, but it appears from those that may be consulted that some, or perhaps many, Carmelites in those difficult centuries continued to believe that Elijah had founded their Order. Claim to historical connection to the spiritual model finally disappeared from works written by members of the Order in the twentieth century. When they recalled the story connecting themselves to Elijah, Carmelites could see that they were united with previous and succeeding generations. The tradition also told them that Elijah's way of life—a life of ascetic purification, love of God, and apostolic service—was their perennial way, too.

Some examples of the claim will be examined here. The articles of Louis-Marie du Christ and Elisée de la Nativité included in volume 2 of *Élie le prophète* published by *Etudes Carmélitaines* in 1956 supply additional ones. The assertion that Elijah founded the Carmelite Order began to surface in documents during the first century of Carmelite residence in Europe. Although the Order soon acquired legitimation from Rome, its members often had difficulty claiming it where they lived at some distance from the Holy See. Their dioceses already having absorbed new Dominican and Franciscan foundations, local bishops tended to look for reasons to reject Carmelites, who rarely arrived in areas before the other two mendicant orders had appeared. The mendicant orders also challenged each other's legitimacy with unfortunate frequency. The fact that Carmelites had no identifiable historical founder often drew the criticism of detractors.

Responding to challenge, medieval and early modern Carmelite constitutions instructed members of the Order to report to outsiders that their way of life began when their "holy fathers" lived as penitents and contemplatives in the solitude of Mt. Carmel from the time of Elijah and Elisha. They were also to say that their way of life continued on the mountain in continuous succession down to the present day. In 1370 *The Institution of the First Monks* repeated what other Carmelite documents had begun to say, that Elijah had founded the Carmelite Order and that the continuous succession of which latter-day Carmelites were living members had included John the Baptist, Obadiah, Jonah, and Carmelite ancestors (occasionally blatantly called Carmelites) who, in the first century, were converted to Christianity and preached alongside the Apostles. Members of the Order made these claims because they trusted the documents in which they read them, which were their constitutions (until at least the beginning of the seventeenth century), the *Institution* (accepted between the fifteenth and the eighteenth centuries to be the original *Rule* of the Order), the 1507 *Speculum Carmelitanum*, and Daniel of the Virgin Maria's 1680 *Speculum Carmelitanum* (both printed anthologies of works dating from the first centuries of the Order. (See Appendix 1 for more details on the dissemination of the *Institution*).

Carmelites were certainly not the only medieval group to declare that it was directly connected to the people and events in sacred history. Nor was the concept of historical succession from biblical figures their invention. As the Dominican Marie-Humbert Vicaire has shown, John Cassian was probably responsible for a tradition, which was repeated for centuries, that said that cenobitic life was directly transmitted by the Apostles to fourth-century Christian monks of the Egyptian deserts and that these, in historical succession, passed that life from generation to generation, bequeathing it to cenobitic groups in later centuries. Corroboration for this can be found in Institute 2:5, where Cassian asserts what others later often repeated on his authority, that the apostle Mark taught the ways of community life of the Church in Jerusalem to the Egyptian monks. Although Carmelites concerned themselves with eremitical life (actually, a modified eremitical life lived in community), their claims of direct contact with Elijah were very similar to Cassian's. Answers to the question, "What moved members of the Order to cling to a historical assertion that was so obviously difficult to prove?" are that it wasn't so difficult to make the claim when they began to make it, and other religious were using the same manner of argumentation to claim similar affiliations for themselves.

It is sometimes implied that all medieval Carmelites believed that the legend was historically true. Well-educated early writers for the Order were careful in handling the claim of the *Rubrica prima* that Elijah and the Carmelite ancestors had had living contact with each other. Where John Baconthorpe says in *Mirror of the Institution of the Order Established for the Cult of the Blessed Mary* that the "order of the Brothers of Carmel appeared to continue the cult of the Blessed Mary" on her mountain, a worship in which "many prophets and kings" participated before them, he says with more caution in his *Compendium* (1324) that "The Order of Carmel began on Mount Carmel, where the prophet Elijah resided, according to Vicentius in the *Speculum Historiali*.... Furthermore, one finds in the *First Constitution* of this same order, published long ago, that from the time of the prophets Elijah and Elisha who inhabited Mount Carmel, certain contemplatives succeeded each other on that same mountain" (Baconthorpe, *Speculum*, ch. 1 in Hendriks, *Élie le prophète*, vol. 2, 43 and *Compendium*, pt. 1 in Hendriks, op. cit., 45). Baconthorpe here finesses the question of continuous succession. He distances himself personally from the claim that Carmelite life began in Elijah's day by remarking not that it is true but that an important document in his Order says that it is true. He neither denies the legend nor asserts that he believes it. *In Praise of Carmelites* (1324), attributed to him, explains that what continued over time on Mt. Carmel was contemplation. No historical links between the mountain's inhabitants and Elijah are mentioned. Regardless of whether or not he wrote the latter document, Baconthorpe's phrasing in the *Compendium* suggests that he had less than full personal commitment to the claim.

A 1374 dispute at Cambridge University between doctors John Stokes, a Dominican, and John Hornby, a Carmelite, caused members to grip their claim to historical succession tightly when confronted by outsiders. Several defenses of the belief were issued shortly after the debate. Stokes's attacking points have not been discovered, but J. P. H. Clark surmises from the record of Hornby's defense that the Stokes attempted to undercut the assertion that Elijah and Elisha had founded the Order. Hornby defended this by pointing to Carmelite occupancy of Mt. Carmel and to parallels between the way members of the Order lived and what the tradition said about Elijah's life. These proofs were more credible then than now. In a later description of the debate, Hornby represents himself as having sawed through the logical legs supporting Stokes's arguments against unbroken succession based on the facts that Carmelites did not wear the same dress as Elijah and that Elijah was not Christian. Clark notes that a simultaneous dispute going on elsewhere "involving the same arguments and with the same 'proofs,'" resulted in the Carmelite John of Hildesheim's *Dialog between a Director and a Detractor* (Clark, 75). Assembling scriptural passages and sayings of the Fathers, Hildesheim pins his argument to the same medieval logic that Hornby used: it is obvious that Carmelites are Elijah's successors because "their life conforms to his." (Jean Leclercq has shown that medieval Benedictines used the same gambit to assert that they were living the life of the Apostles.)

Surely large numbers of Carmelites took the statement of the *Rubrica prima* to their constitutions to mean that the Order was connected to the prophet in unbroken historical as well as spiritual succession. Their relation to their *Rule* affected the ability of *The Institution of the First Monks* to shore up belief in succession. For long believing that the *Institution* was the original Carmelite *Rule* written by John 44 in the fifth century and that Albert's document was a legislative précis of it, members of the Order must have been impressed by its vivid narrative of spiritual succession. The 1370 *Institution* added the important new claim, not seen in earlier documents, that Christ himself started the chain of events that produced the "institution of the first monks," the Carmelite Order, when he called Elijah to imitate him as a hermit. The list of authorities mustered to prove historical, as well as spiritual, relationship to Elijah shifted and lengthened over time, a late believer, Carmelite of the Ancient Observance A. E. Farrington, listing in 1890, for example, "Sovereign Pontiffs," Jerome, John Chrysostom, Cassian, Rupert, Ecclesiasticus, Isidore, Josephus, Philo, Boudon, a revelation to St. Peter Thomas, John 44, 395 writers from every nation and religious body (including 57 Jesuits, 19 Dominicans, 19 Franciscans, 17 Benedictines, and 11

Augustinians), and the 1374 decree declaring that the Carmelites had won the debate at Cambridge (Farrington, 84–87). It appears then that from the fifteenth century onward Carmelites especially relied on the content of the *Institution* to support their belief in Elijah's foundation of the Order.

On the other hand, there always have been members of the Order who refused to pass along the claim of historical connection to Elijah. Several writers who influenced the spirituality of the Order either downplayed the tradition or passed it over in silence. In a passage of his fifteenth-century commentary on the *Rule* cited by Elisée de la Nativité, Soreth dismisses the whole question of historical succession: "We are not sons of the prophets according to the flesh but by imitating their works. Our Redeemer told the Jews who took pride that they were the descendants of Abraham: 'Do the work of Abraham.' The same today should be said to Carmelites: 'Do the works of Elijah'" (cited in Elisée de la Nativité, *Élie le prophète*, vol. 2, 82). Succession was not the issue; imitation was. Neither Teresa of Avila nor John of the Cross cares to defend, or even bring up, historical succession from Elijah.

Others relied on the tradition. Michael of Saint Augustine, a member of the seventeenth-century Touraine reform, writes that the *Rule of St. Albert* is more than a "lively expression of the prophetic life in which the holy Prophets Elijah and Elisha excelled." It also "gives clear testimony" that Carmelites "descend from the holy Prophets Elijah and Elisha through hereditary succession down to our own times."

> St. Albert did not compose our Rule as a new invention, but extracted it from the one which John 44, Patriarch of Jerusalem, gave to those who were dwelling on Mount Carmel around the year of our Lord 400. This latter Rule had been fit to the way of life which Carmelites observed and which they had received by means of a firm and continuous tradition which began in the times of the holy Prophets. At a later time this tradition matched the life our

holy Fathers. Thus it can be concluded that the Rule of St.
Albert harmonizes both with this tradition and with the
life of our holy Founders. (Michael of St. Augustine, 267)

In supporting his claims, Michael of Saint Augustine applies the same
argument that Hornby and Hildesheim did. He explains that historical connection to Elijah is proven by the fact that there are features of
ordinary Carmelite life that resemble details of the patron's legends.

However, he examines the issue of succession more deeply than
did his two earlier confreres. To his way of thinking, it was the *Rule*
that ensured continuous succession from Elijah. The document
shaping Carmelite lives had had the power to knit Carmelites to each
other and to Elijah because it was more than a set of written prescriptions. The Touraine reformer worked out a set of spiritual concor-
dances among the "perfect law of Christ which embraces natural law
and a major portion of the law of Moses," the "law of nature, which
was unwritten" (ibid., 267), Elijah's manner of life, and the Carmelite
Rule. Just as natural law was embraced but superseded by the written
law of Moses, so Elijah's unwritten way of life was captured and
improved upon in *The Institution of the First Monks*. In due time, just
as Christ's perfect law came to embrace natural law and part of the
Torah, so the *Rule of St. Albert* superseded the *Institution*. It became
the most excellent tangible vehicle ensuring the transmission of Elijah's
spiritual life.

Carmelite historian Joachim Smet remarks on the "evangelizing
fervor" and historiographical weaknesses of those who published on
the origins of the Order in the seventeenth century (Smet, vol. 3, pt. 2,
617). Titles of works supporting a historical connection to Elijah continued to surface. The Cordoban Michael Muñoz published a volume
on the nature, origin, and relationship of Elijah to the Order in 1636.
About the same time, the prolific early Discalced writer Joseph of
Jesus Mary of Quiroga penned in 750 folios *The First Part of the
General History, Which Describes the Shining Virtues and Exemplary
Lives of the Saints Belonging to the Carmelite Order from the Time
the Great Prophet Elijah Founded It on Mount Carmel by God's*

Inspiration Until the Infidel Muslims Occupied the Western Shores and Destroyed Their Monasteries. Other cases for the succession have survived as well.

The claim was dealt a serious but not mortal blow by the publication of the *Acta Sanctorum* (*Acts of the Saints*) in Antwerp during the seventeenth century. The *Acta* were published by a team of Jesuits under the guidance of John Bollandus (1596–1665) who sought to establish "scientific" knowledge of the lives of the saints. This especially meant examining the reasonability of the details of old hagiography. The first volume the Jesuits published cast doubt on a claim made by early Carmelite documents that St. Cyril of Alexandria had been a Carmelite (he was, indeed, a legendary figure). In the next volume, Daniel Papebroch disparaged the "little, poorly-sewn together traditions" of Carmelites founded on "pure conjectures, full of anachronisms and contradictions," especially as the traditions were found in *The Institution of the First Monks* (Papebroch, *Acts of the Saints*, cited in Louis-Marie du Christ, *Élie le prophète*, vol. 2, 127). Louis-Marie du Christ relates that Papebroch's critique sought to deny Carmelites their claim of a historical connection to their patron but to allow them the right to claim him as an example of eremitical life, which is what Elijah was to Christians in general. If they relinquished their belief that he had lived like a European member of the Order (which was more or less the Benedictines' claim for Christ's Apostles), Carmelites could indeed claim Elijah as "Author, Inaugurator and Founder," said Papebroch (ibid., 131).

Carmelites rose to the defense, publishing tracts, pamphlets, and larger works that Louis-Marie du Christ notes typically supported their arguments by demonstrating that the Order had existed in each century since the prophet's ninth-century B.C.E. lifetime. In the face of the Bollandists, Calced and Discalced Carmelites continued claiming descent from Elijah. Carmelite of the Ancient Observance Gregory of St. Martin published an *Apology for the Antiquity of the Carmelites, Who Legitimately Maintain Their Origin and Hereditary Succession from the Holy Prophets Elijah and Elisha* in Douay in 1685. Carmelites carved into the base of the statue of Elijah placed in the Vatican basilica in 1727 their claim that Elijah was the founder of the Order. The inscription reads: "The entire Order of Carmelites erected this statue to the Prophet, St. Elias, their Founder."

Michael of St. Augustine's confrere in the Touraine reform Daniel of the Virgin Mary also stood firm in the buffeting winds. His two-volume *Speculum Carmelitanum,* according to Smet, conceived in 1641 but finally published posthumously in 1680, is a major repository of works from the earlier centuries of the Order from which later generations have drawn their knowledge of what Ribot, Baconthorpe, Oller, Grossi, Soreth, and Bostius had said about the legendary founder. Daniel also wrote the *Phoenix of the World, Miracle of Grace and Nature, St. Elijah the Prophet, Princeps of Monastic Religious Life, Patriarch of the Carmelite Order,* which he published in 1670, two years after the Bollandists had discredited the Carmelite claim.

Daniel's caution in approaching his topic is obvious. He dedicates four of the latter volume's five parts to details of Elijah's life found in the Bible, supplemented with long-held Christian beliefs about the prophet, such as that, like Jeremiah, he was sanctified while still in his mother's womb. In the fifth part Daniel discusses additional traditions shared with other monastic orders: Elijah is a perfect mirror of the virtues of poverty, chastity, and obedience. He dedicated himself daily to vocal and mental prayer, psalmody, meditation, and divine contemplation. He modeled the perfect life by his flight from the world, his prudence, justice, fortitude, temperance, faith, charity, and zeal. Only in the appendix does the author tackle the issue of succession. Relying on an intricate assembly of authorities, Daniel lays out the old claim of a historical connection to Elijah. He assembles Scripture that suggests that Elijah instituted eremitical life on Mt. Carmel, arranges it to support the claim that his disciples, the sons of the prophets, joined him in that "conventual" life on Mt. Carmel, and says that Elisha continued the "religious institute." He gathers a host of patriarchs, Church Fathers, the congregation of cardinals, the pope, and

Carmelite writers (ranging from Cheminot to Teresa of Jesus) to testify that Elijah inaugurated the Carmelite Order (Daniel of the Virgin Mary, 370–425).

In 1905, Discalced Carmelite James Rushe was still asserting that "hermits of Carmel" in his own day were still observing the "pious customs" that had been observed on the mountain "from the time of the Prophets" (Rushe, 228). Surely a very late example, the 1927 volume entitled *Carmel: Its History, Spirit and Saints*, whose title page announces that it was "compiled from approved sources by the Discalced Carmelites of Boston and Santa Clara," advances the remark that Elijah "has always been regarded by the Carmelites as the Founder and the first Patriarch of their Order" (*Carmel: Its History, Spirit, and Saints*, 5). It quotes verbatim O. Carm. A. E. Farrington's prickly, authority-laden defense of continuous succession published in 1890. A second answer to the question, "What moved members of the Order to cling to an historical assertion that was so patently difficult to prove?" is simply that trusted writers from within the Order passed it down to them as true.

The critique by the Bollandists did not convince Carmelites to relinquish the claim. Nor did they abandon it when the suppressions of the late eighteenth and nineteenth centuries in their own violent ways diminished hopes for continuous succession from Elijah. It fell to a new group of trusted Carmelite writers to end literal belief in the Elijan succession. Contributors to the change of mind include Bartholomew Xiberta, Brenninger, Zimmerman, Wessels, and Brandsma. The effect of these scholars on the Carmelite family's present-day view of itself has been substantial. During the first decades of the twentieth century, they established an ideal of rigorous scholarship that has continued and that had not existed in the Order at any time before. Results of their research also lay the foundation for study in recent decades. By applying modern standards and techniques of historical inquiry to questions involving the origins of the Order, Carmelite scholars early in this century began to clarify the Order's historical and spiritual sense of itself.

Several Carmelite works directly affected the demise of belief in historical succession. In his influential *Carmelite Mysticism* (published in English in 1936), Titus Brandsma reported the content of *The Institution of the First Monks* but omitted the very obvious claim of the older work that Elijah founded the Order in his ninth century B.C.E. lifetime. Brandsma reported to Carmelite readers (most of whom would not have the opportunity to study Ribot's work, since most of its surviving copies had been gathered into archives or national libraries, and many were in Latin): "It is a record of traditions much older than itself, and was meant to be a definite and permanent guide for monks. In it we read that the guidance which the Holy Ghost gave to Elias and the promises made to him, must be the guiding principles in the life of the hermits on Carmel" as well as monastic life in the centuries that follow (Brandsma, *Carmelite Mysticism*, 13). As Brandsma describes it, the *Institution* appears to be a book that has most to do with Elijah's personal spiritual life as a model for other personal spiritual lives. The *Institution*'s claim that Elijah founded the Order is not mentioned.

Rudolf Hendriks's 1956 edition and translation of selections from early documents that comment on Elijah have helped Carmelites evaluate the claim. His chapter in volume 2 of *Élie le prophète* allows most of the oldest passages describing the beginning of the Order to be studied as a group. Carmelites reading French or Latin can compare the Elijan passages in early documents and can come to their own conclusions concerning the Order's past beliefs about the figure. Important reassessments and new recoveries of Carmelite history have appeared throughout the remainder of the twentieth-century, and some have affected the claim. Adrian Staring, to take a final example, broadened the possibilities Carmelites now have to study the ancient documents of the order with the 1989 publication of *Medieval Carmelite Heritage: Early Reflections on the Nature of the Order*.

Hendriks remarks in a 1964 article, "Elias in the Carmelite Tradition," "Of course the Fathers and the other clerical authors did not mean to say that monasticism as found in the Church was descended in an unbroken historical line from the Old Testament. It was left to the Carmelite authors of a later day [Hendriks refers to Carmelites writing in the thirteenth century] to claim this uninterrupted descent from the times of Elias for their Order. The Fathers meant only a continuity in the Holy Ghost: the same Spirit Who spoke through the Prophets was also at work in the men who laid the foundations of a life of perfection in the Church" (Hendriks, "Elias," 90). Hendriks directs his readers' attention away from historical succession and its perpetual way of life and toward meditation on the continuity in spirit that has been echoed by others. Elisée de la Nativité similarly appeals to the continuity of the spirit in his 1956 contribution to *Élie le prophète*: "The historical details assembled to prove Elijan affiliation lost their effectiveness when they were submitted to a rigorous critique. But the breath that animates these sentences [of the *Institution*] is such that the contemplative soul acknowledges the Voice of the Spirit in them" (Elisée de la Nativité, *Élie le prophète*, vol. 2, 89). In *Prophet of Fire*, published in 1990, Kilian Healy remarks, "It is well to observe that Carmelites today do not speak of an historical succession of the prophet as was so often emphasized in the past. It is the spiritual relationship with Elijah that matters" (Healy, *Prophet of Fire*, 31–32). Echoing John of St. Samson, Healy asks, "Of what value is an historical succession if the spiritual heritage is weak or dead?"

The Order gained and lost when it laid to rest its long-held belief. Relinquishing belief in a historical Elijan succession allowed it to advance in recovering a history of its origins based on reliable facts. When they relinquished literal connection to a prophet who biblical scholars have shown was already the stuff of legend in the sixth century B.C.E., Carmelites could reposition him in their life. The position he had occupied as historical founder of the Order began to be assigned to the flesh-and-blood ancestors whose conditions of life and habits of mind are still being discovered. Once he was displaced from their record of veridical figures and events, Carmelites were better able to think of Elijah as a sign. The demise of belief in historical succession from him allowed these inquiries to happen more easily.

There was, however, something of worth in the traditional story that Carmelites told themselves for so long that was lost once literal belief in it had faded. Regardless of its historical weakness, the legend of Elijah's inauguration of the Order contributed to Carmelite spirituality. It told Carmelites that their way of life was so valid and strong that Carmelites of the past, present, and future would be able to accomplish it and pass it along. Elisée de la Nativité, commenting in 1956, regrets that a "certain scientism" adopted by instructors of theology led these to reject the scriptural, traditional, and popular typologies "that used to nourish the faith, devotion and contemplation of Christians." Elijah, he says, "is one of those types" (Elisée de la Nativité, *Élie le prophète*, vol. 2, 115). In a 1995 article, Antonio Ruiz Molina also remarks concerning early Carmelite legends of the prophet, "The rediscovery of this Elianic heritage has the possibility of being of great spiritual importance for Carmelites, who, too often in modern times, have thought more about the legends than about the spirit that underlay them" (Ruiz Molina, 38). As a spiritual type and as mythic figure, Elijah of Carmelite legend evokes important states of mind. The old legend that the prophet founded an Order whose members imitated his life promoted confidence that a life of prayer could be shared and passed down, despite vicissitudes.

Zeal and Love

Two Carmelite spiritual motifs appear to have converged in the century before Teresa's lifetime, during a period in which leaders of the Order were struggling to overcome religious decline. An earlier chapter discussed details in the Gospels and other works that show that the early Christians transferred Elijah's messianic works to their master. Christians began saying that Jesus Christ, not Elijah, would accomplish the final healing of hearts and acts of purification and judgment that Jews believed the prophet would perform in the final days. Elijah continued to exist in Christian belief, usually associated with John the Baptist, but the great saving actions that the book of Malachi and Jewish tradition assign him were absorbed into Christian belief about Jesus Christ. Beginning in the fifteenth century, Carmelite writers did something of the reverse when they began to say that Elijah was an excellent imitator of Christ, especially in his zealous spiritual love.

Early Carmelites were of course familiar with incidents of Elijah's zeal described in the Bible. There is no evidence, however, that they sought to reenact the prophet's violence. Bruno Secondin notes Elie Wiesel's conclusion that in 1–2 Kings, Elijah is the "'prophet of rage,' susceptible to any provocation" because he addressed King Ahab harshly, shouted and taunted listeners on Mt. Carmel, and raced to Ahab's court to announce impending rain (cited in Chandler, *A Journey with Elijah*, 154). In 1 Kings 18:40, the prophet told the northern Israelites whose hearts he had won back to Yahweh, "'Seize the prophets of Baal; let not one of them escape.' And they seized them; and Elijah brought them down to the brook Kishon, and killed them there." In their essay included in *Élie le prophète*, Michael Hayek and Hervé of the Incarnation remark that the Syriac and Latin Fathers were struck by the biblical record of Elijah's powerful actions; John Chrysostom, for example, said that the prophet's zeal would have destroyed everything if God hadn't removed him from the world, and Jerome commented that etymologically, the prophet's name meant "the force of God."

Although Elijah's sword appears in the Carmelite shield, and the *Rule* since the thirteenth century has called Carmelites to be spiritual warriors in the service of Christ, there is no evidence that members of the Order understood this to involve anything like Elijah's zealous slaughter of the 350 Baalite prophets. Carmelites such as St. Peter Thomas who have been involved with military action are rare (St. Peter was an envoy and emissary of peace). Unless it has happened in their own martyrdom, Carmelites have not been involved in bloodshed. Elijah's extroverted, at times violent zeal is not what inspired medieval Carmelites.

Instead, early members of the Order sought to imitate Elijah's zeal as it was expressed in traditions of the desert. Like Gregory the Great, Cassian, Jerome, or Augustine, they remembered him for his celibacy and for his great feats of fasting, poverty, and penitence. Traces of their admiration of Elijah's full-heartedness are perhaps visible in the insistence of the early documents that the followers of Elijah truly loved solitude, served God very devoutly, shared life with a very holy intimacy, possessed a strong religious fervor, and believed that the holy succession of their spiritual lives was unbroken. The late fourteenth-century prior general Bernard Oller remarks that after Christ began his mission, ancestors (whom Oller calls Carmelites) "were baptized in Christ, piously confessing the universal faith. Then, persevering in the teaching of the apostles, and enjoying wide public acclaim they became faithful messengers of the evangelical truth and legitimate defenders of the Christian religion" (Oller, *Informatio*, art. 1, pt. 3, cited in Hendriks, *Élie le prophète*, vol. 2, 65). Elijan zeal may have been found in any vigorous expression of religious life. Along these lines, John Grossi wrote around 1415 that Elijah withdrew from living among the sons of the prophets into strict solitude on Mt. Carmel because he wanted to live a life that was "more ascetic" than that practiced in community (Grossi, *Viridarium*, sec. 1, cited in Hendriks, op. cit., 68). There is nothing particularly Christian about these descriptions of vigor. Muslim Sufis, for instance, have also truly loved solitude, have served God very devoutly, have been inflamed by religious fervor, and have been linked to their ancestors and descendants in an unbroken spiritual succession. It remained until the fifteenth century for Carmelites to begin to claim a distinctively Christian spirituality for themselves. In this era, they began to write works that attach Elijan zeal to love of Christ.

Albert's *Rule* encourages Carmelites to "live in allegiance to Jesus Christ and serve him faithfully with a pure heart and a good conscience" and to "put on the breastplate of justice so that you may love the Lord your God with your whole heart and your whole soul and your whole strength, and your neighbors as yourselves." Such single-minded dependence and service are identified in the Hebrew Bible with the word, "*ahav*" (love) and in medieval European descriptions of patronage as "*amicitia*" (friendship). When the hermits on Mt. Carmel and medieval Carmelites loved their Lord with their whole heart and soul in the manner in which their *Rule* and their times had taught them, they served him as vassals dependent on him. They especially served, that is, loved Christ with their praise, their imitation of his life, and their commitment to further his mission of converting hearts to God.

In the fifteenth century, Carmelites began to speak of love in an additional way. Surfacing in works such as John Soreth's 1455 commentary on the *Rule* and *The Institution of the First Monks*, a trend in Carmelite spiritual writing developed that Teresa of Jesus and John of the Cross explored more deeply. It began to be said that the Order's way of life at its core involved a love of Christ that was zealous in its self-abandonment. Where in earlier centuries Carmelites wrote about their life as one of service, after the fifteenth and sixteenth centuries, zeal for the glory of God meant for them as well a passionate, daring pursuit of union with God in love. Elijah's great self-statement "*Zelo zelatus sum por Domino Deo exercituum*," could have mystical meaning for members of the Order in time. The inner daring that motivated the prophet's brash actions in 1–2 Kings and that fired the hearts of Carmelite preachers also underlay the terrifying insistence of John of the Cross that union with God in love requires full, irretrievable loss of the egocentric self. These layers of understanding of Elijah's zeal have deepened the particularly Carmelite sense of what it means to love Christ. John of the Cross's disciple John of Jesus Mary Aravalles praised "an excellent spirit, of high quality, full of perseverance and enough power to do violence to the all-powerfulness of God, tearing from heaven fire and water" to novices learning contemplative prayer

(Aravalles, *Instrucción de novicios*, 142, cited in Elisée de la Nativité, *Élie le prophète*, vol. 2, 104). As Carmelite meditation on mystical love of Christ deepened, Elijan fiery zeal became a sign of Christ's overwhelming love.

John Soreth was one of the earliest to connect zeal with love of Christ. In his commentary on Albert's *Rule*, he drew on the works of his countryman, Bernard of Clairvaux, to explain what Christ's double commandment of love in their *Rule* should mean to Carmelites. Others before had explored the meaning of 1 John 4:19, "We love, because he first loved us" (see also 4:10). Following Bernard, Soreth told Carmelites that they should seek to imitate Christ's self-sacrificial love in order to return that love to Christ: "Blessed Bernard says: Seeing that He first loved us, let us love Him tenderly with all our heart, wisely, with all our soul, and fervently, with all our strength. God loved us tenderly by assuming our flesh; wisely, by avoiding sin; fervently, by enduring death" (cited in Deschamp, "Bl. John Soreth," 213). To the long-standing Carmelite understanding of love as service, Soreth added the beliefs that love came from God and that it should be generous and responsive.

The prior general's explanation of how one could return to Christ the love that the Savior first bestowed invokes Carmelite traditions of Elijah and Bernard's emphasis on the vehement love of God: "May the charity of Christ inflame your zeal," he says to his fifteenth-century readers, "may his knowledge instruct you, and may his constancy fortify you." This zeal was only possible for Carmelites because Christ graciously inflamed human hearts with his spirit. "Let your zeal be fervent, circumspect and invincible, may it not be lukewarm, nor lacking in discretion, nor timid" (Deschamp, op. cit., 214). For the general, zeal was more than boldness of those who truly and piously persevered. If Carmelite zeal was true, it was inseparable from the Holy Spirit, the "charity of Christ." In the century that followed, John of the Cross would dwell on the dynamic of reciprocal love between the soul and God, coming very near to saying that love, the Holy

Spirit, and the transformed will become one during mystical exchanges of gifts between the soul and God. The Spanish mystic emphasizes the fullness of the exchange but does not mention Elijah, the great model of full-heartedness in the Order. Soreth as well uses the word "zeal," so reminiscent of the prophet (given the Order's motto), but does not name him.

The Institution of the First Monks also led Carmelites to expand their understanding of love of Christ to include *caritas*, defined as a reciprocal exchange of generous love. In its story, God in the Father, Holy Spirit, and especially the Son "earnestly wished to urge [Elijah], the first and principal leader of monks, and also to urge us his imitators, to be 'perfect as our heavenly Father is perfect' (Matt. 5:48), 'having above all things charity, which is the bond of perfection' (Col. 3:14)." Success in abandonment to the will of God naturally leads to love, both of Christ and of the Father in Christ's love. Such love is the means and the content of divine union. The *Institution* claims that Elijah was the first to be taught to love in this way and first to accomplish it. Indeed, it says that the Carmelite Order sprang from the prophet's wholehearted love of Christ. The previous chapter of this book discussed this in detail.

Historians of the Christian mystical traditions place the sixteenth-century writings of Teresa of Avila and John of the Cross in a spiritual current that they term "affective mysticism" along with writers such as Bernard of Clairvaux and Jan van Ruusbroeck. Soreth's writing and the *Institution* suggest that affective mysticism among Carmelites predated the two great mystics. Other Carmelites than Soreth also spoke of zealous, Christlike, and unitive love as a Carmelite ideal. In 1576, John Baptist Rossi (Rubeo), superior general of the Order, wrote in a circular letter:

> The original and principal ideal of the inhabitants of Mt.
> Carmel, an ideal which every Carmelite must cultivate and
> pursue, is this. Day and night, they must devote all the
> efforts of which they are capable, to uniting their soul and

> their spirit to God by meditation, contemplation and un-
> interrupted love. And this they must do not only in a ha-
> bitual manner, but also by specific acts. (Cited in Barry,
> 126; see also Valabek, 109)

Wilderink has demonstrated as well that the constitutions of fifteenth-
century French nuns strongly encouraged them to cultivate tender-
ness of heart, a heart inflamed by affection, and fervor whose
inspiration and end were the suffering humanity of Christ (Wilderink,
166–167 et passim).

As zealous Christlike love became a benchmark of Carmelite teaching concerning spiritual life, Elijah's name tended to drop away from
discussions of it. Teresa, for example, often mentions the hermits of
Mt. Carmel and often teaches loving zeal but rarely mentions Elijah
by name. Nevertheless his zeal, recast as sacrificial, Christlike love
that is characteristically Carmelite in its wholeheartedness, remains
at the center of the Order. The 1977 *Constitutions and Directory of
the Discalced Brothers of the Order of the Blessed Virgin Mary of
Mount Carmel* puts it this way: "We esteem the venerable biblical
figures, especially the Prophet Elijah contemplating the living God,
and burning with zeal for His glory. We uphold him as the inspirer of
Carmel and take his prophetic charism as the model of our vocation
to hear the word of God deep within ourselves and to share it with
others" (1). The 1995 *Constitutions of the Ancient Observance* agree:
"From Elijah Carmelites learn to be people of the desert, with heart
undivided, standing before God and entirely dedicated to his service,
uncompromising in the choice to serve God's cause, aflame with a
passionate love for God. Like Elijah, they believe in God and allow
themselves to be led by the Spirit and by the Word that has taken root
in their hearts, in order to bear witness to the divine presence in the
world, allowing God to be truly God in their lives. Finally...with Elijah
they learn to be channels of God's tender love for the poor and humble"
(pt. 1, ch. 2, sec. 26, p. 19).

A New Double Spirit

Carmelites over time have added to the traditions they clustered around Elijah. New legends or beliefs do not appear abruptly, nor do they appear as something completely novel. Instead, a new story or new angle on a figure develops when authoritative traditions are re-shaped to speak to a current situation. If the reshaped legend speaks authentically enough, later generations add it to the tradition-stream. *The Institution of the First Monks* ensured the diffusion of certain thoughts about Elijah that Carmelite works from earlier centuries did not mention. It appears to have forged a link between the eremitical practices long associated with the mythic founder and an explicitly Christ-centered life. Most important to present Carmelite spiritual ways, it said that Elijah loved Christ and loved the Father as Christ had. Always seen as full-hearted and zealous, the prophet thereafter for Carmelites became an exemplar of not only passional but passion-ate, Christlike love. Teresa's writings on poverty that appeared a cen-tury and a half later further connected legends of the founder and his first followers to an increasingly Christ-centered Carmelite spiritual-ity. Elijah had always been poor for Carmelites. Teresa explained how that poverty could, or should, carry her sisters and brothers into the depths of Christ's self-offering.

In this century it seems that Carmelites are now establishing a new Elijan tradition. When recent passages commenting on Elijah's "double spirit" are compared, members of both observances can be seen using the new tradition as a way of accepting a certain duality in their life instead of choosing one way over the other. In a talk given at the Provincial Chapter of the Canadian-American Province of Carmelites in 1987 and published the following year in the *Sword*, Discalced Carmelite Constance FitzGerald spoke about the dual pairs she saw operating in the thinking of her sisters and brothers. She asked, "Who are the 'true' Carmelites? The Hermits or the Mendicants? The Nuns or the Friars? The OCDs or the O. Carms? Those 'real contemplatives' who are enclosed or those who minister/preach/ teach?" (FitzGerald, "Place and Journey" 27). FitzGerald spoke of the tendency she saw in herself and in Carmelites she knew to think of such pairs as competitors or as parts of a question with only one right answer. "Yet all the basic values of Carmelite life—the primacy of Christ, community, communion, prayer, the desert, diversity and lack of rigidity, and the mendicant emphasis—are opposed to the comparisons and dichotomies that separate brothers and sisters from one another" (FitzGerald, op. cit., 28). Different balances that affirmed the traditional pairs of Carmelite life instead of splitting them were needed. FitzGerald argued that the pairs should be lived as double affirmations: place and journey, O. Carms and OCDs, women and men.

The new tradition of Elijah's double spirit seems to be helping Carmelites assess a life shaped by the pairs that FitzGerald names. Earlier Carmelite writers occasionally mention Elijah's double spirit, but, as has happened with other features of his 1–2 Kings narrative or his legendary life among Christians in later centuries, the element lay undeveloped. Only in the twentieth century did storytelling about the double portion of spirit that Elisha requests begin to appear in a fuller and more significant way among Carmelites.

Reference to the double portion appears in one of the demonstrations of Yahweh's power over life and death in the story of Elijah in 1–2 Kings. The prophet's movements when Yahweh was about to take him up to heaven by a whirlwind and his disciple Elisha's stubborn refusal to be separated from him (three times the prophet said, "Tarry here," and three times the disciple refused) suggest that both prophets knew God was about to take Elijah away. Others nearby did, too. "The sons of the prophets who were at Jericho drew near to Elisha and said to him, 'Do you know that today Yahweh will take away your master from over you?' And he answered, 'Yes, I know it; hold your peace'" (2 Kings 2:5). "When they had crossed [the Jordan River], Elijah said to Elisha, 'Ask what I shall do for you, before I am taken from you'" (2:9). Elisha asked for the double portion of an Israelite first son, who assumes the responsibilities of the family after his father's death. The request, however, was not for possessions: "'I pray you, let me inherit a double share of your spirit.' And [Elijah] said, 'You have asked a hard thing; yet, if you see me as I am being taken from you, it shall be so for you; but if you do not see me, it shall not be so'" (2:9–10), and, Scripture says, the disciple saw his master ascend. Muslims, Christians, and Jews have been fascinated by God's decision to remove his prophet from the earth before his natural death. In biblical memory, only Enoch, great for his righteousness, had been taken by God in a similar way. Elijah's ascension in a chariot seemed to be an even greater event than Enoch's end. Enoch "walked with God; and he was not, for God took him" (Gen. 5:24). Elijah, astonishingly, was carried from earth to heaven.

Fewer legends worldwide concern themselves with Elisha, who remained below after Yahweh had taken away the master from over him. Attention to the biblical passage has mostly focused on Elijah's departure, on what had happened to him during the ascent, on where he had gone, on when he would come back, and on what he would do once he returned. Like Muslims, Jews, and other Christians, Carmelites in the earlier centuries of the Order rarely made extended comment on Elisha or on the divine gift of the double portion. In his eighteenth-century history of the Order, García Calahorra mentions the double spirit but has nothing to say about it. In the conclusion to his seventeenth-century *Instruction of Discalced Carmelite Novices*, Aravalles alludes to Elisha's gift as he challenges novices to imitate their legendary founder's great spirit:

> Let us imitate our good Father then, our Leader, the sons
> and disciples of whom we flatter ourselves to be, and let
> us demand that he obtain for us from the Lord an excel-
> lent spirit that is perseverant and powerful enough to do
> violence to the omnipotence of God, tearing down from
> heaven fire and water; a vigorous spirit such as Elijah
> obtained by his prayers. Thus showing ourselves worthy

of our ancestors and of the stock from which we descend, God and the angels will bless us, and men will be able to say of us truthfully: Blessed is he who resembles his own people. Who will be astonished to see a doubly-strong spirit among those for whom the obligation is also double? (Aravalles, 142, cited in Elisée de la Nativité, *Élie le prophète*, vol. 2, 104)

Fired by the novice master's thrilling words, young Discalced Carmelites probably understood that a double spirit was a God-given force of will that would help them live up to the great feats of Elijah.

Present-day Carmelites have understood the double spirit differently. They tend to write that the double spirit belonged to Elijah before God gave it to Elisha and that it was an enrichment of spiritual life, not a special aid helping members of a later generation to achieve the deeds of their elders. Mention of the prophet's double spirit began to increase in Carmelite writing in the first decades of the twentieth century. Titus Brandsma's lecture, "In the Spirit and Strength of Elias," delivered in the 1930s and later published and often read in the volumes, *Carmelite Mysticism* and *The Beauty of Carmel,* encouraged the unfolding of the tradition. Brandsma recalled to his readers Elijah's great deeds on Mt. Carmel. After Elijah won back the hearts of the Israelites and lived as a contemplative with his disciples, his "double spirit passed to Eliseus, and from him to the school of the Prophets, and so down through the ages, the life of Elias has been continued in these hermits who ever sought the inspiration in their great exemplar" (Brandsma, *Carmelite Mysticism*, 12). In Brandsma's hands, the double gift was Elijah's active service of his Lord and his inclination to solitude: "The monastic life must follow the lines indicated by [the prophet's] life and experience. It must reflect his double spirit, the life of activity and the exercise of virtue in individual or social activity" (Brandsma, op. cit., 13).

As if opening doors to successive rooms, Brandsma unfolds the implications of Elijah's double spirit to reveal that it includes additional pairs of Carmelite characteristics: "This double spirit has a

three-fold sense…. The first is the double portion of the inheritance
of the Father, the portion of the first-born son, the portion of privileged children" (Brandsma, op. cit., 13). Carmelites asking for
the double spirit must be willing to receive the same responsibilities
that the firstborn Israelite son receives: "Only he who has the intentions of maintaining the noble traditions of the house may ask for this
privileged portion" (14). The second meaning of the double spirit of
Elijah is "the marvelous mixture of contemplative and active life in
the great prophet" (14). Brandsma, like so many of his sisters and
brothers, understands that Carmelite apostolic work needs to be
grounded in contemplation, which is the "higher and better part of
their vocation" (14).

The third level of the double spirit of Elijah that Brandsma unfolds is the symmetry in Carmelite spiritual life described in the famous passage on two goals from *The Institution of the First Monks*.
The double spirit is "the harmonious union of the human exercise of
virtue and the divine infusion of mystical life; the union of the *via
purgativa* and *illuminativa* with the *via unitiva*. It is in this third sense
that the old *Institution* of the Order has taken the double spirit of
Elias and this double spirit we must ask of Heaven [as Elijah told
Elisha, as well]" (14). By the end of his meditation on the double
spirit, the twentieth-century writer has expanded the biblical motif
into a cluster in which more and more traditional features of Carmelite
life are affirmed in a typically Carmelite way. He encourages readers
to see their Order as complex, multileveled, and possessing options.

It must be noted that Brandsma shifts the dynamic of the pair of
Carmelite goals expressed in his last unfolding of the double spirit. In
The Institution of the First Monks, Christ calls Elijah first to ascetic
perfection. The *Institution* teaches that only after heartfelt chastity,
detachment from the world, silence, and seclusion (which will enable
the hermit to offer a pure heart to God) are acquired will apostolic
service be possible. Brandsma instead calls Carmelites to a simultaneous pursuit, and this is the heart of the new Carmelite appreciation

for the double spirit. Brandsma explains the double spirit not as a sequence, in which mystical life follows on virtue or in which apostolic life follows on mystical life, but as a coinherence. The double spirit for Brandsma is the pursuit of virtue and the mystical life, contemplation and action. This simultaneity is the key to the tradition of the double spirit that has appeared among Carmelites in the twentieth century: "the union of the *via purgativa* and *illuminativa* with the *via unitiva*,...virtue in individual or social activity, founded on a life of prayer, and the life of continual practice of meditation, crowned by active contemplation...active and passive contemplation" (Brandsma, op. cit., 14–15).

For recent Carmelite writers, Elijah's double spirit has meant double commitment, double affirmation, and double actions. Contemplation remains the source from which other features of religious life spring, but their handling of Elisha's inheritance of the double spirit suggests that pairs of engagements can exist in one's life simultaneously. The 1940 *Carmelite Directory of Spiritual Life* detects a double affirmation of charisms in earlier traditions:

> Of old, when our fathers led an eremitical life, each one independent of the others, their life like that of all hermits, was purely contemplative. They lived solely for God. They continued in the eremitical life during the first ages after they had been united into some kind of community and had received the Holy Rule from St. Albert, Patriarch of Jerusalem. For they still lived in widely separated cells, meditating day and night on the law of the Lord and watching in prayer. For this eremitical life was written the Rule of John 44 or the book called *De Institutione primorum monachorum*.... Nevertheless at the call of necessity or charity our fathers did not hesitate sometimes to exercise a fervent apostolate and fervently preach the word of God, as is told in the lives of St. Brocard, St. Cyril of Constantinople and St. Angelus. Moreover, they did not hesitate to undergo death to win souls for God. (Brenninger, *Carmelite Directory*, sec. 52, 94)

Neither contemplative life nor the apostolate cancels the other out. God's call resolves potential tensions. The Carmelite contemplative does not hesitate to go out when called.

The outbreak of World War II in Europe that immediately preceded the publication of the *Carmelite Directory* may have affected its remarks on Elijah's double spirit exercised in "most difficult times":

> Carmelites are convinced that this double spirit has been left to them as an inheritance by St. Elias the Prophet, whom they strive to imitate as their Father and Guide. ...A Carmelite, whether he exercises his zeal indirectly by prayer and penance in the contemplative life, or whether he applies himself directly to the priestly ministry should never lose sight of that apostolic zeal that bears the stamp of the spirit of our Holy Father Elias, who in most difficult times preserved faith in the true God for the chosen people. From the abundance of contemplation zeal for God's glory and the salvation of souls must of necessity spring forth. (Brenninger, op. cit., 94–96)

Where once Elijah and Mary emblematized a strongly preferred call to Carmelites to turn away from the world, entering the enclosed garden of the cell, the Carmelite family, regardless of how each community finds its balances, tends to speak now of a more fully double charism, a double spirit.

Among present-day Carmelites, Elijah is now identified with prayer and prophecy, not prayer alone. The 1977 *Constitutions of the Discalced Brothers* declares: "Similarly we esteem the venerable biblical figures, especially the Prophet Elijah contemplating the living God, and burning with zeal for His glory. We uphold him as the inspirer of Carmel and take his prophetic charism as the model of our vocation to hear the word of God deep within ourselves and to share it with others" (Pt. 1, ch. 1, sec. 1, par. 2). The 1971 *Constitutions* of the Ancient Observance sees Elijah in the same way. Healy writes in the introduction: "His love of solitude and prayer (meditating day and night on the law of God), his intrepid zeal in preaching the word of

God that 'burnt like a torch,' is an example and inspiration for us all" (xxix). In 1977 Baudry calls Elijah's spiritual successors to "find a (difficult but necessary) equilibrium between the 'desert' and the 'city'" (Baudry, "Élie et le Carmel," 168). In 1985, Abiven discusses the variety of ways in which different French Carmelite houses are balancing their charisms. In his opening remarks to the World Congress in 1992, Vice-General of the Carmelites of the Ancient Observance John Steneker reminded listeners that the theme of the gathering was "Carmel: A Family of Contemplatives and Prophets" (Steneker, 5).

As part of its general shift in relation to society at large, Carmel at present is meditating on what it means to take a prophetic role in society. Both branches of the Order are thinking about Elijah as an ancient *ish ha-Elohim* (man of God) as they examine their apostolates. Michael Mulhall summarizes recent responses (especially responses of Carmelites of the Ancient Observance) to the patron-prophet: "Elijah has always been the patron of the contemplative life for us. But what has been brought forward today is a sense of contemplation within a dynamic matrix, the threatened human community…mysticism that is lived out 'in the midst of the people'" (Mulhall, 152). Mulhall makes no mention of the double spirit but presumes a Carmelite double commitment to contemplation and action. In a 1997 essay, John Malley as well places "Elijah the 'man of God' in the midst of the people" (Malley, 279). It certainly seems that to the spirituality of his desert solitude, Carmelites have recently added the biblical emphasis on Elijah's spiritual life as a shaper of society. They now assert his double commitment to God and to the well-being of his whole people.

The options for at least some Carmelites now seem not to be contemplation or action, enclosure or apostolate. Both elements in pairs are affirmed. The search for God's presence is to be carried out in complex, not univocal ways. In the remarks he gave to the General Congregation of the Ancient Observance in Caracas in 1992, the Most Reverend Camilo Maccise, Discalced Superior General, explained that Elijah and Mary, great solitary lovers of God that they were, were also models of service to the people. Both observances now find in Elijah a strong call to Christ's life of prophetic contact with people of all walks of life as well as a call to Christ's solitary communion with his father. This was not always so.

In earlier centuries Carmelites probably understood the relation of their interior prayer to their apostolates differently (and viewed differently the other pairs that FitzGerald and Brandsma mention, such as woman and man, or O. Carm. and OCD). The ancient beliefs, inherited from Scripture and the Fathers, that the city marketplaces were dens of iniquity, and that ordinary human contacts inexorably led individuals into what the Apostle Paul lists as the temptations of the flesh—including dissolution, anger, greed and dissension—held for a very long time in Carmel. Ancient understandings visible, for example, in Augustine's struggle to subordinate the earthly side of his nature to God continued to inform medieval and early modern Carmelite writing. Some authors in these centuries conceive that Carmelites who lived their calls of prayer and the apostolate very often were pulled in two different directions by their own divided nature. This was certainly Nicholas of France's worldview, in a more softened form the worldview of the *Institution of the First Monks* and, to a great extent, that of John Soreth and John of the Cross (although the latter obviously trumps the Neoplatonic dichotomy between body and spirit, world and God, with love, which overcomes division). It is a worldview that was originally inherent in the vow of cloister that Carmelite women began taking when Soreth instituted the Second Order.

Following proponents of the worldview who said that everything is divided into two different, competing planes, many Carmelites for centuries (along with other Christian religious) believed that the spirit by nature would always pull the soul toward God and that the flesh—which was understood to include the body, the emotions, one's children, one's family ties, one's civic or national loyalties, and one's personal fears and hopes—would by nature pull the soul away from God. Influenced by this worldview, there was no need to ask whether Mary or Martha had the better part. The life of Martha, that is, the life of the apostolate, was either lesser in value or more dangerous because it was more liable to the leveling influence of the flesh, in the Pauline sense of that word. In the old Neoplatonic view of the human being, which can be supported from some scriptural passages but not from others, spirit and flesh were expected to struggle against each other until, by heroic effort and the grace of God, the flesh was tamed.

Not all Carmelites believed or taught this (the comparison of John of the Cross' preference for Mary with Teresa's insistence on both Mary and Martha is illuminative), but very many of the writers in earlier centuries who remark on Elijah do so in order to promote the unworldly, unenfleshed spirit. For centuries Elijah was an ideal figure who called Carmelites to become completely spiritual in the seclusion of the desert. This was considered the better part. Until the twentieth century, the spirit/flesh dualism underlay many written Carmelite discussions of the identity of the Order. If the few details we have of the lives of medieval and early modern Carmelites are examined, and not the legends of their writers, a tension seems to emerge. The Order has always attracted those who are genuinely called to contemplation. It very often (paradoxically, in the old worldview) drew those, who, like St. Teresa, simultaneously felt the call to bring other human beings toward God's saving presence. This, according to the Neoplatonic dualism of spirit and flesh, was at least a paradox and at most a conflict between two opposing tendencies, one of which was better. Thus, although in the past Carmelites have devoted themselves sincerely to pastoral and missionary work, they very frequently wrote (and probably spoke) to themselves in ways that suggested that their contemplation, but not their apostolate, was their spiritual life. They acknowledged the pair but valued one element more than the other. Until recently, Elijah has been for Carmelites what he was to the desert fathers, a sign of withdrawal from the world into intimacy with God. His legendary purity of heart was accomplished in Neoplatonic ways: he detached himself from his family, from certain self-preoccupied feelings, and from bodily satisfaction that would imprison and drag him down.

In many ways, societies at large are no longer as binary as they once were. People tend to distrust categorization. The concepts that underlay belief that body and spirit oppose each other are no longer generally accepted. Many living today acknowledge the unstable and rapidly changing human experience that *Gaudium et Spes* pondered in the late sixties. Under the impact of recent events in history, Christian theological inquiry is now being pursued in multiple paradigms, and the paradigms themselves are being critiqued for their political implications. The Carmelite tradition of Elijah's double spirit seems to have appeared during the cultural unsettlement that followed World War II in Europe. Its greatest usefulness may be that it allows members of both observances to affirm their great traditions without constructing them as oppositions in an era when life is nothing if it is not complex.

More inquiry is needed into the matter, but there are also signs that the tradition of the double spirit of Elijah appeared as Carmelite writers began saying more about the Spirit of God. As has been noted, in the first half of the twentieth century, Carmelites began to explain that what connected Carmelites to Elijah was the Holy Spirit, not historical events. If this is so, the emphasis on the Holy Spirit that Adrian Hastings relates was added to the final 1965 draft of *Perfectae Caritatis*—the document of Vatican II that addressed renewal of the religious life—possibly made its contribution to the developing Carmelite tradition of the double spirit. The content of the decree certainly has affected how members of the two observances have understood the double spirit of late. According to *Perfectae Caritatis*, religious life should be a sign of salvation to the world. It should be a deliberately chosen way of fulfilling baptism. It is a ministry to other human beings that can be carried out authentically in more than one way. The spirit of the founder and the community's traditions, although important in renewal, are secondary to the fundamental criterion of religious renewal, which is following Christ.

John Abiven speaks of a new form of religious life that first surfaced in Europe in the sixteenth century, "founded on the Incarnation" that "situates the experience of God in presence within the world" (Abiven, 159–160). Observances such as his own, begun before this definition of apostolic life found its expression in the Society of Jesus and in many missionary ventures, feel authentic tension between pursuit of vocation in the world and pursuit of it "within the domain of silent prayer and ascetic practices" (Abiven, 162). Abiven acknowledges that different Carmelite communities have maintained a variety of balances between these poles of religious life. A son of his tradition and of his century, Abiven affirms the balances.

For Further Reading

Brandsma, Titus, O. Carm. *The Beauty of Carmel*. Dublin: Clonmore & Reynolds, 1955. Or, *Carmelite Mysticism*. 1936; rpt. Faversham, England: Carmelite Press, 1980.

Chandler, Paul, O. Carm., ed. *A Journey with Elijah*. Rome: Institutum Carmelitanum, 1991.

Cicconetti, Carlo, O. Carm. *The Rule of Carmel: An Abridgement*. Translated by G. Paulsback. Edited by P. Hoban. Darien, Ill.: Carmelite Spiritual Center, 1984.

FitzGerald, Constance, OCD. "Place and Journey in Carmel, " *Sword* 58 (1988): 2:27–48.

Giordano, Silvano, OCD, ed. *Carmel in the Holy Land: From Its Beginnings to the Present Day.* Arenzano: Il Mesaggero di Gesù Bambino, 1995.

John of the Cross. *The Collected Works of St. John of the Cross.* Translated by K. Kavanaugh, OCD and O. Rodriguez, OCD. Washington, D.C.: ICS Publications, 1991.

Mulhall, Michael, O. Carm., ed. *Albert's Way: The First North American Congress on the Carmelite Rule.* Rome: Institutum Carmelitanum, 1989.

Paul-Marie of the Cross, OCD. *Carmelite Spirituality in the Teresian Tradition* (1953). Translated by K. Sullivan, RSCJ. Washington, D.C.: ICS Publications, 1997.

Smet, Joachim, O. Carm. *The Carmelites: A History of the Brothers of Our Lady of Mount Carmel.* 5 vols. Darien, Ill.: Carmelite Spiritual Center, 1976–85; vol. 1 revised in 1988.

Sullivan, John, OCD. "Carmelite Spirituality and the New Evangelization," *Spiritual Life* 41 (Summer 1995): 2:67–78.

Teresa of Avila. *The Collected Works of St. Teresa of Avila* (1976). 3 vols. Translated by K. Kavanaugh OCD and O. Rodriguez OCD. Washington, D.C.: ICS Publications, 1985–1987.

Vella, Alexander, O. Carm. "Elijah's Wilderness Journey and the 'Desert Ideal,'" *Carmelus* 37 (1990): 3–37.

Appendix 1
A Note on the Dissemination of *The Institution of the First Monks*

Myths and beliefs endure by consent, not by legislation. New legends appear, and old ones fade in a subtle process. Sociopolitical conditions that encourage particular traditions may be identified at times, but living a richly mythic life is never explained by any material pressure. Traditional beliefs refer most to the inner realms of human existence and to original questions. They are not easily traceable.

This easily admitted, several things may be said about how the Carmelite Order managed to safeguard its beliefs concerning Elijah to later generations. One method Carmelites used was described in the previous chapter. Those seeking change in the Order deliberately linked what they were promoting to earlier traditions. Reformers reached back to the values and stories associated with Elijah and fit them to their own time. Paul-Marie of the Cross has a further thought about how works such as the *Rule*, the *Rubrica prima,* Soreth's commentary, and *The Institution of the First Monks* have been able to convey the ethos of the Order to Carmelites throughout the centuries. In his opinion, certain works are more reminders or manifestations than they are sources of the Carmelite charism. If they are Carmelites, readers catch the scent or feel the melody of what they deeply know when they read these works, says Paul-Marie of the Cross. Thus a story about Elijah, if it is told in a certain way, awakens the memory of something in the Carmelite reader. There are certain things that we know so deeply that we only need to be reminded of them.

Those same influential texts, including the list of works that matter to Elijah's place in the Order—First and Second Kings in the Bible, the *Rule*, the *Rubrica prima,* works by Hildesheim or Cheminot, Soreth's commentary, Bostius's work lauding the Virgin, the works of the Discalced reformers and those of the Touraine reform, and spiritual commentaries by Titus Brandsma and Paul-Marie of the Cross—have also been material bridges spanning gaps in time and space. Passed from hand to hand, copies of constitutions containing the *Rubrica prima* made their way into houses at great distances from each other, each reliably communicating to early Carmelites that Elijah had lived as a contemplative hermit on Mt. Carmel. Able to be copied and small enough to be safeguarded, volumes containing the *Rule* and its commentaries, or containing histories of origin, could bear legends from one era to the next. If a house were secure enough, a book could remain in its library generation after generation. When printing ensured identical copies, a widely distributed work such as *The Institution of the First Monks* had multiple opportunities to cross distance and time to affect Carmelite thought.

The Institution of the First Monks is now claiming the attention of scholars in the Order. As is by now clear, it is one of the greatest written repositories of tradition that the Carmelite family possesses. Whether its influence is visible because later Carmelite writers cite it or whether its content affects Carmelite life more implicitly, it can be safely said that it is superseded as a written deposit of traditions in the two observances only by the Bible, the *Rule*, and the writings of Sts. Teresa of Avila and John of the Cross. As a source of traditions concerning Elijah, it has no peer except Scripture among Carmelites.

Details recently uncovered about the distribution of the work indicate that it made its way into many community libraries, and so it is possible to think that many Carmelites between the fourteenth century and the Enlightenment knew its story of Christ's call to Elijah to achieve the two goals of the spiritual life. The Catalan provincial Felip de Ribot circulated the *Institution* in 1390 in a collection that he claimed contained original historical and legislative documents of the Order. Some, he claimed, were very ancient, dating to the dawn of Christian monastic life. Thomas Netter's request for a copy of it in 1425 suggests that manuscripts of the *Institution* may have spread throughout Europe rather quickly. Some manuscripts of the work have survived. Otger Steggink reported finding a considerable number of them in libraries in France, England, Germany, Italy, and Belgium. Its inclusion in the printed 1507 *Speculum Carmelitanum,* an anthology of Carmelite historical, devotional, and juridical documents, widened its distribution. Other editions of the *Institution* were published by Thomas of Jesus in 1599, by Peter Wasteels in 1643, by John Baptist Lezana in 1643, and by Daniel of the Virgin Mary in his 1680 *Speculum Carmelitanum.* Gabriel Wessels, a pioneer of modern Carmelite historical research, published the first book of the *Institution* in 1914–1916.

Its impact on the Order was also aided by its translation into several languages by the sixteenth century. For example, a bilingual Latin-Spanish manuscript of the *Institution* belonged to the monastery of the Incarnation during Teresa of Avila's years there. More recently, Norman Werling's translation of the first book and part of the second made that portion of the *Institution* available to English readers in this century, as did Brian Deschamp's publication of the first book in *Carmel in the World* in the 1970s.

Carmelites have also absorbed content of the *Institution* from influential writers in the Order who have described its ethos, its storyline involving Elijah and the Order, and its spiritual teachings. Soreth, for example, encouraged readers of his commentary on the *Rule* (which appears to have had some circulation beyond France) to join him in seeking perfection and in obtaining the glory promised by God, the two goals of spiritual life announced by the *Institution,* by "practicing with all our strength the form of life given by Heaven to our Father Elijah." (Deschamp, Exposition, vol. 2, p. 3–4). The Belgian Arnold Bostius repeated the arguments and some of the scenes of the *Institution* in his 1479 *De patronatu et patrocinio Beatissimae Virginis Mariae in dicatum sibi Ordinum*. Additional references to its title or content appear throughout the fifteenth and sixteenth centuries. Several scholars believe that Sts. Teresa and John knew the work. (Otger Steggink recently has made a closely argued case for this in a 1995 issue of the French journal, *Carmel*). Jerónimo Gracián told its story in a sermon delivered to celebrate the founding of a Carmelite church in Brussels in 1611, citing as his source the 1507 *Speculum Carmelitanum*. The Hieronymite Bishop Diego de Yepes retold its narrative to prove that Teresa's reform was only the latest evidence that God intervened from time to time to nurture the spirituality of the Carmelite Order. According to Elisée de la Nativité, traces of the *Institution* may be found in John of St. Samson's commentary on the *Rule* published in 1658.

It is difficult to track the influence of the *Institution* during the eighteenth and nineteenth centuries, an era in which the Carmelites suffered repression and dispersal. In the first decades of the twentieth century, scholars in the Order turned to the *Institution* and to past writers who had been nourished by it. Gabriel Wessel's decision to extract only the first of its seven books for publication has had the effect of suggesting to many that its teachings on detachment, what Wessels calls its *pars ascetica,* are the heart of *The Institution of the First Monks*. This ignores too much the whole work. The statement of the two goals of the spiritual life cited in full in the previous chapter has also been commonly said to be a summary of the *Institution*. In its preface, the 1940 *Carmelite Directory* says to members of the Ancient Observance: "We are…of the opinion that nothing would be of greater advantage in our explanation of the Carmelite life, than following the Rule of John 44, as it is called, and establishing two parts—one, by which we show the way to perfect purity of heart; the other, by which we explain prayer, although we are not unaware that no one can attain purity of heart without prayer" (Brenninger, *Carmelite Directory*, xix–xx). In his 1953 *Carmelite Spirituality in the Teresian Tradition* that became a formation document for Discalced Carmelites, Paul-Marie of the Cross cites the passage in which Christ conveys to Elijah the two goals of the spiritual life to describe the life of the first hermits of Carmel.

Carmelites often mention the *Institution* in print and often cite the two-goals passage from its first book to explain their identity. The reclamation of the whole work as an articulation of Carmelite spirituality was begun only recently. It appears that the time has now come to explore the implications of Wessel's remark that the *Institution* was the principal book of spiritual reading in the Order until the works of the two Discalced saints Teresa and John appeared. Titus Brandsma's assessment of *The Institution of the First Monks* published in the 1930s has also encouraged a present-day return to it as an important articulation of Carmelite spiritual identity. Certainly through its wide dissemination and the respect with which it was held in the fifteenth through the eighteenth centuries, the work has played a significant role in the handing down of the traditions concerning Elijah's attainment of purity of heart and love. The critical edition of the full text, being prepared for publication by Paul Chandler, O. Carm., will make the whole work more accessible for study.

Appendix 2
Trends in Recent Carmelite Study of Elijah

Several trends in scholarship have influenced Carmelite study of Elijah. The very important work that Carmelites such as Gabriel Wessels and Benedict Zimmerman conducted in the first decades of the twentieth century established a tradition of study within the Order from which both branches are still benefiting and which has affected the way Elijah is now studied. Wessels, for example, published facsimile editions of Cosmas de Villiers' eighteenth-century *Bibliotheca Carmelitana* in 1927. He also reprinted and edited Touraine reformer Michael of St. Augustine's *Introduction to the Interior Life*. Joachim Smet remarks that the latter event "opened a window on the Order's spiritual heritage" that allowed present-day Carmelites from both branches to understand that the Order "encompassed something more than scapular devotion" (Smet, *The Carmelites*, vol. 4, 217). Carmelite scholars working in the first decades of the twentieth century were particularly concerned to retrieve the spiritual heritage of the Order. Their labor began a tradition of scholarly recuperation of the past in both observances. Smet's comprehensive history of the Order, published between 1976 and 1985, exemplifes the later success Carmelites have had in prolonging and refining the scholarly initiatives of the first decades.

Carmelite studies of Elijah issued in the last few decades have also been influenced by the recent opening up of possibilities for understanding how old texts may be meaningful to a later age and the dissemination of new knowledge about the culture and history of the Bible. Carmelites have chosen to write about their patron in terms of his biblical contexts. In print, at least, members of the Order have paid much less attention to the Elijah of their own monastic and eremitical tradition. The inclination to comment about the biblical, not the medieval, Elijah appears as early as the *Beauty of Carmel,* produced by Titus Brandsma in the thirties, and as late as the 1989 article "Probing the Elijah Cycle," written by Sister Robin Stratton, who in 1989 used Jungian and literary theory to demonstrate that the biblical prophet is an archetypal hero. Also signaling the trend to consider the biblical Elijah are Alexander Vella's 1990 article, "Elijah's Wilderness Journey and the 'Desert Ideal,'" and the number of biblically based articles on the figure included in *Journey with Elijah,* the volume that resulted from the 1991 consultation on the relation of Elijah to the Order held in Washington, D.C.

Although there are notable exceptions, such as the collection of essays on Elijah published in the two-volume 1956 *Élie le prophète* (issued by *Études Carmelitaines*) and Kilian Healy's commentary on *The Institution of the First Monks* in *Carmel in the World* 21 (1982):3, the disinclination to write about Elijah's well-developed figure in earlier (that is, in medieval and early modern) Carmelite traditions is striking. On first thought, this is no mystery. Scripture is more easily accessible to Carmelites than have been the old documents of the Order, which often remain in Latin, Spanish, Italian, or French, and generally remain archived. Full texts of medieval documents are rarely available for communities to study together. In other words, the recent choice of Carmelite writers to return to the scriptural, not their own traditional, Elijah may have been affected by accessibility. The Bible and tools for its examination are generally available. Early documents of the Order have not been.

Nevertheless, the attention to the biblical more than the medieval Carmelite Elijah probably cannot be explained by such practicalities alone. Carmelite life in community is of course biblical, but it is also profoundly monastic and traditional. Elijah's Carmelite profile may be fainter in the daily influences of liturgy, iconography, sermons, or storytelling than is his biblical profile, but members do have regular contact with features of collective memory about him. The motif of zealous love that received comment in the final chapter of this book is an ordinary part of Carmelite mindset, for example. The fact that both medieval Carmelite and biblical traditions of the prophet still influence present-day community life sharpens the question: Why do those who have chosen to write about Elijah in recent decades prefer to dwell on Scripture, and not, for example, on the *Rubrica prima* or what the early Discalced friars, such as Thomas de Jesus or leaders of Touraine reform, say about him?

Perhaps the trend among biblical scholars of the sixties and seventies to read emotions and mentalities into scriptural scenarios affected the choice (see, for an example, Aharon Weiner, *The Prophet Elijah in the Development of Judaism,* 1978). During those decades scholars studying the anecdotes about Elijah found in 1–2 Kings often speculated about the prophet's inner drama. Biblical scholars came to widely varying conclusions concerning the prophet's spiritual states in episodes such as the encounter at Mt. Horeb. Some detected fear and collapse where others saw a process of divine transformation. Many conjectures about what was going on inside Elijah when he heard the "still, small voice" have been published. It is attractive to ponder the unspoken, interior states of great figures in narratives, but far too often, those who wrote about Elijah in the sixties and seventies did not discipline their thought concerning the biblical Elijah's interior life with the same rigor and clarity of analysis found in the 1969 article "The Figure of Elijah in the Old Testament," by Roland Murphy, O. Carm., in *Ascent,* a journal for Carmelite sisters. The eminent scholar there declined to "read into" the Elijah passages a set of present-day feelings and concerns, even present-day Carmelite feelings and concerns. Instead, he helped the ancient texts about Elijah speak in their own idiom to present-day readers. Fr. Murphy concluded in 1969 that "it is these [biblical] traditions about the prophet—his jealousy before the Lord, his theological clarity, his prophetic courage—that surely belong to the Elijah heritage of Carmelites, and they stand before today's Carmelites as a challenge to renewal" (15). Murphy's thoughts about the prophet's motives were much more solidly grounded in features of the ancient stories themselves than were other remarks being published about Elijah's feelings and thoughts by scholars outside the Order. In 1991, Murphy offered additional expertly grounded biblical commentary to challenge, not reinforce, prior Carmelite generalization about the Order and Elijah in his contribution to *Journey with Elijah.*

Carmelites have been inclined to consider their patron's inner experience in episodes described in the Bible, but on the whole they have not wanted to amplify it with haggadot. In its 1979 report, the Council of Provinces of the Ancient Observance restated obvious scriptural features in its conclusion that "God dominates [Elijah's] whole life and unifies it so completely that the prophet is with God [at all times]. He feels very strongly the necessity to keep himself constantly open to the action of God in continuous contact with the source of revelation" (cited in Mulhall, "Elijah," in *A Journey with Elijah*, 144). Writers in the Order tend not to invent an inner life for the biblical Elijah but to engage in spiritual confrontation with Scripture. They ask not "what must have been going on in the prophet?" but St. Anthony's question, "what needs to happen in our life before we may say—in a biblically Elijan way—'The Lord lives before whom I stand'?" First and Second Kings seem to have been the major locus of Carmelite attention. The Elijah of the book of Malachi and the Gospels, who is the forerunner of the Lord in the last days, has not drawn the attention of Carmelite writers.

Carmelite interest in writing about their patron as a prophet has turned their attention to Scripture and has led it away from earlier Carmelite traditions about Elijah. Beginning with the desert fathers, Christians had seen Elijah as a withdrawn and detached holy man, not as a public one. Where the Bible describes him as a messenger of God sent to recapture the heart of his entire nation, in Christian tradition he became the member of a spiritual elite, who was expected to affect others as an example of repentance, ascetic discipline, and prayer, but not by direct contact. Medieval Carmelites declined to associate Elijah's biblical prophetic activities with their mendicant apostolate, and Carmelites in later centuries have followed suit. *The Institution of the First Monks* strongly associates Elijah with monastic and eremitical life. It handles the pastoral apostolate as a necessary topic to be slipped over rather quickly. With few exceptions, Elijah's prophetic service described in Scripture does not appear in earlier Carmelite storytelling. The Middle Ages did not bequeath a connection between Elijah and pastoral work to the present, nor did the intervening centuries.

Given what has just been said, it is no surprise that members of the Order have more easily turned to the biblical, not the medieval, Elijah for help in meditating on their apostolic charism. Michael Mulhall saw an early example of Carmelite attention to the Old Testament prophet in a 1967 circular letter in the Ancient Observance that declared that the prophet was a contemplative and a prophetic example to the Order. In his entry in *Journey with Elijah*, he concluded that Carmelites have recently seen their patron as "a man whose interior life was so intense that it pushed him into action at the exterior level," which he reports that the General Congregation (of O. Carms.) defined in 1974 as "adequate spiritual direction." Summarizing changes in Carmelite response to Elijah between 1970 and 1990, Mulhall remarks: "Elijah has always been the patron of the contemplative life for us. But what has been brought forward today is a sense of contemplation within a dynamic matrix, the threatened human community...mysticism that is lived out 'in the midst of the people.'"

Discalced Carmelites are thinking about Elijah and his prophetic charism as well. The 1977 *Constitutions and Directory* of Discalced friars declares, "We uphold him as the inspirer of Carmel and take his

266 Elijah, Prophet of Carmel

prophetic charism as the model of our vocation to hear the word of God deep within ourselves and to share it with others." Superior General Camilo Macisse, OCD, relied on the biblical profile of Elijah to explain how the prophet and Mary were models of service to the people in a speech he delivered to the General Congregation of the O. Carm. Order in Caracas in 1992. In an article published the same year, Michael Dodd, OCD, commented on the relation of contemplation and service. Speaking of Discalced men and Secular Order Carmelites, Dodd said, "We are not called to total withdrawal from the society we have left. Friars and Secular Order members live out their vocations in the midst of the world, and that must be different [from the vocation of cloistered Carmelite nuns]. In some ways we are called to look, rather than to the nuns [a positive example of contemplation in seclusion], to that figure in Carmelite tradition who most strongly represents for us the mixture of prayer and action, the prophet Elijah" (Dodd, 102). Once again, it is the biblical, not the medieval, Elijah who draws current interest.

Medieval and early Modern traditions of Elijah did not provide much anchorage for meditation on him as a paragon of "mysticism lived out in the midst of the people," to quote Mulhall again (152). There are, however, possibilities for such meditation in the tradition that arose of Elijah, the Christed lover, who zealously reciprocated the generous love bestowed upon him. The reader is referred to the portion of the previous chapter that discusses this. During the fifteenth and sixteenth centuries, Carmelites found ways to connect Elijah's full-hearted zeal for the Lord God of Hosts with the full-hearted love of the Father that caused Christ to plunge into the preaching mission recorded in the Gospels and to set his face toward Jerusalem. The connections earlier Carmelites found between Elijah and Christ may be able to speak to those pursuing the apostolate.

Nevertheless, older Carmelite traditions of Elijah do seem to be coming back under study. The seminar on the prophet that resulted in the volume, *Journey with Elijah*, included essays by those interested in his biblical profile and those who sought to see him in the light of the earlier patristic and Carmelite tradition. The introduction to the volume reported that participants "concluded that there exists a fruitful tension between the biblical figure of Elijah and the image of him which the first Carmelites draw from their ecclesial and geographic milieu" (9). Other signs of the shift in attention to the Elijah of Christian monastic and Carmelite tradition are the study week on *The Institution of the First Monks* held in 1996 in Washington, D.C., the 1995 volume by Discalced sister Eliane Poirot entitled *Élie Archetype du Moine* (*Elijah, Archetype of the Monk*), and a 1995 issue of the French journal *Carmel*, dedicated to exploring his traditions.

Reconnection with earlier Carmelite views of Elijah should yield rich results. There is much potentially to be seen in the passages in earlier works that speak of relations among Elijah, the Virgin Mary, and Christ. Present-day Carmelite study of the Order's earlier views of Elijah may consider the medieval philosophy and theology underlying attitudes toward the relation of the body and soul that are expressed in old eremitical traditions. Knowing these should begin to open up what medieval Carmelite writers meant when they praised Elijah's eremitical virtues. Probing older theologies and worldviews underlying old traditions, present-day Carmelites may discover that, in some cases, they retain medieval views, but in other cases, their mindset differs from the one at work in the old traditions. Examining old mindsets would contribute to thought about how best to dwell in the present.

Bibliography

Abiven, Jean, OCD. "Vie religieuse apostolique et tradition Carmélitaine." *Carmel* 38, no. 2 (1985): 158–164.

Ackerman, Jane. "Stories of Elijah and Medieval Carmelite Identity."
History of Religions 35, no. 2 (1995): 124–147.

Ahlgren, Gillian T. W. *Teresa of Avila and the Politics of Sanctity*.
Ithaca, N.Y.: Cornell University Press, 1996.

Alberto de la Virgen del Carmen, OCD. "Doctrina espiritual del 'Libro
de la institución de los primeros monjes.'" *Revista de espiritualidad*
19, no. 77 (1960): 427–446.

Allchin, A. M. *Solitude and Communion: Papers on the Hermit Life*.
Reprint, Fairacres, England: SLG, 1983.

Alvarez, Tomás, OCD; A. Fortes; F. Antolín; S. Giordano; S-M.
Morgain; and B. Velasco, O. Carm. *Constituciones de las
carmelitas descalzas, 1562–1607*. Rome: Teresianum, 1995.

Appleby, Joyce, Lynn Hunt, and Margaret Jacob. *Telling the Truth
About History*. New York: Norton, 1994.

Arenal, Electa and Stacey Schlau. "'Leyendo yo y escribiendo ella': The Convent as Intellectual Community." *Journal of Hispanic Philology* 13, no. 3 (Spring 1989): 214–229.

Athanasius. *The Life of Antony and the Letter to Marcellinus.* Classics of Western Spirituality. Translated by Robert C. Gregg. New York: Paulist, 1980.

Barnestone, Willis, ed. *The Other Bible.* New York: Harper Collins, 1984.

Barry, Gabriel, OCD. *Historical Notes on the Carmelite Order.* Darlington, England, 1980.

Baudry, Joseph, OCD. "Elie et le Carmel." *Carmel* no. 2 (1977): 154–168.

———. "L'Imitation d'Élie au *Livre premier de l'Institution des premiers moines." Carmel* 2, no. 76 (1995): 39–56.

———. "Solitude et fraternité aux origines du Carmel." *Carmel* 5 (March 1971): 84–106.

———. "Thomas de Jésus, OCD, et l'origine des Saints Déserts." *Carmel* 78, no. 4 (1995): 31–44.

Boaga, Emanuele, O. Carm. *Nello spirito e nella virtù di Elia: Antologia de documenti e sussidi.* Rome: Comissione Internazionale Carmelitana per lo Studio del Carisma e Spiritualità, 1990.

———. "La statua si S. Elia Profeta nella Basilica Vaticana." *Carmelus* 25, no. 2 (1978): 353–379.

Boyce, James J., O. Carm. "Cantica Carmelitana: The Chants of the Carmelite Office." Ph.D. diss., New York University, 1984.

———. "The Feasts of Saints Elijah and Elisha in the Carmelite Rite: A Liturgico-Musical Study." In *Master of the Sacred Page: Essays and Articles in Honor of Roland E. Murphy, O. Carm.*, edited by Keith Egan, T.O. Carm; Craig Morrison, O. Carm.; and Michael Wastag, O. Carm., 155–189. Washington, D.C.: The Carmelite Institute, 1997.

———. "The Medieval Carmelite Office Tradition." *Acta Musicologica* 62, no. 2/3 (May 1990): 119–151.

Brandsma, Titus, O. Carm. *The Beauty of Carmel*. Dublin: Clonmore & Reynolds, 1955.

———. *Carmelite Mysticism*. 1936. Reprint, Faversham, England: Carmelite Press, 1980.

Brenninger, John, O. Carm. *The Carmelite Directory of the Spiritual Life*, 1940. English translation, Chicago: The Carmelite Press, 1951.

Bright, John. *A History of Israel*. 3d ed. Philadelphia: Westminster, 1981.

Brinner, William M., trans. *The History of Al Tabari*. Vol. 3 of *The Children of Israel*. Albany, N.Y.: SUNY, 1991.

———. "Prophets and Prophecy in the Islamic and Jewish Traditions." In *Studies in Islamic and Judaic Traditions II*, edited by William Brinner and Stephen Ricks. Atlanta, Ga.: Scholars, 1989.

Brown, Peter. *The Body and Society: Men, Women and Sexual Re-nunciation in Early Christianity*. New York: Columbia University Press, 1988.

———. "The Rise and Function of the Holy Man in Late Antiquity." *Journal of Roman Studies* 61 (1971): 80–101.

———. *The Making of Late Antiquity*. Cambridge, Ma.: Harvard University Press, 1978.

———. *Society and the Holy in Late Antiquity*. Berkeley, Calif.: University of California Press, 1982.

Bynum, Carolyn Walker. *The Resurrection of the Body in Western Christianity, 200–1336*. New York: Columbia University Press, 1995.

Calciuri, Nicola. *Vita Fratrum del Sancto Monte Carmelo del P. Nicola Calciuri, O.C. (+1466)*. In *Ephemerides Carmeliticae*, edited by Graziano di S. Teresa, OCD, 241–531. Rome: Teresianum, 1955.

Carlson, R. A. "Élie à l'Horeb." *Vetus Testamentum* 19 (1969): 416–439.

Carmel: Its History, Spirit and Saints. Compiled from approved sources by the Discalced Carmelites of Boston and Santa Clara. New York: P. J. Kenedy & Sons, 1927.

Carmelite Constitutions, 1995. Rome: Carmelite Communications, 1996.

Carroll, R. P. "The Elijah-Elisha Sagas: Some Remarks on Prophetic Succession." *Vetus Testamentum* 19 (1969): 400–415.

Cassian, John. *Conferences*. Classics of Western Spirituality. Translated by Colm Luibheid. New York: Paulist, 1985.

————. *The Institutes*. Ancient Christian Writers. Translated and annotated by Boniface Ramsey, O.P. New York: Newman, 2000.

Chandler, Paul, O. Carm., ed. *A Journey with Elijah*. Rome: Institutum Carmelitanum, 1991. [Given the importance of this publication, all of its contributions are listed]:

Benjamin, Don C., O. Carm., "The Elijah Stories," 39–54.

Boaga, Emaneuele, O. Carm., "Elia alle origini e nelle prime generazioni dell'Ordine Carmelitano," 85–110.

Chandler, Paul, O. Carm., *"Princeps et examplar Carmelitarum:* The Prophet Elijah in the *Liber de institutione primorum monachorum,* 111–134.

Mulhall, Michael, O. Carm., "Elijah the Portrait of a Contemplative Become Liberator: A Survey of Order Documents on Elijah, 1960–1990," 135–152.

Mesters, Carlos, O. Carm., "A caminhada do profeta Elias," 163–182.

Murphy, Roland, O. Carm., "The Biblical Elijah: A Holistic Perspective," 21–28.

Pidyarto, Henricus, O. Carm., "Elijah in the New Testament," 55–64.

Secondin, Bruno, O. Carm., "Interpretare il profeta Elia, per ispirare la vita," 153–162.

Vella, Alexander, O. Carm., "Elijah, Man of the Desert," 29–38.

Waaijman, Kees, O. Carm., "The Elijah-Stories in the Jewish Tradition," 65–84.

Cicconetti, Carlo, O. Carm. *The Rule of Carmel: An Abridgement.* Translated by Gabriel Pausback. Edited by Paul Hoban. Darien, Ill.: Carmelite Spiritual Center, 1984.

Clark, J. P. H. "A Defense of the Carmelite Order by John Hornby, O. Carm., A.D. 1374." *Carmelus* 32, no. 1 (1985): 73–106.

Cogan, Mordechai and Hayim Tadmore. *II Kings.* In *The Anchor Bible* 11. New York: Doubleday, 1988.

Constitutions and Directory: Discalced Brothers of the Orders of the Blessed Virgin Mary of Mount Carmel. Holy Hill, Wis.: Provincial Office, 1977.

Coote, Robert, ed. *Elijah and Elisha in Socioliterary Perspective.* SBL Semeia Studies. Atlanta, Ga.: Scholars, 1992.

Corbin, Henry. *Creative Imagination in the Sufism of Ibn 'Arabi.* Translated by Ralph Manheim. Bollingen Series 91. Princeton, N.J.: Princeton University Press, 1969.

Craghan, John, C.SS.R. *Love and Thunder: A Spirituality of the Old Testament.* Collegeville, Minn.: The Liturgical Press, 1983.

Cyr, Terrence, O. Carm. "Carmelites and the Charism of Prophecy." *Carmelite Digest* 7, no. 3 (Summer 1992): 27–39.

Daniel of the Virgin Mary, O. Carm. *Phoenix Seculorum Gratiae, et Naturae Miraculum S. Elias Propheta, Religiosae Monasticae Conversationis Princeps, Patriarcha Ordinis Carmelitani.* Frankfurt: Joannem Baptistam Schönvvetterum, 1670.

Dan, Joseph, ed. *The Early Kabbalah.* Classics of Western Spirituality. New York: Paulist, 1986.

Deschamp, Brian, O. Carm. "Bl. John Soreth *Commentary on the Carmelite Rule.*" *Carmel in the World* 10, no. 3 (1971): 209–215 and 11, no. 1 (1972): 76–81 (Deschamp's translation of passages from Soreth's *Commentary.*)

———. *The Expositio Sacratissimae Religionis Fratrum of Blessed John Soreth (+1471) on the Carmelite Rule.* Ph.D. diss., Katholieke Universiteit te Leuven, 1973.

———. "The Institution of the First Monks." The Text of Book 1 of the *Institution. Carmel in the World* 13 (1974): 69–75, 152–161, 245–260.

Diego de Yepes. *Vida de Santa Teresa de Jesús.* Paris: Garnier, 1847.

Documenta primigenia: Volumen I, 1560–1577. Rome: Teresianum, 1973.

Dodd, Michael, OCD. "In the Heart of the World, I Will Be Hope: The Discalced Carmelite Charism Today." *Spiritual Life* 38, no. 2 (Summer 1992): 99–106.

Douglas, Mary. *How Institutions Think.* Syracuse, N.Y.: Syracuse University Press, 1986.

Dupré, Louis. "The Christian Experience of Mystical Union." *Journal of Religion* 69, no. 1 (1989): 1–13.

Egan, Keith J., T.O. Carm. "Carmelite Spirituality." In *The New Dictionary of Catholic Spirituality*, edited by Michael Downey. Collegeville, Minn.: The Liturgical Press, 1993.

———. "Medieval Carmelite Houses, England and Wales." *Carmelus* 16 (1969): 142–226.

———. "The Spirituality of the Carmelites." In *Christian Spirituality II: High Middle Ages and Reformation*, edited by Jill Raitt, 50–62. New York: Crossroad, 1989.

Efrén de la Madre de Dios, OCD. "El ideal de Santa Teresa en la fundación de San José." *Carmelus* 10 (1963): 206–230.

Efrén de la Madre de Dios, OCD, and Otger Steggink, O. Carm. *Santa Teresa y su tiempo*. 3 vols. Salamanca: Biblioteca de la Caja de Ahorros, 1982.

Élie le prophète. 2 vols. *Études Carmélitaines*. Paris: Desclée de Brouwer, 1956. [Given the importance of this publication, all of its contributions are listed]:

Volume 1:

Bardy, Gustave, "Le souvenir d'Élie chez les Pères Grecs," 131–158.

Boismard, Émile, OP, "Élie dans le Nouveau Testament," 116–130.

Botte, Bernard, OSB, "Le culte du prophète Élie dans l'Église chrétienne," 208–218.

Hayek, Michel, "Élie dans la tradition syriaque," 159–178.

Hervé de l'Incarnation, OCD, "Élie chez les Pères Latins," 179–207.

Paul-Marie de la Croix, OCD, "Hauts Lieux élianiques," 9–52.

Spasky, Théodosy, "Le culte du prophète Élie et sa figure dans la tradition orientale," 219–232.

Steinmann, Jean, "La geste d'Élie dans l'Ancien Testament," 93–115.

Volume 2:

Bruno de Jésus-Marie, OCD, with the collaboration of Charles Badouin, Carl-Gustav Jung and René Laforgue, "Puissance de l'Archetype," 11–33.

Dorothée de Saint-René, "'In spiritu et virtute Eliae,'" 190–198.

Élisée de la Nativité, OCD, "Les Carmes imitateurs d'Élie," 82–116.

Hendriks, Rudolf, O. Carm., "La Succession héréditaire," 34–81.

Kallenberg, Pascal, O. Carm., "Le culte liturgique d'Élie dans l'Ordre du Carmel," 134–145.

Lambert, Pierre, "Hérésies élianiques," 293–300.

Louis-Marie du Christ, OCD, "La Succession élianique devant la Critique," 117–133.

Massignon, Louis, "Élie et son rôle transhistorique, *Khadiriya*, en Islam," 269–289.

Michel-Marie de la Croix, OCD, "Un Prophétisme dans l'Église," 151–189.

Moubarac, Youakim, "Le prophète Élie dans le Coran," 256–268.

Stiassny, Marie-Joseph, NDS, "Le Prophète Élie dans le Judaïsme," 199–255.

Farrington, Andrew E., O. Carm. *St. Elias and the Carmelites*. Dublin: James Duffy, 1890.

Ferrand, Daniel, OCD. "Le culte liturgique d'Élie dans les deux traditions carmélitaines." *Carmel* 76, no. 2 (1995): 101–109.

Filippo della Trinità, OCD. "Teresa di Gesù, Carmelitana." *Rivista di vita spirituale* 17 (1963): 405–419.

"Final Document: Carmel: A Place and a Journey into the Third Millenium" (of the General Chapter 5–28, September 1995). *Analecta Ordinis Carmelitarum* 46, no. 1–2 (Jan–Dec. 1995): 236–251.

Fishbane, Michael. "Biblical Prophecy as a Religious Phenomenon." In *Jewish Spirituality from the Bible through the Middle Ages*, edited by Arthur Green, 62–81. New York: Crossroad, 1988.

FitzGerald, Constance, OCD. "Impasse and the Dark Night." In *Women's Spirituality: Resources for Christian Development,* edited by Joan Wolski Conn. New York: Paulist, 1986.

———. "Place and Journey in Carmel." *Sword* 48, no. 2 (1988): 27–48.

Fitzgerald-Lombard, Patrick, O. Carm. *Carmel in Britain: Essays on the Medieval Carmelite Province.* Vol. 2: Writings and Theology. Rome: Institutum Carmelitanum, 1992.

Flannery, Austin, OP, gen. ed. *Vatican Council II: The Conciliar and Post Conciliar Documents.* Vol. 1. Revised edition, Northport, N.Y.: Costello, 1987.

Fortunato de Jesús, OCD, and Bede of the Holy Trinity, OCD, eds. *Constitutiones Carmelitarum Discalceatorum, 1567–1600.* Rome: Teresianum, 1968.

Francisco de Santa María, OCD. *Historia profética de la órden de nuestra Señora del Cármen.* Madrid: Díaz de la Carrera, 1641.

François de Sainte-Marie. "Saint Elias in Patristic Literature." *Sword* 11, no. 3 (August 1947): 224–228.

Frankfurter, David. *Elijah in Upper Egypt: The Apocalypse of Elijah and Early Egyptian Christianity.* Minneapolis, Minn.: Fortress, 1993.

Friedman, Elias, OCD. *The Latin Hermits of Mount Carmel: A Study in Carmelite Origins.* Rome: Teresianum, 1979.

García Calahorra, Manuel, O. Carm. *Breve compendio del orígen y antiguedad de la sagrada religión del Carmen.* Madrid: Manuel Martín, 1766.

García Oro, J., OFM. "La reforma del carmelo castellano en la etapa pretridentina." *Carmelus* 29, no. 1 (1982): 130–148.

Garrido, Pablo María, O. Carm. *El hogar espiritual de Santa Teresa: En torno al estado del Carmelo español en tiempos de la Santa.* Rome: Institutum Carmelitanum, 1983.

———. *La "reforma" teresiana y la órden del Cármen: ¿Ruptura o complemento?* Rome: Institutum Carmelitanum, 1991.

Gellrich, Jesse M. *The Idea of the Book in the Middle Ages: Language Theory, Mythology and Fiction.* Ithaca, N.Y.: Cornell University Press, 1985.

Ginzberg, Louis. *The Legends of the Jews.* 7 vols. Philadelphia: JPS, 1938–1942.

Giordano, Silvano, OCD, ed. *Carmel in the Holy Land: From Its Beginnings to the Present Day.* Arenzano: Il Mesaggero di Gesù Bambino, 1995.

Gracián, Jeronimo, OCD. *Obras del P. Jeronimo Gracian de la Madre de Dios.* Vol. 2. Edited by Silverio de Santa Teresa, OCD. Burgos: Tipografia de "El Monte Carmelo," 1933.

Gray, John. *I and II Kings.* Philadelphia: SCM, 1963.

Gruenwald, Ithamar. *Apocalyptic and Merkavah Mysticism*. Leiden: Brill, 1980.

Gutmann, Joseph. *Hebrew Manuscript Painting*. New York: George Braziller, 1978.

Hastings, Adrian. *A Concise Guide to the Documents of the Second Vatican Council*. Vol. 2. London: Darton, Longman and Todd, 1969.

Healy, Kilian J., O. Carm. "Elijah Spiritual Father of Carmel—IV." *Carmel in the World* 21, no. 2 (1982): 85–102.

———. *Methods of Prayer in the Directory of the Carmelite Reform of Touraine*. Rome: Institutum Carmelitanum, 1956.

———. *Prophet of Fire*. Rome: Carmel in the World Paperbacks, 1990.

Hendriks, Rudolf, O. Carm. "Elias in the Carmelite Tradition." *Carmel in the World* 4, no. 1 (1964): 87–100.

Heschel, Abraham. *The Prophets*. 2 vols. New York: Harper, 1962.

Idel, Moshe. *Kabbalah: New Perspectives*. New Haven, Conn.: Yale University Press, 1988.

Jean de Saint-Samson (John of St. Samson). O. Carm. *Prayer, Aspiration and Contemplation*. Translated and edited by Venard Poslusney, O. Carm., New York: Alba House, 1994.

John of the Cross. *The Collected Works of St. John of the Cross*. Translated by Kieran Kavanaugh, OCD, and Otilio Rodriguez, OCD. Washington, D.C.: ICS Publications, 1991.

Jotishky, Andrew. "Gerard of Nazareth, John Bale and the Origins of the Carmelite Order." *Journal of Ecclesiastical History* 46, no. 2 (April 1995): 214–236.

Justin Martyr. *Dialogue with Trypho, a Jew*. In *The Apostolic Fathers with Justin Martyr and Irenaeus*. Vol. 1 of *The Ante-Nicene Fathers*. New York: Charles Scribner's Sons, 1926.

King, Archdale A. *Liturgies of the Religious Orders*. London: Longmans, 1954.

Knowles, David. *The Religious Orders in England*. 2 vols. Cambridge: Cambridge University Press, 1961.

Lawrence, Clifford H. *Medieval Monasticism: Forms of Religious Life in Western Europe in the Middle Ages*. London: Longman, 1984.

Le Goff, Jacques, ed. *Medieval Callings*. Translated by Lydia G. Cochrane. Chicago: Chicago University Press, 1990.

Leclercq, Jean, OSB. *La Vie Parfaite: Points de Vue sur l'Essence de l'État Religieux*. Turnhout, Belgium: Brepols, 1948.

Leyser, Henrietta. *The New Eremitical Movements in Western Europe, 1000–1150*. New York: St. Martin's, 1984.

Longchamp, Max Huot de. "Élie a l'Horeb, ou l'expérience mystique." *Carmel* 76, no. 2 (1995): 91–100.

Maccise, Camilo, OCD. "The Contribution of the Carmelite Charism to the Work of the New Evangelization." In *Evangelization for Carmelites Today*. Melbourne, Australia: Carmelite Communications, 1992.

Malley, John, O. Carm. "The Emphasis on the Word of God in Carmel in Recent Years." In *Master of the Sacred Page: Essays and Articles in Honor of Roland E. Murphy, O. Carm.* Edited by Keith Egan, T.O. Carm. and Craig Morrison, O. Carm. Washington, D.C.: The Carmelite Institute, 1997.

Matías del Niño Jesús, OCD. "Manuscritos carmelitanos en la B.N. de Madrid." *Ephemerides Carmeliticae* 8 (1957): 187–255.

McGinn, Bernard, trans. and ed. *Apocalyptic Spirituality: Treatises and Letters of Lactantius, Adso of Montier-en-Der, Joachim of Fiore, the Franciscan Spirituals, Savonarola.* Classics of Western Spirituality. New York: Paulist, 1979.

———. *Visions of the End: Apocalyptic Traditions in the Middle Ages.* New York: Columbia University Press, 1979.

———. *The Foundations of Mysticism: Origins to the Fifth Century.* New York: Crossroad, 1991.

———. *The Growth of Mysticism: Gregory the Great through the Twelfth Century.* New York: Crossroad, 1994.

McMahon, Patrick, O. Carm. "Pater et dux: Elijah in Medieval Mythology." In *Master of the Sacred Page: Essays and Articles in Honor of Roland E. Murphy, O. Carm.* Edited by Keith Egan, T.O. Carm. and Craig Morrison, O. Carm. Washington, D.C.: The Carmelite Institute, 1997.

Meisel, Anthony C. and M. L. del Mastro, trans. *The Rule of St. Benedict.* New York: Image, 1975.

Melka, John, OCD. "Interview with a Hermit." *Carmelite Digest* 1, no. 4 (1986): 58–62.

Michel de Saint Augustine (Michael of St. Augustine), O. Carm. *Introducción a la vida interna y práctica fruitiva de la vida mística*, 17th century, edited by Gabriel Wessels and translated by E. M. Bañon Torres. Spanish translation, Barcelona: José Vilamala, 1936.

Moses of León, R. *Zohar: The Book of Splendor.* Edited by Gershom Scholem. New York: Schoken, 1949.

Mulhall, Michael, O. Carm., ed. *Albert's Way: The First North American Congress on the Carmelite Rule*. Rome: Institutum Carmelitanum, 1989.

Murphy, Roland, O. Carm. "Élie (le prophète)." In *Dictionnaires de Spiritualité*. Vol. 4, cols. 564–572. Paris: Beauchesne, 1960.

———. "The Figure of Elijah in the Old Testament." *Ascent* 1 (1969): 8–15.

———. "Israel and Moab in the Ninth Century B.C." *Catholic Biblical Quarterly* 15 (1953): 409–417.

Neusner, Jacob, trans. *The Talmud of Babylonia: An American Translation. I: Tractate Berakhot,* Brown Judaic Studies 79. Chico, Calif.: Scholars, 1984.

Nicholas of France. "*The Flaming Arrow (Ignea Sagitta)* by Nicholas, Prior General of the Carmelite Order, 1266–1271." Translated by Bede Edwards, OCD. *The Sword* 39, no. 2 (June 1979): 4–52.

Pantin, William A. "Two Treatises of Uthred of Boldon on the Monastic Life." In *Studies in Medieval History Presented to Frederick Maurice Powicke,* edited by Richard Hunt, William Pantin, and R. Southern, 363–385. Reprint, Westport, Conn.: Greenwood, 1979.

Patai, Raphael. *The Messiah Texts*. Detroit, Mich.: Wayne State University Press, 1979.

Paul-Marie de la Croix (Paul-Marie of the Cross), OCD. *Carmelite Spirituality in the Teresian Tradition*, 1953. Translated by Kathryn Sullivan, RSCJ. Washington, D.C.: ICS Publications, 1997.

Peters, Cosmas. "Élie et l'Ideal Monastique." In *Dictionnaire de Spiritualité*. Vol. 4, pt. 1, cols. 567–571. Paris: Beauchesne, 1960.

Proper Offices of the Saints Granted to the Barefooted Carmelites. Translated from the Latin for the Carmelite convent in Boston. Boston: John Cashman, 1896.

Querol Sanz, José Manuel. "Helyas, Elías y los cisnes: notas sobre la transmisión de una materia poética." *Carmelus* 44, no. 1 (1997): 105–124.

Rahman, Fazlur. *Prophecy in Islam: Philosophy and Orthodoxy*. Chicago: Chicago University Press, 1958.

Rappoport, Angelo. *Myth and Legend in Ancient Israel*. Vol. 3. New York: Ktav, 1966.

Regla primitiva y constituciones de los religiosos descalzos de la orden de nuestra madre Santísima la Bienaventurada Virgen María del Monte Carmelo, de la primitiva observancia. Madrid: Joseph Doblado, 1788.

Roefs, Victor, O. Carm. "The Earliest Evidence Concerning the Carmelite Order." *Sword* 19 (1956): 224–245.

Rose, André. "Élie dans la tradition patristique et liturgique de l'Église." *Carmel* 76, no. 2 (1995): 57–69.

Rossi, John Baptist. *Constitutiones fratrum ordinis beatissimae Dei genitricis Mariae de Monte Carmeli.* Rome: Franciscum Zannettum, 1586.

Rushe, James P. *A Second Thebaid: Being a Popular Account of the Ancient Monasteries of Ireland.* Dublin, London, and New York: Sealy, Bryers and Walker, 1905.

Ruiz Molina, Federico, O. Carm. "La Mémoire du Prophète Élie chez les premiers Carmes." *Carmel* 2, no. 76 (1995): 17–38.

Saggi, Ludovico, O. Carm. *Los orígenes de los carmelitas descalzos (1567–1593): Historia e historiografía.* Seville, 1990.

———. *Saints of Carmel.* Translated by Gabriel Pausback, O. Carm. Rome: Carmelite Institute, 1972.

———. "Santa Teresa 'Carmelitana.'" *Carmelus* 18, no. 1 (1971): 42–63.

Sawyer, John. *Prophecy and the Biblical Prophets.* Revised, Oxford: Oxford University Press, 1993.

Schimmel, Annemarie. *Mystical Dimensions of Islam.* Chapel Hill, N.C.: North Carolina University Press, 1986.

Scholem, Gershom. *Kabbalah.* New York: New American Library, 1974.

———. *Origins of the Kabbalah.* Translated by Allan Arkush. Princeton, N.J.: Princeton, 1990.

Smet, Joachim, O. Carm. *The Carmelites: A History of the Brothers of Our Lady of Mount Carmel.* 5 vols. Darien, Ill.: Carmelite Spiritual Center, 1976–1985; vol. 1, revised 1988.

————. *Cloistered Carmel: A Brief History of the Carmelite Nuns.* Rome: Institutum Carmelitanum, 1986.

Smith, Jane Idelman and Yvonne Yazbeck Haddad. *The Islamic Understanding of Death and Resurrection.* Albany, N.Y.: SUNY, 1981.

Staring, Adrianus, O. Carm., ed. *Medieval Carmelite Heritage: Early Reflections on the Nature of the Order.* Rome: Institutum Carmelitanum, 1989.

Steggink, Otger, O. Carm. "Élie dans la tradition du Carmel thérésien primitif." *Carmel* 76, no. 2 (1995): 71–89.

————. "L'enracinement de Saint Jean de la Croix dans le tronc de l'Ordre Carmélitaine." In *Actualité de Saint Jean de la Croix.* Brussels, 1970.

————, ed. *Juan de la Cruz, espíritu de llama: Estudios con la ocasión del cuarto centenario de su muerte, 1591–1991.* Rome: Institutum Carmelitanum, 1991.

————. *La reforma del Carmelo español: La visita canónica del general Rubeo y su encuentro con Santa Teresa, 1566–1567.* 2d ed. Avila: Institución 'Gran Duque de Alba,' 1993.

Stefanotti, Robert, O. Carm. *The Phoenix of Rennes: The Life and Poetry of John of St. Samson, 1571–1636.* New York: Peter Lang, 1994.

Steneker, John, O. Carm. "Welcome to the Congress." *Carmel in the World* 31, no. 1–2 (1992): 4–6.

Stock, Brian. *Listening for the Text: On the Uses of the Past*. Baltimore, Md.: Johns Hopkins, 1990.

Stratton, Robin, OCD. "Probing the Elijah Cycle." *Sword* 49, no. 1 (April 1989): 29–34.

Sullivan, John, OCD. "Carmelite Spirituality and the New Evangelization." *Spiritual Life* 41, no. 2 (Summer 1995): 67–78.

Teresa de Jesús (Teresa of Avila). *The Collected Works of St. Teresa of Avila*, 1976. 3 vols. Translated by Kieran Kavanaugh, OCD, and Otilio Rodriguez, OCD. Washington, D.C.: ICS Publications, 1985–1987.

Torrey, Charles C. *The Lives of the Prophets: Greek Text and Translation*. Journal of Biblical Literature Monograph Series 1. Philadelphia: SBL, 1946.

Valabek, Redemptus Maria, O. Carm. "Prayer Among The Carmelites of the Ancient Observance." *Carmelus* 28, no. 1 (1981): 68–143.

Velasco Bayón, Balbino, O. Carm. *El Carmelo español 1260–1980*. Vol. 4 of *Los Carmelitas: Historia de la órden del Cármen*. Madrid: Biblioteca de Autores Cristianos, 1993.

Vella, Alexander, O. Carm. "Elijah's Wilderness Journey and the 'Desert Ideal'" *Carmelus* 37, no. 1 (1990): 3–37.

Vicaire, Marie-Humbert, OP. *L'Imitation des Apotres: Moines, Chanoines, Mendiants, IVe–XIIIe Siècles*. Paris: Éditions du Cerf, 1963.

Voragine, Jacobus de. *The Golden Legend: Readings on the Saints.* Translated by William G. Ryan. 2 vols. Princeton, N.J.: Princeton University Press, 1993.

Waaijman, Kees, O. Carm. and Hein Blommestijn, O. Carm. "The Core of the Carmelite Identity According to the Rubrica Prima." In *The Carmelite Family: Documents of the XIII Council of Provinces of the Order of the Brothers of the Blessed Virgin Mary of Mt. Carmel.* Edited by the Carmelites of Nantes, France. Melbourne, Australia: Carmelite Communications, 1994.

Wanroij, Marcus van, O. Carm. "The Prophet Elijah Example of Solitary and Contemplative Life?" *Carmelus* 16, no. 2 (1969): 251–263.

Welch, John, O. Carm. *The Carmelite Way: An Ancient Path for Today's Pilgrim.* New York: Paulist, 1996.

Werling, Norman, O. Carm. "The Date of the Institution." *Sword* 13, no. 2 (1949): 275–334.

————. "The Book of St. John, 44th" *Sword* 7, no. 4 (1943): 347–354.

White, Marsha C. *The Elijah Legends and Jehu's Coup.* Atlanta, Ga.: Scholars, 1997.

Wiener, Aharon. *The Prophet Elijah in the Development of Judaism: A Depth-Psychological Study.* London: Routledge, 1978.

Wilson, Robert R. *Prophecy and Society in Ancient Israel.* Philadelphia: Fortress, 1980.

Wilderink, Vital, O. Carm. *Les Constitutions des Premières Carmélites en France*. Rome: Institutum Carmelitanum, 1966.

Zimmerman, Benedict, OCD. *Carmel in England: A History of the English Mission of the Discalced Carmelites, 1615–1849*. London: Burns & Oates, 1899.

———. "Les réformes dans l'Ordre de Notre-Dame du Mont-Carmel." In *Mystiques et Missionaires*. Vol. 2 of *Études Carmélitaines*, 155–195. Paris: Desclée de Brouwer, 1934.

Zumthor, Paul. "Intertextualité et mouvance." *Littérature* 41 (1981): 8–16.

Carmelite Ritual for Spanish Congregation, 1788

jane-ackerman@utulsa.edu

The Institute of Carmelite Studies promotes research and publication in the field of Carmelite spirituality. Its members are Discalced Carmelites, part of a Roman Catholic community—friars, nuns, and laity—who are heirs to the teaching and way of life of Teresa of Jesus and John of the Cross, men and women dedicated to contemplation and to ministry in the Church and the world. Information concerning their way of life is available through local diocesan Vocation Offices or from the Vocation Directors' Offices:

5345 S. University Avenue, Chicago, IL 60615

2131 Lincoln Rd., NE Washington, DC 20002

P O Box 3420, San Jose, CA 95156-3420

5151 Marylake Drive, Little Rock, AR 72206